American eight-week-old puppy. Sturman's **Park Place Fair Weather at Ambleside.** (Breeder: Barbara Wood)

The Cavalier King Charles Spaniel

Bruce Field

ROBERT HALE · LONDON

ISBN 0 7090 5644 3

Robert Hale Limited
Clerkenwell House
Clerkenwell Green
London EC1R 0HT

2   4   6   8   10   9   7   5   3   1

Photoset in Times by
Derek Doyle & Associates, Mold, Clwyd.
Printed in Great Britain by
St Edmundsbury Press Ltd, Bury St Edmunds, Suffolk.
Bound by Hunter & Foulis Ltd, Edinburgh.

Contents

This book is dedicated to my four young granddaughters

Katie
Sarah
Carley
and Louise.

They are already very keen animal lovers. I hope this love of animals will continue throughout their lives and that the pleasure they give to, and receive from, animals will be immense.

'Whenever man is unhappy, God gives him a dog.'

Lamartine

Acknowledgements

I thank those Cavalier enthusiasts worldwide who have kindly assisted me with information. They are too numerous to mention individually, but I have received rather special help from several individuals and wish to acknowledge my indebtedness to them. They are: Jane Bowdler; Susan Burgess; Dr Bruce M. Cattanach; Dr Peter G.G. Darke; Bet Hargreaves; Moira Jones; and Roy Robinson. I am also grateful to Fiona Bunce for her lovely drawings and to Sylvia Lea for typing the manuscript.

I would like to thank the Cavalier King Charles Spaniel Club of the USA for allowing me to quote extracts from its Breed Standard. The UK Breed Standard and extracts from the Kennel Club glossary are reproduced with the kind permission of the Kennel Club, London.

PICTURE CREDITS

C.S. Tatham: p.2. Jim Meager: pp. 43, 208. David Dalton: pp. 44, 61, 79, 164, 175, 204. Tracy Morgan: pp. 46, 52, 102 (*bottom*), 110, 160, 189, 202, 236. Joy Stanley: p. 70. F. Bunce: p. 73 (*top*). Thomas Fall: pp. 73 (*bottom*), 102 (*top left*). Carol Ann Johnson: p. 75. Hartley: p. 76. Nyby (Sweden): p. 83. G. Inglis: pp. 90–1 (*top*), 170. David Bull: p. 91 (*middle right*). Peter Lodge: p. 100. M.A. Booth: p. 102 (*top right*). Eunice M. Field: p. 137. Rob Dix: p. 147. Russell Fine Art: pp. 156, 200. Lionel Young (of Bristol): p. 172. Panther Photographic: p. 179. D.J. Lindsay: p. 182. A. Periam: p. 187. Mikron Photos Ltd: p. 198. B.G. Hubrich: p. 215. C.S. Photography: p. 219. McFarlane: p. 233.

Valerie Watson's **Beatrice** and royal coach

Introduction

Persons who have not had on-going involvement with animals, particularly dogs, have missed out on one of the most rewarding of relationships.

From a very young age I remember the frequent visits to my grandparents' farm and being with the variety of lovely animals that gave me so much pleasure. I believe that relationships with animals and a nearness to nature and the countryside are character forming in the most positive sense.

The particular advantage of dogs, when compared with other animals, is that most dogs allow a closer, more satisfying relationship right through from birth 'till death us do part'. Cavaliers not only expect such a relationship; they work hard and affectionately to bring it about and make it mutually rewarding. The pleasure and companionship they give is truly enormous. Their faithfulness and eagerness to please are outstanding. Their role in life has always been the giving of pleasure and being a companion. They are wonderful with children.

Eunice, my wife, and I look back with pleasure upon thirty years' association with the breed. We have deliberately kept our number of Cavaliers small so that our relationship with them has been very close, personal and meaningful (we have never employed kennel staff). We have known each dog intimately as an individual – appreciated their idiosyncrasies and recognized when they were a little off-colour or when puppies were ready for their 'mad half hour playtime'. We have experienced disappointments, and at times real heartache, but overall the sense of fulfilment we have received from our Cavaliers has formed a most important part of our life.

In our early days of working with Cavaliers we were fortunate to visit Amice Pitt, the founder of the breed, at her home. She was kindness itself, spending several hours with us. She was most helpful in providing and sharing information and was quite forthright in her expectations of those involved with Cavaliers.

She held a principled view of what was best for the breed in the long term, and stressed the need for breeders to accept the responsibilities and avoid any gimmicky or risky short cuts. Her advice is still sound and relevant today.

This book tells my story of Cavaliers. It describes what I have witnessed in the growth and development of the breed and gives my assessment of the current state of Cavaliers. I describe some of the great characters I have encountered, both canine and human. I have endeavoured to provide interesting and stimulating information, whether it relates to establishing your own successful blood-line, heart disease, choosing and caring for a puppy, exhibiting, judging or whatever. The intention is that the book will be an absorbing read but also, in the longer term, provide a reference point.

Cavaliers are now well established and thriving throughout the world, and the English Cavalier Club has members in twenty-four overseas countries. I have recently judged the breed in Australia, New Zealand, Sweden and America, and I was very pleased with the many lovely, typical and sound Cavaliers that were brought under me. I particularly value the many friendships formed with Cavalier enthusiasts on these overseas trips. My aim, therefore, has been to give this book an international appeal and relevance.

1

History and Evolution of the Breed

The evolution of the Cavalier King Charles Spaniel has been fascinating. For several centuries it was popular as a toy spaniel; then it lost favour and became virtually extinct, requiring great efforts by a small band of devotees to revive it. Now success has been achieved beyond their wildest dreams, as Cavaliers are one of the most popular breeds.

I propose to deal with the breed's evolution in two parts – pre-1925 and post-1925 – because I regard 1925 as a watershed year when dedicated enthusiasts began to make the effort to bring back to life the true Cavalier King Charles Spaniel, as distinct from the short-faced, round-skulled King Charles Spaniel. The effort needed was considerable and lengthy. It took twenty years hard work before the Kennel Club agreed, in 1945, to accept separate registrations for Cavalier King Charles Spaniels. Even so, Amice Pitt said she felt that separate registration for Cavaliers probably came too soon, after the much curtailed breeding during the 1939–45 war because the new breed had too narrow a base upon which to build.

Both periods, pre-1925 and post-1925, have had prominent persons, including Royals, playing vital roles. There are many lovely stories, some factual and some legendary. For those who are particularly interested in the historical development of dogs (all types, not just Cavaliers) as seen through beautiful paintings, there is a gem of a book called *Dog Painting 1840–1940* by William Secord.

History before 1925

Toy spaniels have been part of the rich historical tapestry of European and British life for more than 500 years, and Royal involvement has been substantial.

One of the first depictions of small spaniel-like dogs is contained in the magnificent religious portrait of a group of animals in *The Vision of St Eustace* painted by Antonio Pisano, called Pisanello, in 1440. William Secord reproduces it in his book *Dog Painting* and comments: 'Note the pair of small spaniels in the left foreground, no doubt ancestors of our present-day King Charles Spaniels.'

In the early 1500s the Venetian artist Tiziano Vecellio, known as Titian, painted the *Uffizi Venus*, which includes a red and white spaniel curled up on a bed. Paolo Veronese (1528–88), in his painting *Hermes, Herse and Aglauros*, shows a small red and white spaniel-type dog with domed skull, short compact body and rather short nose. This painting is also reproduced in Secord's book.

When Mary Queen of Scots was beheaded on 8 February 1587, she was wearing her state robes of black velvet stamped with gold, and a petticoat of crimson velvet. In the life of Mary Queen of Scots it is recorded that 'her little favourite Lap-Dog (a small black and white spaniel) which had affectionately followed her, and unobserved, had nestled among her clothes, now endeavoured by his caresses to restore her to life and would not leave the body till he was forced away. He died two days afterwards, perhaps from loneliness or grief.'

Charles I, whose reign began in 1625 and ended on 30 January 1649 when he was beheaded at Whitehall, had a spaniel called Rogue. Charles II (reigned 1660–85), from whom the name of the breed derives, regularly had several small spaniels (commonly known as 'Little Cocking Spaniels') in close attendance. There are various reports from Samuel Pepys and others that Charles was so obsessed with his spaniels that at times they adversely affected his attention to his Royal duties. The first Parliament of Charles II was, coincidentally, known as The Cavalier Parliament. Charles II's youngest sister Henrietta d'Orleans was a lover of toy spaniels, particularly small ones. A painting by Pierre Mignard in 1660 shows Henrietta cradling in her arms a tiny spaniel which is wearing earrings. James II, the brother and successor to Charles II, was also very fond of the small spaniels with their lovable disposition.

The first Earl of Marlborough, John Churchill, played a

significant role in breeding and developing the Blenheim type of toy spaniel. His residence, Blenheim Palace, was the birthplace of many generations of the variously called Blenheim, or Marlborough, spaniel.

There is a delightfully romantic story attributed to Sarah, Duchess of Marlborough, relating to the origins of the lozenge, or spot, on the head of Blenheim Cavaliers. Legend has it that she was so anxious whilst awaiting news about the battle of Blindheim (or Blenheim), which took place in Germany on 13 August 1704, that, unwittingly, she gently pressed her thumb on the skull of an in-whelp bitch she was nursing. It is said that coinciding with news of the mighty victory by the Duke at Blenheim the bitch gave birth to five lovely puppies, all bearing the lozenge, or thumbprint, of the Duchess. If only it was so easy!

The Marlborough Blenheims seem to have been larger and more robust than the very small toy spaniels depicted in the paintings of the Old Masters Rembrandt, Van Dyck and Gainsborough, and the more recent ones of Fragonard, Boucher and Landseer. The Frenchman Jean-Honoré Fragonard (1732–1806) in his painting *The Love Letter* depicts a charming toy spaniel with a lovely Cavalier-type head with flat skull, large and dark widely-spaced eyes, high-set ears, and a soft expression (reproduced in Secord's book). By contrast, in the 1816 painting *Blenheim King Charles Spaniel in a Landscape* by Henry Bernard Chalon, the Blenheim shown looks to be a sizeable dog. The Duke of Marlborough always said that Blenheims should be able to keep up with a horse, and Mrs Pitt agreed with this view. Marlborough, a great soldier, was so fond of his spaniels that he is said to have taken one with him on his campaigns as a mascot.

A writer who said she had her first King Charles Spaniel in 1901 stated in a Cavalier Club paper of 1957 that 'Before the first War (1914–18) there was a fifth variety in our midst, the Marlborough Blenheim, the pride of Woodstock and the old Duke, and they were bred at Blenheim Palace. A very handsome fellow this dog was, with sound action and swagger, good marking and profuse feathering. The nose was long but ended "blunt", the eyes large and dark.'

The Duke of Norfolk also kept the Blenheim type, but additionally had his exclusive King James Spaniels which were coloured black and tan. The Duke maintained his exclusive ownership of his black and tan strain by feeding any surplus puppies to his eagles. An interesting point regarding black and tan toy spaniels was made by Mrs Neville Lytton in her book *Toy Dogs*, published in 1911. She suggested they had water spaniel blood in their early ancestry and that this was confirmed by the fact that toy spaniel puppies were still 'very often' born with webbed feet. Mrs Lytton stated 'I have five dogs now in my possession which, have these webbed feet.' I have discussed this with 'Bunty' Green (Heatherside), who has no recollection of any Cavalier having been born with the slightest inclination towards webbed feet.

Queen Victoria at the time of her coronation in 1838 had a delightful small tricolour called Dash, and he features in several paintings by Landseer. Her Majesty was given Dash as a present in February 1833, when she was thirteen years old. Dash died in 1840 and was buried in the gardens at Adelaide Lodge. On his memorial stone is this deeply moving epitaph.

> Here lies DASH The Favourite Spaniel of Her Majesty, Queen Victoria, By Whose Command this Memorial was Erected. He died on 20th December in his 9th year.
> His attachment was without selfishness.
> His playfulness without malice.
> His fidelity without deceit.
> READER if you would live beloved and die regretted profit by the example of DASH.

Queen Victoria's great love of dogs is legendary, and many artists painted her faithful pets, including Gourlay Steell, Charles Burton Barber and Maud Earl, but the most famous of all was Edwin Landseer (1802–73). Landseer's head portrait of Dash is one of the most widely copied dog paintings of all time.

Apart from figuring attractively in many famous paintings, the toy spaniel was also included in the first illustrated edition of Shakespeare's *The Taming of the Shrew*. There were several colours of toy spaniels, including black and white, black and tan, tricolour, Blenheim and, from about 1850, the ruby.

However, from about 1840 the Cavalier type, i.e. the flat-skulled, longer muzzled, toy spaniel, began to lose favour. Instead there developed an increasing attraction towards Pugs and toy spaniels with the King Charles type of head i.e. domed, with low set ears and a much shorter muzzle, well turned up between the eyes. Naturally breeders increasingly sought to breed this desired type of head. Differing views have been expressed as to whether or not breeders used other breeds, e.g. Pugs and Bulldogs, in the second half of the nineteenth century in order to achieve the shorter muzzle more quickly.

In 1885 the Toy Spaniel Club was formed. Four colours were recognized, each with a separate name under the all embracing title of toy spaniels. The separate names for the different colours were:

King Charles	– Black and tans
Prince Charles	– Tricolours
Blenheims	– Rich chestnut, or ruby red markings, on a pearly white background
Rubies	– Rich chestnut red

In 1903 the name King Charles Spaniel was adopted to include all the four colours, and the name of the Toy Spaniel Club was changed to the King Charles Spaniel Club. This change of name was only accepted by the Kennel Club after the personal intervention of King Edward VII (again showing the Royal involvement with the breed).

The King Charles Spaniel with its domed head, low set ears and upturned muzzle gradually ousted the earlier type with the flat skull and longer muzzle. By 1925 the longer muzzle type was almost extinct and it was in that year that a really significant event occurred.

History from 1925 onwards

In 1925 Mr Roswell Eldridge from Long Island, New York, visited England and was disturbed that he could no longer find the old type of toy spaniel with the flat skull and longer nose.

Mr Eldridge, a multi-millionaire, visited England several times a year and became a familiar sight hunting with the West Somerset Hunt. He was intrigued with pictures of old type spaniels and wished to buy a breeding pair to take back to the States but was unable to do so. He therefore resolved to do something about it. He arranged that two special classes for the type should be included at Crufts in 1926 and the ensuing four years, with a special prize of £25 for the winner of each class. The prize money in those days was substantial and well worth winning. The classes also acted as a challenge to some of the breeders of the time.

The Cruft's catalogue details were as follows:

The Blenheim Spaniel of King Charles II Time

The desired type of spaniel was then illustrated by Sir E. Landseer's painting of a pair of long-nosed King Charles

Spaniels. This was followed by a written description of what was required.

BLENHEIM SPANIELS OF THE OLD TYPE

as shown in pictures of Charles II's time, long face, no stop, flat skull, not inclined to be domed, with spot in centre of skull. The First Prizes in Classes 947 and 948 are given by Roswell Eldridge, Esq., of New York, and will be continued for five years. The Prizes go to the nearest to type required.

There were only two entries in each of the dog and bitch classes but this was hardly surprising the first year. Mrs Treleaven's Ferdie of Monham won the dog class and Mrs A.M. Raymond-Mallock's Flora was successful in the bitch class. The judge was Mrs Prowett Ferdinands and she also judged Pugs. It is interesting that the owner of the bitch class winner, Mrs A.M. Raymond-Mallock, wrote the 1915 book *Toy Dogs* and judged Cavaliers at Crufts in 1936.

In 1927 there were three entries in each class and Mrs Hewitt-Pitt won first prize in the bitch class with Waif Julia. Incidentally, the catalogue shows that this bitch was available for sale at a price of £50.

In 1928 entries increased substantially, with five in the dog class

Ann's Son

and nine in the bitch class. The famous Ann's Son, owned and bred by Miss K. Mostyn Walker, won the dog class, and Mrs Amice (or Hewitt) Pitt again won the bitch class, but this time with Hentzau Sweet Nell bred by Mrs Elkins.

In 1929 the number of entries were six dogs and six bitches. Ann's Son again showed his quality by winning the dog class and also won three other general King Charles classes. The bitch winner was Flora, who had previously won the class in 1926.

In 1930 (the last of the five years) there were three entries for the dog class and eight for the bitch class. The dog class was again won by Ann's Son, making it three wins in consecutive years for him.

The Crufts Show of 1930 was immediately followed in the same building on the same day by the Cavalier King Charles Spaniel Club Show. There were five classes plus brace, team and litter. Ann's Son won all three classes for which he was eligible. It can therefore be said he had quite a successful day!

Ann's Son had already proved his outstanding quality by his three consecutive wins at Crufts in the years 1928, 1929 and 1930, but then, amazingly, after being retired from the show-ring, he was brought out again at Crufts in 1936 at the age of nine and took Best of Breed. The highly regarded judge in 1936 was Mrs A.M. Raymond Mallock, whose Flora had won the first £25 special bitch class at Crufts in 1926 and repeated the win in 1929.

Ann's Son was never beaten in his show career and also contributed greatly to the development of Cavaliers in two other ways. First, through his stud work (fee three guineas or £3.15). Second – and this was undoubtedly Ann's Son's outstanding bestowal to Cavaliers – he was chosen as the live model upon which the Breed Standard was formed in 1928.

In the Cavalier Club Bulletin of Christmas 1955 there was the following description of Ann's Son.

A FEW FAMOUS DOGS OF THE PAST
by
Speedwell Massingham

Christmas is a season both of remembrance and rejoicing, and as I look back over past scenes, beautiful dogs I have loved and admired, move with old friends before my mind's eye.

The first to come is Ann's Son, the wonderful tiny Cavalier born in 1927 and bred by Miss Mostyn Walker whom I knew well. Imagine him! Never Beaten! Winner of the £25 Prize awarded I believe by an American. He had everything. A toy dog of 13 lbs. short in the back, entirely flat head, streaming ears to his legs, large dark eyes wide apart, nose long with white blaze running from it right up the forehead tipped with jet to match his dark eyes, thick soft silky coat like early pictures, a lightly marked red-gold and silver Blenheim and as sound as a bell. He was supreme!

But looking at the photograph of him as I write I realise it was not only all the perfect points that gave him his glory. It was the overall quality which this exquisite little dog had and which shines out of his face in the picture, that made him the 'Best Ever Born'. His breeder told me of his enchanting temperament and how he was mated to lots of bitches as everyone wanted this little wonder repeated. But, alas, not one of his many descendants has been his equal. All the same he lies in pedigrees of most kennels and perhaps one day a perfect tiny gold and silver descendant with his quality will trot into the ring. I only hope if this happens that the dog will be recognised as a paragon and not passed over!

Mrs Pitt acknowledged that Ann's Son was 'very mean under the eyes and he was poor in hindquarters' but nevertheless stated 'he was an outstanding dog'.

There is a little vagueness as to the history of Ann's Son. Views have been expressed that his sire may not have been a King Charles Spaniel but was in fact a Papillon (see page 23). There are also differing reports as to when he was born. Mrs Pitt, in a report written in 1955 and reproduced later under the heading *How it All Began*, said he was born in 1924. There is additionally on the front sheet of a leaflet produced, I believe, by the Cavalier Club about 1960, a photograph of Ann's Son (the one showed earlier) and underneath is printed 'ANN'S SON 1926'. But it seems likely that he was born in April 1927. According to the Kennel Club Breed Supplement and the Crufts catalogue of 1928 his date of birth was 29 April 1927. Also Speedwell Massingham in his article gave the year as 1927. Then, immediately following Ann's Son's Best of Breed at Crufts 1936, his owner, Miss Mostyn Walker, said he was 'in his ninth year'. The Crufts judge Lillian C. Raymond Mallock stated 'this dog carried all before him as a youngster seven years ago and then retired protem'. The weight of evidence, therefore, seems to favour that he was born in 1927.

His date of birth is important because he is said to have sired the famous Daywell Nell in 1939. Siring a litter at twelve years of age is possible, whereas if he was born in 1924 this would have made him fifteen, which would have made his siring the litter improbable.

We need to be as accurate as possible in our knowledge of Ann's Son because he was the foundation stone on which the breed was built. From him came Daywell Nell, and from her came Champion Daywell Roger, the first champion in the breed and the sire of eleven champions. Most Cavaliers go back to this line.

It is interesting that Ann's Son in his younger days was sold to an actress for £100, but he proved so destructive that he was returned and exchanged for a Pomeranian.

Miss Mostyn Walker, the breeder and owner of Ann's Son, died in June 1952.

It was in 1928 that the Cavalier King Charles Spaniel Club was first established. Founding the Club sounds easy but in fact it was very difficult to collect sufficient people to form a meeting, there being only eight present at the inaugural meeting. A tremendous role was played by the indefatigable Amice Pitt in getting things moving. She worked vigorously and continuously to get the breed established along appropriate lines. Although it was a long hard slog she persevered, and the breed's growth and current success owe much to her.

It is important to understand the mammoth difficulties that breeders wishing to produce the Cavalier type faced in the early years. For their initial breeding stock they often had to depend upon long nosed rejects from the King Charles breeders. Some King Charles breeders did not wish to be helpful because they saw the Cavalier type as being a retrograde step, a deviation from the desirable type. The stock that was available to use was therefore extremely limited and sometimes not of the best quality.

The early concentration by Cavalier breeders had to be on long noses and flat skulls. Other characteristics, be they soundness, size or whatever, had to receive a lower degree of priority. The early focus had to be on achieving a completely different head type to that of the King Charles Spaniel.

In a show critique published in October 1935, D. Fowler of Braemore states:

CAVALIER SPANIELS

I was particularly impressed with the marked improvement in this variety of Toy Spaniels – even though I am sure everyone agrees that breeders of these spaniels have such a lot of work in front of them before they succeed in establishing or re-establishing the type of the spaniel of long ago, but notwithstanding all that, there is no doubt that a good start has been made, and that the exhibits were far more level in type and size than I have ever seen them before, and quite a number had level mouths and consequently much less 'stop' than they used to have, and size is decidedly reduced.

The stud dogs that realistically could be used were very small in number. This was particularly so during the 1939–45 war, when so many dogs had to be put down because of the grave shortage of food for humans, never mind dogs. Also, petrol was rationed, and travelling for any reason was not easy. Thus a long trip to a stud dog would not have been regarded as having a high priority. Older readers will remember the wartime posters with the stern question: 'Is your journey really necessary?'

As a result, there were some extreme examples of repeat matings and some close 'in-breeding'. For instance between August 1939 and December 1943 Mme J. Harper Trois-Fontaines' Blenheim bitch Freckles of Ttiweh had seven litters, totalling thirty-nine puppies, by the same dog, namely Plantation Banjo, her own black and tan. Banjo also sired two litters, totalling thirteen puppies, by his own daughter, Princesse Celia de Fontenay, in March and October 1943. Another of his daughters, Princesse Bianca de Fontenay, had one puppy by him in January 1943. A full brother and sister mating, namely Prince Carol de Fontenay and Princesse Bianca de Fontenay, produced three puppies in May 1944.

It has to be clearly pointed out that close in-breeding such as this should only be practised by breeders with considerable experience and who know their stock's genetic make-up very thoroughly. Whilst there can be advantages, the dangers are considerable. One can understand in those early days in the breed the need to try and 'fix' particular features by in-breeding. Less understandable is the frequent mating of poor Freckles – such a practice would rightly be frowned upon today.

Katie Eldred described Madame J. Harper Trois-Fontaines in the following way:

> She was a wealthy, somewhat forceful lady who spoke English with a pronounced Belgian accent and owned a School for Models in London. She was also a well-known breeder of Great Pyrenees when she 'took up' Cavaliers. Although she did some strange things in her breeding program, the breed has to be grateful to her for keeping it alive during World War II when most of the rest of us were doing war work, or having babies, or both, and couldn't find the time – or the food – to maintain a kennel of dogs.

On in-breeding in the early years, and her intentions of taking up breeding again after the 1939–45 war, Amice Pitt wrote the following in an article dated Christmas 1957.

When the Second World War was over and Dog Shows and breeding started again, I too started to look round for the dog that I wanted to lead my kennel. I saw and heard of many but most of them had been so inbred on both sides to both Plantation Banjo and Cannonhill Richey that they were of little use to me. Both these sires were influential in the breed but were used to every bitch, and this before the Kennel Club divided the King Charles Spaniel from the Cavalier King Charles Spaniel, so that any amount of good blood that could have been used was neglected leaving us with a very inbred line. So it was obvious that if I were to start again I must do so by going right back to the first Cavalier who was something more than a 'nosey' short-face, so back to Ann's Son. Mrs Brierley sent me a dog puppy out of Daywell Nell, herself a daughter of Ann's Son and out of a bitch by Ann's Son so that fixed that side of the family for me.

This puppy, who cost fifteen guineas (£15.75), grew into Champion Daywell Roger, the first champion in Cavaliers,

Champion Daywell Roger, born 7.10.45

winning eight CCs including Crufts 1948. He went on to sire eleven champions.

Mrs Pitt later described him thus:

Daywell Roger was a medium-sized dog, heavily marked and certainly not the best Cavalier on Show points but he had tremendous presence – large dark kind eyes and extremely sound with the rather bustly quick action of a pony or toy dog. He was full of character. Bold, yet kind and full of the spirit of adventure – no creepy crawly here, always gay and with a great awareness of his importance. He kept all the younger dogs in their place and insisted on his rights.

He had various adventures during his twelve years of life, nearly losing an eye by too friendly an advance on a strange cat, and secondly when he was found unconscious by an over-turned kitchen table. He was unconscious for two hours on this occasion and I suppose he was lucky to get over this. A third adventure was when I first came to Ascott Earl and I thought Roger was in a fit. Inspection showed that he had sat on a cactus. This last adventure inspired a rather ribald poem from one of his admirers!

Time goes fast, so quite a few of the modern Cavalier enthusiasts never saw Champion Daywell Roger but nearly everyone will find him in the pedigrees of their dogs.

Ch. Daywell Roger was the first male champion in the breed when he obtained his third Certificate under Mr Tom Scott. He, of course, had been transferred to my daughter and it was a big thrill to her. He won his laurels quickly and rapidly established himself as the leading sire of the breed. He won the stud dog cup every year until his 10th year and finished his Show career at the Jubilee Show 1956. If I forget some of his successes at stud it is because I have no records with me.

His sons: Champions Harmony, Jupiter, Hillbarn Alexander of Ttiweh, Pargeter Jollyean of Avoncliffe, Pargeter Thundercloud of Ttiweh, Hillbarn Desmond, Mingshang Sir Roger.

His daughters: Champions Prologue of Ttiweh, Mathilda of Ttiweh, Polka of Ttiweh, Dolores of Hillbarn.

His grandchildren and his own winning children are many and he has been tremendously influential in our pedigrees and is the perfect example of a dominant sire.

Not every champion is as influential as this dog. In all breeds there are these key sires as there are in the cattle and horse pedigrees, and these sires stamp their progeny and bring out the best in their mates. It isn't only one mating that is a success but all bitches brought seem to be suitable for the dominant sire. They are historical facts in the history of our breed and blood lines and must never be forgotten when we plan for the future.

Dogs of Daywell Roger's quality are not hung on every tree or bought two a penny – there are champions, super champions and lucky champions – some manage to sire a few winners, some none and are worthless to the breed and some like Daywell Roger have that bit extra which makes a great dog. He was a laster too, gay and in perfect health up to the day of his death and was the sire of a litter of five promising puppies in his twelfth year.

Look back in admiration at this great dog.

Since the late 1920s there have been vague rumours about other breeds possibly having been used to improve Cavaliers, although it has to be said this was not recommended by the Cavalier Club. The breeds mentioned include Welsh Springers, Cocker Spaniels, Papillons and Dachshunds. I find it difficult to believe that anyone would have contemplated using a Dachshund, simply because of the problems likely to arise from short legs and long bodies. A Welsh Springer cross would have had more to offer with its similar rich Blenheim colouring, long nose and some similarities of type, but surely its size would have been a drawback. In fact size was a great problem in the early days. Hearsay, but from a source I respect very highly, has it that one Welsh Springer Spaniel was almost certainly used.

Mrs Pitt said Ann's Son was probably bred by a Papillon sire. Two other breeders of the time, one of them a great friend of Miss Mostyn Walker – the breeder and owner of Ann's Son – said categorically that Ann's Son was the offspring of a tricolour bitch and a Papillon. Ann's Son certainly had the daintiness and prettiness to justify a connection with Papillons, and we know that Miss Mostyn Walker did keep and breed Papillons. But as 'Bunty' Green points out in a personal communication, Ann's Son 'must have been more Charlie than Papillon. Where else would he have obtained those lovely eyes?'

We know that Cavaliers had been granted separate registration in 1945. In that year Mrs Pitt, Mrs Eldred and Mme Harper Trois-Fontaines were asked to discuss which dogs could be taken from the King Charles Spaniel registers and be appropriately known as Cavaliers. The three ladies met at the Kennel Club and carefully perused several large books of King Charles Spaniel registrations. They selected the names of all dogs that were Cavaliers or Cavalier-type, and they also included the names of King Charles Spaniels of both sexes that were known to produce 'nosey' puppies. From the list they compiled, every Cavalier in the world today (with just a few exceptions) is descended. It was, however, still possible, with Kennel Club approval, to breed Cavaliers back to King Charles Spaniels for several years after 1945. Katie Eldred explains it in the following way: 'During those first post-war years, breeders had occasionally to go back into short faced blood to avoid too much in-breeding. This was permitted by the Kennel Club, the progeny being registered as Interbred; after three generations of breeding back to Cavalier stud dogs, the third generation was eligible for the Cavalier Register.'

Celandine of Littlestream, born 1946 (the grand-dam of Champion Pargeter Patron, born 1950), was an inter-bred. Her sire was Flash Gordon, a King Charles Spaniel. As Barbara Keswick pointed out: 'In those days, owing to the lack of Cavalier sires, certain King Charles dogs were allowed by the Kennel Club.'

There was also inter-breeding between other varieties of spaniels. In the old papers of Amice Pitt is a partially damaged, undated, unsigned but headed letter which appears to have been written by Miss Mostyn Walker in 1949 or 1950 and which reads in part:

> Dear Mrs Pitt,
> Very interested in yr Cavalier notes this week.
> In any case I was going to write you.
> First of all if it interests you come along, have a spot of lunch & take a squint at a gorgous wee golden spaniel.
> Mother 'of ware' cocker, small type snipey. Sire a short face blenheim dog who sires very cobby pups, very small. I bred two litters from different little old fashioned cockers all took type from Mother, & small cobby bodies profuse ears etc from Dad, result perfectly lovely wee dogs.
> I got the idea from Lloyd, have you read his book Cocker Spaniels & how they came from blenheims, its a good try out worthy of the best, far far better than any Cavalier present day. You can see the little golden bitch she is my shadow. I tried to buy back her litter brother, no money can get him so as I have Dam & sire shall have another try.

For those who know little about Cockers, the 'of Ware' kennel owned by Mr H.S. Lloyd was extremely famous and won Best in Show at Crufts a magnificent six times between 1930 and 1950. Mr Lloyd died in January 1963. The Blenheims referred to in the letter are believed to be Duke of Marlborough Blenheims. John Scott in his *Sportsman's Cabinet* (1803) wrote '... the smallest spaniels passing under the denomination of Cockers is that peculiar breed in possession and preservation of the Duke of Marlborough and his friends.'

It has been possible to trace a link up with Miss Mostyn Walker and 'the wee Cockers' she mentions. A Miss I.E. Neal, now living in the Norwich area, 'having known and viewed the pedigree dog scene seriously since 1938', remembers taking one of her pocket Cockers to mate with a flat-faced bitch of Miss Walker's. Also, Miss Walker bought '2 tiny pups (pocket Cockers)' from Miss Neal. Miss Neal states: 'At the end of the War 1945–46 I knew Miss Mostyn Walker well and we often had long discussions on Cavaliers and small spaniels in general!' In addition to her miniature Cockers, Miss Neal also had inter-breeds resulting from King Charles Spaniels and pocket Cocker matings. Miss Neal has very early photographs and one can see the Cavalier resemblance in some of the stock. One photo shows a Blenheim long-nosed bitch, said to be of Ttiweh breeding, in whelp to Miss Neal's Mr Pepys (a miniature Cocker × King Charles Spaniel cross). Miss Neal describes a small dog she bought which was registered as a Cocker. However, she says as it matured it became obvious it was a Welsh Springer × Cocker cross. Miss Neal used him at stud several times, including twice to her small inter-bred bitches. The puppies that resulted included two very small ones 'ending up so like the old Ann's Son type spaniel'.

Miss Neal states: 'I finally ended up with 7 generations of miniature spaniels, some I outcrossed with King Charles ... [with] ... quite pleasing results as one got the sturdy body with Cavalier type head.' Miss Neal in her reminiscences of the late 1930s states 'It was all so different then, not so commercialised.' In considering small spaniels about the time of Ann's Son, she says 'I'm pretty sure the small Old English and Norfolk Spaniels (now extinct) were used in these very early strains.'

We also know that a Cocker Spaniel was used, with Kennel Club approval, to improve Cavalier stock in the 1950s. In a personal communication, Miss M.D. Barnes informed me that she talked to top Cavalier breeders before doing so, and was particularly seeking to improve certain characteristics such as soundness, mouths, flat skulls, dark eyes and pigment. Her mother's black and white cocker bitch Suntop Joyful was mated to Miss Barnes' black and tan reserve Challenge Certificate winning Cavalier dog, Crest of Candelight. Miss Barnes feels the mating was successful, as witnessed, four generations later, by reserve Challenge Certificate winning dogs in all four colours, the desired characteristics having been achieved and 'fixed'. Miss Barnes further states that the good health and long lives of her mother's Cockers also benefitted the Cavaliers. The Cockers were all home bred but had 'of Ware' ancestry. Sadly, Miss Barnes was unable to show two breeds in different groups at championship shows and therefore gave her Cavaliers to the late Betty 'Kenavon' Mingay, and concentrated on her very successful

English Setters. Miss Barnes says she is unaware whether there are descendants still about (possibly in Scotland) from Suntop Tuffet, Ada, Pargeter Evelyn, etc.

Mrs Pitt stated in 1962 that she would like to see the Kennel Club lift the four generation Interbred Rule so that, without losing the King Charles descent, a really fresh source of blood could be introduced (she suggested as a possibility the Papillon).

If anyone has knowledge of any other breed being used in this way then I would be glad to hear, so that I could try to add a little more to the evolutionary jigsaw of the Cavalier King Charles Spaniel. It truly is a fascinating subject.

Suntop Spillikin born 1952 – Ruby 18 lb

Left **Suntop Joyful** born 1949 – Cocker Spaniel grand-dam of Suntop **Spillikin** above. *Centre* **Suntop Red Riding Hood** born 1952 – 14 lb. Reserve Challenge Certificates. *Right* **Suntop Peggoty** born 1954 – sired by **Suntop Spillikin** above.

Phenomenal Growth in Registrations

Although in 1945 separate registration of Cavalier King Charles Spaniels was approved by the Kennel Club, in fact a litter of three was separately recorded under King Charles Spaniels (Cavalier) in the Kennel Club Gazette of August 1943. Born 5 July 1943, there were two rubies and a tricolour, bred by Mme J. Harper Trois-Fontaines. The sire was Plantation Banjo and the dam Snow White of Ttiweh. However, it was not until 1945 that Cavaliers were separately shown in the Kennel Club annual registration statistics.

To say that the growth in registrations has been spectacular is not overstating the case. I wonder whether Mr Roswell Eldridge now has a satisfied smile on his face, or whether he is continually turning in his grave through disbelief and concern at the results which have stemmed from his initiative.

The facts speak for themselves:

1945	60 registrations
1950	314 registrations (a five-fold increase in five years)
1960	1,150 registrations
1970	3,192 registrations (a fifty-fold increase in twenty-five years)
1980	8,898 registrations
1985	10,090 registrations
1988	8,658 registrations
1989	15,953 registrations (84% increase on previous year)
1990	16,823 registrations (the peak so far)
1991	15,514 registrations
1992	13,918 registrations
1993	13,705 registrations

There was a considerable surge in registrations in 1989. This is, however, easily explained as in 1989 it became necessary to register each and every puppy in a litter, whereas previously it had been possible to just register the litter as one entity or, alternatively, to register selected puppies from the litter.

In 1990 there was a further increase to 16,823, but between 1991 and 1993 registrations have reduced by 3,118 or 18.5%. What do these reductions indicate? Is it a temporary respite before further increases, or have we now reached a plateau with further increases being unlikely? My crystal ball is cloudy! However, my hope is that it is a stabilizing plateau with more emphasis for the future on breeding top quality stock rather than vast numbers of mediocre dogs.

Amice Pitt, in her Chairman's Letter in the Cavalier Club Year Book for 1966, wrote: 'Cavaliers are going ahead by leaps and bounds, with larger registrations, more Challenge Certificates and increased popularity. Unfortunately with all this tremendous success the usual pitfalls of a popular breed have crept in – ambition, greed and a lack of real idealism.... I feel that this commercialism is very close to us now.... Cavalier Breeders can do almost anything with perseverance, unity and idealism.'

How correct was Mrs Pitt's prediction about commercialism all those years ago. Commercialism has long since overtaken the breed in a vast way. Oh for more, much more, of the idealism and unity that Mrs Pitt requested.

Some people who have bought a Cavalier feel that as they have been given a pedigree, and the dog or bitch is Kennel Club registered, that it must be good quality and therefore ought to be bred from. If it also seems to offer the opportunity of making them some money, that helps to persuade some owners to go ahead. As a result some very poor specimens have been used for breeding and the breed has suffered. Breeders who sold them the puppy in the first instance have sometimes colluded in this thinking, especially if it has resulted in a stud fee for them.

It is also believed that some persons involved with other breeds have started to breed Cavaliers and have cashed in on their popularity, not through genuine interest but simply as a way of subsidising their original breed or breeds.

Cavaliers would be helped if there was a greater emphasis on quality rather than quantity. Breeders who really care for the breed, along with Cavalier Breed Clubs, can together encourage this aim for quality. It is a simple matter for breeders to have registration certificates for poor specimens endorsed 'Progeny not eligible for Registration'. If this has not been done at the time of sale, owners of poor quality stock can be gently and tactfully advised that only really good specimens should be used for breeding.

However, it may not be easy, and sometimes it may be unsuccessful. Let me relate an example from my own experience. I received a phone call enquiring 'Could my stud dog be used today?' The reason for this last minute approach was that the bitch had 'missed' from its last mating to a well known dog. Another mating had been promised but the dog concerned was now seeking its third Challenge Certificate and was attending a show the following day. The stud dog owner therefore did not wish him to be used just prior to the show. It all seemed very reasonable. The bitch was brought to my home and it was an awful specimen, being so untypical. My wife and I spent the whole afternoon gently explaining and persuading that the bitch should not be bred from. We pointed out that her offspring would be unlikely to be a credit to the owner, or to the breed. After several cups of tea and biscuits the bitch's owners seemed to accept the logic of what we had said and left about 5 p.m. to return home. The bitch was taken to another breeder that same evening and mated!

Nevertheless, I still feel that established and knowledgeable breeders should advise appropriately when it is patently obvious that a particular Cavalier should really not be used for breeding. I believe that an increasing number of responsible breeders are now supporting this view.

Thirty years ago it was rare to see another Cavalier, but now they seem to be everywhere. When out walking with Cavaliers it is usual to meet several others. The breed is so popular, and rightly so. But this surely puts a responsibility on established breeders to do all they can to maintain good quality in the breed and to not allow it to be spoiled through increased production. The Code of Ethics gives helpful guidelines which we can use positively.

Growth in Cavalier Clubs

Whilst we have nowhere near the same number of breed clubs as some other breeds e.g. German Shepherds and Cocker Spaniels, nevertheless the growth in Cavalier breed clubs has been significant. The table below shows the dates when different Cavalier clubs were established.

1928   Cavalier King Charles Spaniel Club (the Parent Club)
1946   Three Counties Peke and Cavalier Club
1957   West of England Cavalier King Charles Spaniel Club
1959   Scottish Cavalier King Charles Spaniel Club
1959   Cavalier King Charles Spaniel Club of Ireland
1969   Northern Cavalier King Charles Spaniel Society
1975   Eastern Counties Cavalier King Charles
           Spaniel Society
1976   Midland Cavalier King Charles Spaniel Club
1978   Northern Ireland Cavalier King Charles Spaniel Club
1979   Southern Cavalier King Charles Spaniel Club
1982   South and West Wales Cavalier King Charles Spaniel
           Club
1985   Humberside Cavalier King Charles Spaniel Club

Some Cavalier enthusiasts do not appreciate the length of time that some of the overseas Cavalier clubs have been in existence. For instance the American club was established in 1956, the New South Wales Club of Australia in 1968, the Swedish and Finnish clubs were both established in 1972 and the Canadian Club in 1973 i.e. before some regional British clubs.

There is an annual liaison meeting of the United Kingdom Cavalier Clubs – an excellent idea, but it is as yet at an elementary stage. However it did good work in reaching broad agreement on the important Code of Ethics, which is very much to its credit.

A considerable advantage of having several Cavalier breed clubs is that they can show individual initiative and action, but Cavaliers will also benefit considerably if, on the important matters affecting the breed, the clubs can agree upon concerted action at the liaison meeting.

I know that Mrs Pitt expressed anxieties about any further expansion in the number of breed clubs when there were only five or six in Britain, as she was worried about possible problems associated with fragmentation. I believe that some of her fears have been realized, but that these can be overcome if there is a willingness by all clubs to share information and to work together on important matters.

Entries at Championship Shows

As one would expect, the number of Cavaliers entered at Championship Shows has grown tremendously over the years, commensurate with the growth in popularity of the breed.

The judge of the Cavalier King Charles Spaniel Club's first Championship Show was Mrs B. Jennings of the Plantation Cavaliers. There were thirteen classes for individual dogs, plus classes for litter, brace and team. A total of thirty-eight dogs were entered (not twenty-eight as stated in some reports), plus three litters aged between six weeks and three months. There were 109 entries, plus nine pairs in the brace class and three teams in the team class ('three or more exhibits belonging to the same exhibitor'), making a total of 121 entries. The thirty-eight dogs and three litters that were entered belonged to eighteen exhibitors, none of whom, surprisingly, lived north of Shropshire. Where were the northern Cavalier enthusiasts at this, the first breed championship show held at Stratford-upon-Avon?

The front cover of the catalogue indicates that the Show Secretary and Manager was Mr A.O. Grindey, who also acted as

Secretary to the massive Birmingham All Breeds Championship Show from 1948 to 1984. Add Amice Pitt as Chairman and what an unbeatable brace you had to run the first Cavalier Championship Show. It was the same Mr Grindey who, twenty-seven years later in 1973, set the Cavalier world alight by awarding Hall and Evans' Alansmere Aquarius Best in Show at Crufts.

The Show Regulations in 1946 allowed for equal first prizes to be awarded, but in fact a clear decision was made in each class. Some of the classes were for both sexes. Bitch Challenge Certificate and Best of Breed was Eldred's Belinda of Saxham.

In the Cavalier Club Bulletin of Christmas 1955 Mrs Speedwell Massingham described Belinda of Saxham:

> The one most like him (i.e. Ann's Son) I have ever seen was the lovely Belinda of Saxham, his grand daughter. She was larger and heavier but she had all the points, plus that rare thing 'quality' in excess. She too was Blenheim and had the entirely flat head, and ears about eight inches long – like a Charles the Second wig – which framed her sweet face. She had the great dark eyes set wide apart and long face perfectly shaped capped by the black nose. Perhaps her coat was a touch longer than that of Ann's Son. Her legs were richly frilled and her feet deeply bedded in long silver fringes.
>
> Belinda lived in the hard times of the War and before we had Challenge Certificates she collected many Firsts. She was the first Cavalier to win a Challenge Certificate when they were granted to the breed. Only misfortune prevented her from winning her Third Certificate to seal the Champion she really was ... Belinda had a sweet and gentle disposition matching her beauty. She was by Duke's Son out of Lu Lu and her father was out of Ann's Son by Nightie Night. She has many descendants, Champion Little Dorrit of Ttiweh being one and I have her son James of Turnworth, brother of Champion Little Dorrit, and there are others who are well known winners. Belinda's lucky owner was Mrs Eldred who was wartime Secretary of our Club.

Overleaf is one of the first Challenge Certificates awarded at the very first championship show for Cavaliers – on 29 August 1946.

Katie (Jean) Eldred, the owner of Belinda of Saxham, gave further information about the lovely bitch.

> Thus Jane (Pitt, now Bowdler) and I were the proud owners of the winners of the first Challenge Certificates ever offered for the breed. I still have that Challenge Certificate, together with the second which Belinda won the following August under Mr William Worfolk, a well-known all round judge ... Belinda was due to be

Bitch Challenge Certificate and Best of Breed **Belinda of Saxham**

shown under Mrs Rennie at the Ladies Kennel Association show in 1948 and I was fairly confident of winning the third and qualifying Challenge Certificate as I knew Mrs Rennie liked her. Alas! Five days before the show Belinda had a massive heart attack and had to be euthanized to save further suffering. She was whelped on July 17 1939, was seven years old when she won her first Challenge Certificate and was almost nine when she died. She had been bred twice ...

Dog Challenge Certificate winner was the famous Daywell Roger (described earlier) owned by Miss J. Pitt, now Mrs Jane Bowdler. Daywell Roger took the Challenge Certificate after coming third in Puppy Dog or Bitch, Blenheim or tricolour class, having been beaten by two bitch puppies. Other winners at this first championship show who became well known were Little Dorrit of Ttiweh, Comfort of Ttiweh, Plantation Banjo and Young Pretender of Greenwich. Two not quite so well known winners were Tweetie and Pin-Up Peggie. Regrettably, Standsure

Kissmequick was only awarded a third prize despite the judge describing her thus: 'useful type, good shape, well marked, moves well, nice body and legs'! What a pity we do not have romantic, inviting names like these nowadays. Amongst the special prizes awarded was one for 'Best Mouth'.

The judge's critique included the following comments:

> The bitches generally were a stronger selection than the dogs. I was struck by what appeared to be a wide diversity of type and weight, the latter appearing to range between 10 and 18 lbs. Competition was keen. I was delighted to see the quality of some of the exhibits. Quite a number conformed to the standard absolutely, and only a few of the streamlined, undocked tail variety were present. Most of the exhibits were true spaniel type, compact in body, active in movements, good in heads and mouths; in fact good specimens of what we earlier breeders had worked hard to get and produced just before the war broke out. There were very few black and tans or tricolours present.

In 1956, for the first time, separate judges were appointed for dogs and bitches at the Cavalier Club Jubilee Championship Show. Mrs V. Rennie judged dogs and Mrs Rothwell Fielding judged bitches. Thereafter one judge officiated for both sexes until 1970, since when we have always had two judges at the Cavalier Club Championship Show.

Two judges are now a vital necessity, because of the enormous entries received. At the Club Golden Jubilee Championship Show in 1978 there were 617 dogs entered. Miss P. Turle judged dogs and Mrs V. Preece judged bitches, while the referee was Mrs A. Pitt (fifty years with the Club!). At the Ruby Anniversary of Championship Shows in 1986 there was an even bigger entry of 665 dogs. The judges were Mr Ellis Hulme for dogs and the late Brigadier Jack Burgess for bitches. At the Diamond Jubilee Championship Show in 1988 there were yet more dogs – 760. Judging commenced in both rings at 8.30 a.m., and by 6.00 p.m. Mrs Susan Burgess and Miss Caroline Gatheral were agreed that Caroline of Homerbrent was Best in Show.

Times had changed considerably from the early days. In the late 1940s the small number of Cavalier enthusiasts had shown their dogs tirelessly wherever the breed was scheduled, and especially in variety classes, in order to bring the breed to the notice of the dog world fraternity. Prominent kennels at that time included Mrs Pitt's Ttiwehs, which took the leading role in taking the breed forward; the Hillbarns, owned by Mrs Helen Pilkington; the Crustadeles (Mrs Daphne Murray); and the kennels of the two sisters – the Mingshangs (Miss Phyllis Mayhew) and the Heathersides (Mrs I.J. ('Bunty') Green), who recently judged a massive entry at the Cavalier Club Championship Show and also at Crufts. Over the next decade the Pargeters (Mrs Barbara Keswick), the Sunninghills (Miss Pam Turle) and the Eyeworths (Lady Mary Forwood) came into prominence.

These early pioneers have been succeeded in more recent times by other great breeders. It is a fascinating exercise to try and predict who will be the top successful breeders over the next twenty-five years.

Going back to 1956, the Cavalier Club then had a total membership of 109, which was not large considering the Club had been established 28 years earlier. Five members came from Eire, seven from more distant shores (two from South Africa, two from Holland, one from the USA, one from New Zealand and one from Finland) and 97 came from the United Kingdom, including two from Scotland.

It is interesting to compare the Club's current membership. Total membership just exceeds 2,000, of which 438 are overseas members from 24 countries.

Austria	4	Holland	7
Australia	43	Iceland	1
Barbados	3	Kenya	2
Belgium	1	Malta	1
Brazil	1	Norway	13
Canada	30	New Zealand	23
Denmark	8	South Africa	6
Finland	25	Singapore	1
France	26	Spain	1
Germany	5	Sweden	45
Greece	1	Switzerland	4
Hong Kong	1	USA	186
		TOTAL	438

There are, of course, many more Cavalier enthusiasts in overseas countries. The above list only shows those who are members of the English Cavalier King Charles Spaniel Club.

2

The Breed Standard

The original Breed Standard was drawn up in 1928. Members of the Cavalier Club committee had before them as a live model the Blenheim Ann's Son, who was generally accepted to be the outstanding Cavalier at that time. Additionally, members of the committee had brought all the reproductions they could find of pictures of the sixteenth, seventeenth and eighteenth centuries which contained toy spaniels. Mrs Pitt wrote during the 1930s that in forming the Standard the club decided to aim at the Dutch type of spaniel that appears in paintings of about 1630. The club decided against other types of spaniels of the same period and also against the Landseer types of the 1830s (although a Landseer painting was used to illustrate the special classes funded by Roswell Eldridge at Crufts 1926–30).

Mrs Pitt explained the choice in the following way:

It is continually mentioned by the Hon. Mrs Lytton (in her book *Toy Dogs and Their Ancestors* published in 1911) that there existed several different types of Toy Spaniel even in the 17th century and that the different types have through the years been continually crossed and recrossed by specialist and experimenting breeders. The Cavalier Club, in its wish to breed a type of King Charles Spaniel without some of the modern disadvantages (a dog that could, even when a show specimen, whelp and rear its own puppies without outside help and interference; a dog that could go rabbiting with the best and which needed no coddling; a dog as fitted for a hard country life as to be a lap dog, and also one which did not 'snore' quite so enthusiastically) had several to choose from. The French-Italian type of pretty little Spaniel, with its rounded head, shortish nose, with decided stop, or the plainer Dutch style of Spaniel, with its longer pointed nose, flat head and very little stop. The latter type was chosen at the Club meeting.

Mrs Pitt said that examples of such dogs can be found in paintings reproduced in Mrs Lytton's book, and she mentioned particularly the following:

Page 10 Lady Washing Her Hands – G. Ter Borch about 1650
Page 38 Children of Charles I – Van Dyck about 1632
Page 42 Dutch Picture about 1660
Page 62 Picture at Crabbet Park about 1670
Page 140 Wife of Philippe Le Roy – Van Dyck about 1623
Page 220 Marlborough Blenheims of about 1750–1800

The second painting mentioned above, plus another by Van Dyck featuring the children of Charles I with a toy spaniel and an enormous mastiff, are reproduced in William Secord's book. These are delightful paintings. All the dogs depicted are well broken in colour. With one exception they all have flat skulls, and the exception's slightly rounded skull is probably over-emphasized by low set ears. Their noses are certainly longer and more tapered than present day Cavaliers, but the first Standard clearly stated 'about 1½ inches'.

After long deliberations the Standard, quite brief in its content, was agreed. Mrs Pitt, looking back in 1961, wrote:

> A lot of elasticity was allowed and was necessary when we started as, if the Standard had been too tight, few specimens would have come anywhere near the desired ideal. We all knew we had a long way to go, and also, that given the chance breeders would level out the difficulties.

It says much for the wisdom and foresight of the committee that the basics of the Standard have remained substantially unchanged.

This was the original 1928 Standard:

Drawn up by the Committee of Cavalier King Charles Spaniel Club

STANDARD

Points of old type
Cavalier King Charles and Blenheim Spaniels

	Points
General Appearance and Soundness	
Active, Sporting, Fearless	15
Head. Almost flat between ears no dome spot desired	15
Eyes. Dark, large and round, but not prominent	10
Nose. Slight stop about 1½ inches. Black	10

Muzzle. Pointed	10
Texture of Coat. Long Silky	10
Colour. All recognised	5
Chest. Moderate	
Ears. Long and feathered, high set	10
Tail. Longish, docked	5
Legs and Feet. Moderate bone, feet well feathered	5
Weight. 10 to 18 lbs	5
Faults. Under shot, light eyes	
	100

Disqualifications

The Committee were in accord with the following:

As this was a new and tremendous opportunity to achieve a really worthwhile dog, it was agreed that as far as possible the dog should be guarded from fashion, and there was to be no trimming. A perfectly natural dog was desired, and was not to be spoiled to suit individual tastes, or as the saying goes 'carved into shape'.

In the early 1960s Mrs Pitt said the original Standard 'was left very loose as we knew that we had not got the dogs, but the idea was a small dog of about 16 lb and as you probably know they weigh very heavy, but essentially a toy dog full of quality. That was the aim.' It is interesting that in the original Standard minimum weight was 10 lb; all colours were recognized; and tails were required to be docked.

A later Standard of Points, believed to be 1948 or 1949, was more detailed and the points allocated differed very slightly. The mouth was now required to be level; docking of tails was optional; and the requirements regarding colours were now more tightly drawn in that, apart from the four current colours, the only other colour allowed was black and white, which was said to be 'permissible but not desirable'.

This later Standard of Points reads as follows:

Cavalier King Charles Spaniel Club

STANDARD OF POINTS

GENERAL APPEARANCE - an active, graceful, well-balanced dog. Absolutely fearless and sporting in character and very gay and free in action . . . 15

HEAD - almost flat between the ears, no tendency to dome 15

NOSE - shallow stop, length from base of stop to tip about 1½". Nostrils should be well developed and the pigment black 10

EYES - large, dark and round, but not prominent. The eyes should be spaced well apart 10

MUZZLE - well tapered to the point - level mouth, and lips well covering, but not hound-like 10

EARS - long and high set with plenty of feather 10

BODY - should be short-coupled with plenty of spring of rib - back level - chest moderate, leaving ample heart room - neck should be well set on and shoulder not too straight 5

TAILS - the docking of tails is optional - if short, only one-third to be removed - if long, the length of the tail should be in balance with the body 5

COAT - long and silky - free from curl - slight wave is permissible. Plenty of feather 5

FEET AND LEGS - moderate bone - straight. Feet compact and well-cushioned 5

WEIGHT - 10 to 18 lbs. A small well balanced dog well between these weights is desirable. Classes are provided for miniatures 5

COLOURS - Black and tan - raven black with tan markings above eyes, on cheeks, inside ears, on chest and legs and underside of tail. Tan should be bright . . . .

Ruby - whole-coloured rich red. . . . .

Blenheim - rich chestnut markings well broken-up on a pearly white ground. The markings should be evenly divided on the head, leaving room between the ears for the much valued lozenge mark or spot, a unique characteristic of this breed . . . .

⎫
⎬ 5
⎭

Tricolour - black and white, well spaced and broken-up, with tan markings over the eyes, on cheeks, inside ears, inside legs and on underside of tail . . . .

Black and white - permissible but not desirable . . . .

100

FAULTS - light eyes. Undershot and crooked mouths and pig jaws. White marks on whole coloured specimens. Coarseness of type. Putty noses. Flesh marks. Nervousness.

FOR NOVICES ONLY - In the Cavalier we have a little dog of ideal temperament for nearly all purposes. He is sporting - many of them have been successfully trained to the gun - he is an excellent child's companion; always ready to play - he is equally happy as the much loved and spoiled house pet. In breeding we want to remember this and to try never to lose this delightful happy nature. In so many show breeds that were immune from nerves one now sees nervousness amounting in many cases to panic and snappiness, and therefore we Cavalier breeders have been warned in time and must not let this happen to our breed. The Cavalier is also extremely hardy and must never be allowed to become anything else. Avoid all physical structural weaknesses, shelly bodies, cramped hind quarters with restricted action, pinched pelvises, narrow terrier heads with small mean eyes - all are hereditary faults, easier to breed in than out. The Club will always be willing to give helpful advice to novices through the Secretary.

Although the above states 'Classes are provided for miniatures', Mrs Bunty Green (Heatherside) informs me there never were any classes arranged for 'miniatures'. There were, and still are, occasional classes of 'not exceeding 15 lb' and 'not exceeding 18 lb' in order to try and encourage people to breed to the correct weights.

Ttiweh Champions 1954. *Left to right:* **Jupiter, Alexander, Harmony, Little Dorrit, Comfort, Daywell Roger, Amanda Loo** (black and tan) and **Trilby**

The Standard has since been further revised on two grounds: first, in order to clarify; and second, the Kennel Club has attempted to standardize the format and requirements of all Breed Standards, wherever possible and reasonable. As a result the current Kennel Club Standard takes the following form:

Cavalier King Charles Spaniel

General Appearance Active, graceful and well balanced, with gentle expression.

Characteristics Sporting, affectionate, absolutely fearless.

Temperament Gay, friendly, non-aggressive; no tendency to nervousness.

Head and Skull Skull almost flat between ears. Stop shallow. Length from base of stop to tip of nose about 3.8 cms (1½ inches). Nostrils black and well developed without flesh marks, muzzle well tapered. Lips well developed but not pendulous. Face well filled below eyes. Any tendency to snipiness undesirable.

Eyes Large, dark, round but not prominent; spaced well apart.

Ears Long, set high, with plenty of feather.

Mouth Jaws strong, with a perfect, regular and complete scissor bite, i.e. the upper teeth closely overlapping the lower teeth and set square to the jaws.

Neck Moderate length, slightly arched.

Forequarters Chest moderate, shoulders well laid back; straight legs moderately boned.

Body Short-coupled with good spring of rib. Level back.

Hindquarters Legs with moderate bone; well turned stifle - no tendency to cow or sickle hocks.

Feet Compact, cushioned and well feathered.

Tail Length of tail in balance with body, well set on, carried happily but never much above the level of the back. Docking optional. If docked no more than one-third to be removed.

Gait/Movement Free moving and elegant in action , plenty of drive from behind. Fore and hind legs move parallel when viewed from in front and behind.

Coat Long, silky, free from curl. Slight wave permissible. Plenty of feathering. Totally free from trimming.

Colour Recognised colours are:-

Black and Tan Raven black with tan markings above the eyes, on cheeks, inside ears,on chest and legs and underside of tail. Tan should be bright. White marks undesirable.

Ruby Whole coloured rich red. White markings undesirable.

Blenheim Rich chestnut markings well broken up, on pearly white ground. Markings evenly divided on head, leaving room between ears for much valued lozenge mark or spot (a unique characteristic of the breed)

Tricolour Black and white well spaced, broken up, with tan markings over eyes, cheeks, inside ears, inside legs, and on underside of tail.
Any other colour or combination of colours highly undesirable.

Size Weight - 5.4-8 kgs (12-18lbs). A small well-balanced dog well within these weights desirable.

Faults Any departure from the foregoing points should be considered a fault and the seriousness with which the fault should be regarded should be in exact proportion to its degree.

Note Male animals should have two apparently normal testicles fully descended into the scrotum.

Changes introduced included:

Muzzle	previously 'well tapered to the point' now 'well tapered'
Shoulder	previously 'not too straight' now 'well laid back'
Weight	previously '10 to 18 lbs' now '5.4–8 kgs (12–18 lbs)
Gait/Movement	mentioned under a separate heading for the first time
Faults	previously – were specified now a general statement. It is believed this may have been introduced to discourage 'fault judging'.

Interpretation of the Standard

It is obvious that this relatively brief Standard can only provide a guide. Nevertheless, it contains the essentials which breeders should be aiming for, and judges should be looking for.

The Cavalier King Charles Spaniel Club in 1992 produced a brief and rather useful booklet entitled *Interpretation of the Breed Standard*. This aims to add a little meat to the skeleton of the Breed Standard, and thus assist in achieving a rather fuller understanding. It has been criticized for being far too brief and therefore not giving sufficient information. It is, however, difficult to hit the happy medium and please everyone with a publication of this sort. Within its limitations it makes a useful contribution and provides a concise revision note for anyone about to undertake their first judging appointment.

I propose to look in detail at each part of the Cavalier through the current Standard, and then in the next chapter consider some very important broader issues such as type, soundness and balance. All these matters are inextricably linked and need to be considered together if success is to be achieved with Cavaliers.

But first, before completing this introduction to Cavalier Breed Standards, it is worthy of note that whilst all Standards across the world are based closely on the English version, some go into greater detail and are more precisely defined. For instance the American Standard is more than double the length of the English one, and also has some slight differences in content. For example it specifies an ideal height of twelve to thirteen inches at the withers; it states that whilst a scissor bite is preferable a level bite is permitted; and the nose should be *at least* 1½ inches. The fuller detail of the American Standard can be appreciated by comparing the following sections with those of the English version.

Eyes – Large, round and set well apart; colour a warm, very dark brown, giving a lustrous, limpid look. There should be slight cushioning under the eyes, which contributes much to the sweet, gentle expression characteristic of the breed. Faults: small, almond shaped, prominent or light eyes; white surrounding ring.

Ears – Set high, but not close, on top of the head. Leather long with plenty of feathering and wide enough so that when the dog is alert, the ears fan slightly forward to frame the face.

Body – Short coupled with ribs well sprung but not barrelled. Chest moderately deep, leaving ample heart room. Back level, leading into strong, muscular hindquarters. Slightly less body at the flank than at the rib, but with no tucked-up appearance.

Legs – Forelegs straight and well under the dog, bone moderate, elbows close to the sides. Hindlegs moderately muscled; stifles well-turned; hocks well let down. The hindlegs, viewed from the rear, should parallel each other from hock to heel. Pasterns strong and feet compact with well-cushioned pads. The dog stands level on all four feet. Faults: loose elbows, crooked legs; stifles turned in or out; cow hocks, stilted action, weak pasterns; open feet.

Since its formation in 1956 the Cavalier King Charles Spaniel Club USA has built up a long, proud and considerable experience in Cavaliers. There are now also several regional Cavalier King Charles Spaniel Clubs in the USA.

Many Cavalier breeders from the United Kingdom have judged abroad, and now some Cavalier specialists from other countries are judging in Britain, which is to be welcomed. Whatever the

Chuck Minter's **Fair Oaks Fairfield Poseidon** winning USA 1994 National Speciality Show at Atlanta, Georgia with the judge, George Donaldson (Scotland). (Breeder: Christine Meager)

country of origin, there is little if any difficulty with the various Standards, which in essence are very similar.

Let us now consider how the Standard should be interpreted. To help us to do so the following skeletal diagram of a Cavalier is shown.

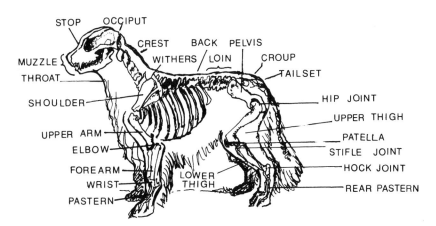

GENERAL APPEARANCE: Active, graceful and well-balanced, with gentle expression.

Much of the history of the breed relates to being a lap dog and comforter. These are important functions, but they do not mean that a Cavalier should sit all day on someone's lap, or on a silk cushion. A Cavalier is an active dog and needs to be exercised daily. Some owners can only manage to take their Cavalier a mile around the local streets or park, but other Cavaliers I know love to accompany their owners on fourteen mile (22 kilometre) hikes, up hill and down dale in the Lake District. A few do some work in the shooting field, flushing and retrieving small game. When in the countryside Cavaliers are alert, busy and active, but when their owner stretches out on a grassy bank to rest the Cavalier is sure to come running back and snuggle up close.

The overall picture of the Cavalier is that it should be graceful and well-balanced with a gentle expression. It needs, therefore, to be well-proportioned and for all parts of the body to fit together into an attractive, harmonious, symmetrical shape that tends to make people say 'What a lovely dog'. A well-balanced Cavalier will be very slightly longer from the withers to the tail than withers to the ground. Whilst no height is mentioned in the British Standard, the height at the withers is usually twelve to

Briggs and Harker's **Champion Emsmere Royalist**

thirteen inches and this is in fact specified in the American Standard. The tail is an important part of the overall picture and should always be wagging happily from side to side.

The gentle expression completes the overall picture. It is often described as a soft melting expression, one that seems to establish an instant friendly rapport. It is the Cavalier's passport to anyone's heart.

The description given is for a mature Cavalier. A puppy, or an immature junior, may still be a little leggy, or not fully 'knit together' and balanced. But with time the poise, balance and gracefulness appear. Some have more of these qualities than others, and they are often the future show winners.

CHARACTERISTICS: Sporting, affectionate, absolutely fearless.

TEMPERAMENT: Gay, friendly, non-aggressive; no tendency to nervousness.

These two categories are best considered in unison, because together they describe the desired personality.

A Cavalier should be gentle and affectionate, of a sunny disposition, eager to please and friendly to all, be they human or canine. It should be a pleasure to meet and be with, because its main role is as a companion dog. A Cavalier loves everybody, particularly its family, and is loved by all. It is especially gentle and affectionate with children. It should not be nervous but in fact be fearless so that it will happily go into any situation, but without being aggressive.

In order to be this agreeable companion it must not be yappy, noisy, demanding or tiresome to be with. Similarly, it must not in any way be sullen, sulky, disagreeable or standoffish.

There is no excuse for a bad-tempered Cavalier. One with a suspect temperament is untypical of the breed, and many would say it should be put down. It certainly should *never* be bred from. The biggest asset and attraction of the breed is its temperament. There can be no compromise or fudging. A Cavalier must be gentle, affectionate, happy, friendly, eager to please and a pleasure to live with.

A Cavalier should be able to fit in with any setting, be it country manor, small terraced house or flat, and with any combination of companions. The American Standard sums up well what is required: '... bad temper and meanness are not to be tolerated and shall be considered disqualifying faults. It is the typical gay temperament, combined with true elegance and 'royal' appearance, which are of paramount importance in the breed.'

For those who have any doubt, however slight, about the importance of breeding to maintain first class temperament, I suggest you read about Tugger, an Irish Terrier, in the American book *The Puppy Report* by Larry Shook. Shook writes of 'a crisis now affecting America's dogs and people who love them' and he is referring specifically to temperament. I am indebted to Pat Winters for sending me a copy of the book.

HEAD AND SKULL: Skull almost flat between ears. Stop shallow. Length from base of stop to tip of nose about 3.8 cms (1½ inches). Nostrils black and well developed without flesh marks, muzzle well tapered. Lips well developed but not pendulous. Face well filled below eyes. Any tendency to snipiness undesirable.

Head study of Briggs and Harker's **Champion Emsmere Royalist**

In the early Standard of Points (page 36) 55 out of 100 were allocated to the total head, i.e. including ears, eyes, muzzle and nose, thus expressing the importance attached to an attractive head. Whilst the points system has long since fallen into disuse a correct and attractive head is still regarded very highly. The head is naturally the first feature one is drawn to. In fact some judges are criticized for going overboard on heads and not paying sufficient attention to other parts of the body when making their assessment.

The skull needs to be almost flat between the ears, and most heads today fulfil this requirement. Breeders have successfully bred away the 'well domed skull' of the King Charles Spaniel. The ears need to be set high, otherwise the almost flat skull image is lost. The skull also needs to be wide enough to enable the eyes to be 'spaced well apart'. If the skull is narrow, the width necessary for the eyes is lost, and this tends to provide a mean expression. On the other hand, if the skull is too wide it can make the head look coarse. Either of these two extremes would make the head untypical. A puppy may have a prominent occiput i.e. back point of the skull which will provide the necessary width when the head 'breaks' as the puppy gets older.

The stop should be shallow. Some persons find this difficult to understand. It does not mean as shallow as with some breeds, e.g. Collie, but shallow when compared with the King Charles Spaniel. The latter has a well-defined stop with its very short nose upturned to meet the skull. When compared to this the Cavalier's stop has to be much shallower. Half-way between the Collie and King Charles Spaniel would be about right.

The length of the nose from base of stop to tip of nose is 'about 3.8 cms (1½ inches)', whereas the American Standard says at least 1½ inches. Mrs Pitt observed in the 1950s: 'It is always a disappointment to me to see a short-faced Cavalier winning high honours as it shows a lack of appreciation of the beauty of the real type, and the years of work which went to make it.'

Nostrils should be black and well-developed without flesh marks. Black nose pigment is something that many breeders are currently finding difficult to achieve. It is not a new problem, as Susan Burgess noted when she judged Crufts in 1979: 'One of the biggest problems appeared to be pigmentation. The majority of the Blenheim and rubies, some tricolours and at least one black and tan had off-colour noses, which was horrifying. The weather has not helped but when tricolours and black and tans are affected surely this is a danger signal we cannot ignore.'

I have found that if a puppy has pink skin showing through the hair under the nose, and on the chin, then the likelihood is that nose pigment will not be a strong black, and with time is likely to deteriorate. Too many Cavaliers have 'off-colour' noses ranging from not quite jet black, through shades of grey and brown, to a fawn, all of which detract from the desired expression.

It has always been known that the nose pigment of some

bitches will vary slightly as they come into season, or when they have a litter, and pigment is therefore felt by some to be related to hormones. It is also known that nose pigment in some dogs and bitches deteriorates in the winter. Whilst there is little authoritative information written about pigmentation, the rather poor nose pigment found today in many Cavaliers suggests it is a matter not receiving sufficient attention in breeding programmes. Bitches with poor pigment are being used for breeding, and it seems likely that some are being mated by dogs from lines with poor pigment, thus compounding the problem. Doubling up on a fault is a sure way of perpetuating, and indeed increasing, the problem.

Products like seaweed and elderberry, and certain homoeopathic concoctions, do not improve pigment, despite the claims made. The only way to improve pigmentation is by using breeding stock which has jet black pigment. Under no circumstances consider using false colouring to the nose – it is misleading and it is against Kennel Club rules and the Cavalier Club's Code of Ethics. Unfortunately, a few unscrupulous exhibitors are believed by some experienced judges to be cheating in this way. They need to be winkled out through having occasional spot checks on suspect dogs. Perhaps this is a matter which could be discussed at the annual Liaison Meeting of Breed Clubs and a strategy determined.

Nostrils should also be well developed and without flesh marks. Some young Cavaliers with small flesh marks may lose them as they mature, and when these small areas 'black in' they usually are dense black, and the pigment often remains good for the future. Those Cavaliers with larger flesh marks which remain into adulthood give an unfortunate 'odd look'. Flesh marks seem to be more prevalent in certain lines. It therefore seems risky to breed from a mature Cavalier still showing flesh marks as there is a likelihood that the fault will be reproduced in some progeny, possibly extending beyond the next generation. Incidentally, for those not conversant with the phrase, 'a butterfly nose' is sometimes used to describe flesh marks.

The muzzle is to be 'well tapered'. Some newcomers find this a little difficult to grasp. The muzzle should not be box like, or pinched, but nicely tapered without being pointed.

The lips should be 'well developed but not pendulous'. In other words, the lips should not hang below the lower jaw as with hounds. The Standard does not mention colour of the lips, but if they are black they complement the dark features of the nose and eyes and add to the attractiveness of the head. There should be no throatiness, double chin or thick hanging jowls.

The head should be well filled below the eyes. This is often referred to as cushioning and is important because it gives a nicely rounded look. The cheeks, however, must not be too full as they can then contribute towards a coarse looking head. Neither should there be any tendency to snipiness i.e. the contour of the face should not fall away too quickly beneath the eyes. The correct degree of cushioned, or padded, effect gives added appeal to the head and expression. A puppy often takes time to develop the cushioning.

When considering the head we are therefore seeking the individual features to be well balanced, so that they fit together harmoniously, thus providing the sweet, gentle and soft expression which is so important in Cavaliers.

A dog's head should be slightly broader, with a more masculine tone, than the head of a bitch, which will be slightly smaller, more feminine and pretty.

The drawings overleaf illustrate the points that have been made about the head.

EYES: Large, dark, round but not prominent; spaced well apart.

Judges often drool and wax lyrical over really nice eyes in Cavaliers.

It has already been stated that eyes need to be spaced well apart. They should also be large, round and dark brown. Although large, they should not appear bulbous or protruding because such eyes can appear to give a terrified expression and look awful. Small eyes, almond shaped eyes, or those that are too light, being hazel or even yellow tinged, can contribute to a hard, mean expression, whereas the Standard demands a 'gentle expression'. The rims to the eyes should also be dark but today there are many Cavaliers, even big winners, with white rims. Certainly the dark surrounding ring helps to give the total eye that lustrous, limpid look required by the American Standard.

Correct eyes do so much to bring about the desired soft, gentle expression. In her judge's critique for the Bath Championship Show of 1956 Mrs Pitt said: 'I should like to comment on the light eyes which were very prevalent. Breeding in a fault like this is a fault we have inherited from certain big winners and we shall have to be firmer in our breeding programmes as it is ugly to say the least.' The problem was still present to a certain extent fifteen years ago but has lessened in recent years. Light eyes are now rather the exception. This is good news and shows what can be done by skilful breeding.

There have been problems with some eyes being too small. As

Correct head and correct ear
placement

Domed head. Incorrect ear
placement

Correct stop

Too deep

Too shallow

Correct muzzle and cush-
ioning under eyes

Too snipey. No cushioning
under eyes

Too much cushioning under
eyes

Hound lips and throatiness

Correct lips and throat

long ago as 1957, after judging the Cavalier Club Open Show Miss M.D. Barnes wrote: 'Is there a tendency for eyes to be getting smaller? Big dark eyes are imperative or we shall lose the true gentle expression.' In 1965 C.G.E. Wimhurst in *The Book of Toy Dogs* stated: 'there is a tendency for the large eye to shrink in size.' This problem is still with us today to a certain extent, and I believe it is rather more prevalent amongst tricolours. However, the recent reports of some judges suggest that the situation may now be starting to improve very slightly. Let us hope that this progress can be maintained because eyes can make or mar the expression and head – they are that important.

Hull's **Telvara Karbon Kopy**

EARS: Long, set high, with plenty of feather.

Ears are required to be set high in order to enhance the almost flat skull. If they are set too low they make the skull appear rounded, even if it is not. When a Cavalier hears an unusual sound, or is alert, it is often possible to see the ears lift higher on the head, and they then tend to fan forward nearer to the eyes and cheeks, giving a picture frame effect.

The ears of all four colours of Cavaliers should have long feathering. In practice it is often found that tricolours have particularly long feathering, followed closely by black and tans, with the Blenheims and rubies being a little less profuse.

Cavalier ears being of the penchant type, wide and heavily feathered, they need regular attention to keep them clean and free from wax and mites (for more information see Chapter 8).

MOUTH: Jaws strong, with a perfect, regular and complete scissor bite i.e. the upper teeth closely overlapping the lower teeth and set square to the jaws.

Very important changes have taken place in the Breed Standard relating to mouths, viz:

1928 Standard:	made no mention of mouths under points, but faults included 'Undershot'.
1948–1970:	'Mouth – Level' but faults included 'Undershot'.
1970–1985:	'Mouth – Level; scissor bite preferred'.
1986 onwards:	'a perfect, regular and complete scissor bite'.

These changes are understandable because breeders have had since 1925, or certainly since 1945, to produce the distinctive Cavalier head and mouth. It is appreciated that breeding a particular type is undoubtedly a long term project. But approximately fifty years from 1945, or seventy years from 1925, is a reasonable period during which it can be expected that we should have substantially achieved the desired mouth. That is, I believe, the reasoning behind the important changes made to the Standard.

The fact remains that we still have something of a problem with Cavaliers being produced with incorrect mouths. We therefore still have progress to make in breeding this out. Bad mouths are hereditary, so as long as breeders continue to use stock for breeding which have incorrect mouths, or come from lines with this fault, the problem will continue. It will haunt such breeders – if not in the first generation, the probability is that it will recur in the second and subsequent generations. Some breeds, e.g. Bull Terriers, have not paid sufficient attention to this problem and have paid dearly for it over a long period.

Many see a bad mouth as a structural fault of some importance. Therefore it is no surprise that in many breeds a bad mouth is a complete bar to success in the show ring. I believe this applies almost completely to Cavaliers. This seems both understandable and reasonable, in view of the changes made to the Breed

Standard over the years, and in view of what is so clearly expected now. Therefore I am surprised by the 'Interpretation of the Breed Standard' published by the Cavalier King Charles Spaniel Club in 1992 which states: 'A slightly undershot or level bite in a young pup could be overlooked as many will come correct by 18–24 months.' I believe this is flawed in two ways.

First, a judge has always been expected to judge what he sees before him on the day. It is unrealistic to expect him to be able to foresee whether an undershot mouth will have changed to a scissor bite in six or twelve months' time. No one can guarantee that, not even the breeder who knows the line well. I suspect that a considerable majority of undershot mouths remain undershot, and it is only a small, possibly a very small, minority that change to a correct scissor bite.

Second, by stating that an incorrect mouth can be overlooked in a young pup there is an implied suggestion that incorrect mouths are not as important as the developmental changes in the Breed Standard would indicate. The current Standard clearly states 'a perfect, regular and complete scissor bite', and I believe judges and breeders should stick to that requirement. If an exhibitor shows a puppy with an incorrect mouth, the exhibitor should not expect any clairvoyant allowances from the judge. If the owner is convinced the mouth will come right the sensible solution is that the puppy is held back from the show-ring until the 'bite' is correct.

The scissor bite, as the name implies, requires the upper teeth to close tightly over the lower teeth as they overlap. When a faulty mouth is found in a Cavalier it is usually that the upper teeth do not overlap, and in fact drop in behind the lower set. This is when the mouth is said to be undershot. A mouth may also be level, i.e. have a pincer bite, which occurs when the upper set of teeth rest on top of the lower set. That is also classed as an incorrect mouth. An overshot mouth is when the top teeth overlap the bottom teeth, and there is a gap between them. The gap can vary from slight to substantial, as with a pig or a parrot, and these descriptive terms are sometimes used. Of course though some pet Cavaliers may be either undershot or overshot, their owners will have realized that they eat perfectly successfully.

A badly overshot Cavalier is a rarity. However I well remember at Birmingham Championship Show an exhibitor storming out of the ring, fuming. She thrust her dog at the friend to whom I was talking and demanded, 'Have a look at him. The Judge said he could not place him higher than third because he is overshot.' The dog was a junior with several recent firsts to his credit at Championship Shows. When my friend opened the dog's mouth there was quite a definite gap between the two sets of teeth and the dog was indeed overshot. But earlier judges had either not spotted the condition or, alternatively, had regarded it of little importance.

I have noticed that a small number of adult Cavaliers now have quite tiny teeth, almost like weak baby teeth. I cannot see them being of much use in chomping up food. Perhaps such dogs only eat sloppy food. A full set of good, strong teeth provide a useful set of tools to any dog. A Cavalier should have forty-two teeth made up of twelve incisors; four canine, eye or fang teeth; sixteen pre-molars; and ten molars. The incisor teeth at the front are used for slicing, hence the importance of the scissor bite; the fangs are for gripping, hence their greater length, pointedness and strong roots; and the molars are used for grinding. Pre-molars are general purpose teeth. The whelping bitch uses the incisors to release newly born puppies from the foetal sac, and the molars to grind and sever the strong umbilical cord.

Judges on the Continent often pay much greater attention to teeth than British judges and have been known to count them. I have seen a number of Cavaliers with only ten instead of twelve incisors. I am not sure of the reason for this. Possibly it is because the dog has a slightly narrow jaw with insufficient space for twelve incisors, or there may be a hereditary factor involved.

A wry mouth is fortunately an extreme rarity with Cavaliers. A wry mouth is when one of the jaws, usually the lower, is twisted to one side and is out of line with the upper jaw. It is inadvisable to breed from a Cavalier with a wry mouth.

Occasionally, one sees owners playing a game with their dog. It is a kind of tug of war with a piece of rope, cloth, or a specially purchased plastic toy. Sometimes the game extends beyond the tug of war to swinging the dog off its feet, and twirling round and round with the dog off the ground. Some stronger jawed breeds may be able to take this without damage to their teeth or jaw, but for a Cavalier, especially a young one, I would regard it as the height of folly. I suspect considerable damage might be caused to the teeth or the set of the jaw.

This section has needed to be fairly detailed and the following drawings will provide a kind of recap and illustrate correct and faulty mouths.

NECK: Moderate length, slightly arched.

An attractive arched neck of the correct length, flowing from the

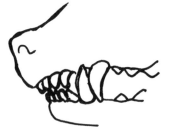

(a) Correct scissor bite

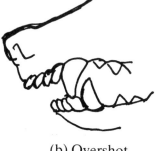

(b) Overshot

(c) Undershot

skull into a level back, helps considerably in providing a picture of beauty and elegance, both standing and on the move. The neck needs to be sufficiently long for the head to be carried proudly high, which contributes to the elegance, and also enables true, unrestricted, stylish front movement.

If the neck is too short the Cavalier looks stuffy and heavy around the neck and shoulders and loses much of its elegance. Too short a neck is often accompanied by too straight shoulders, and the dog not only looks unbalanced but movement usually suffers as well. Whilst the arched topline of the neck should flow in a graceful line, similarly the lower neckline should also be 'clean' with the skin fitting snugly at the throat.

The need for the neck to be of 'moderate length and slightly arched' is of course not just for aesthetic reasons. The area around the arch of the neck is the anchor point for many muscles, ligaments and tendons – the arch acts similarly to the keystone in an archway and is the strength point. The moderate length also permits rather longer muscles than would be possible in a short, stuffy neck. These rather longer muscles contribute to better movement because longer muscles tire less quickly than short, heavy ones. The length of the neck obviously needs to be in balance with the remainder of the Cavalier.

Hill and Webber's **Phloxcarn Spring Bluebell at Montcolly**. (Breeder: Jean Newell)

FOREQUARTERS: Chest moderate, shoulders well laid back; straight legs moderately boned.

The chest needs to be moderately wide and in balance with the overall size of the particular Cavalier. Sufficient chest and body width is needed to provide ample room for the heart and lungs, and for the front legs to be appropriately distanced from each other.

Some dog experts rate shoulders as being the most important part of any dog. This is not surprising as correct shoulders can give so many positive benefits. I have mentioned earlier the importance of correctly angled shoulders in order to obtain a good reach of neck, flowing outline, balance and natural long-striding movement.

It is generally agreed a good lay back of shoulder blade (or scapula) is required. But what does this mean and how is it measured? This matter needs to be considered carefully as substantially differing views have been expounded. Let us first consider what the breed standards state. An earlier British Standard, believed to have been introduced in 1948 or 1949, stated 'shoulder not too straight'. But the current British

Standard states 'shoulders well laid back'. However the American Standard states: 'Shoulders – should slope back gently with moderate angulation.' We are not just concerned with semantics, because there are *now* two quite differing views of the correct lay back of the shoulder.

In the past many respected authorities, including R.H. Smythe, MRCVS, McDowell Lyon, and Lawrence M. Kalstone, stated categorically the correct inclination of the shoulder blade should be 45 degrees to the ground. Faulty, i.e. too upright, shoulders were said to be angled at 55 to 60 degrees to the ground. There was general agreement about these so called 'facts'. For instance Lyon in *The Dog in Action* emphatically stated that a shoulder blade angled at 45 degrees was much more efficient than one of 60 degrees. He said the 45 degree blade is longer and wider with larger supporting muscles. It gives far better lift, length of stride and therefore better locomotion generally, which is less fatiguing to the dog. If there is strong drive from behind, i.e. from the rear legs, as required in the Cavalier, then the front assembly, of which the shoulder blade is the foundation, has to be able to accommodate this rear drive and respond to it. Lyon states the 45 degree shoulder can work much more effectively than the 60 degree shoulder.

Lyon advised not to underestimate the importance of correctly laid shoulder blades in small dogs (like Cavaliers), making the point that they are vital to every dog for efficient comfortable movement. Consider also that a Cavalier jumping from a chair receives more concussion to its joints, relatively, than a horse jumping fences in the Grand National.

Lyon suggests that when assessing the slope or angle of the shoulder blade one should feel the raised ridge in the centre of the blade and relate this as an angle to the ground.

But in 1983 Rachel Page Elliott's book *The New Dogsteps* appeared. It was an impressive, persuasive publication as the author had used ordinary x-rays and cineradiography (moving x-rays) in her observations. She made the point that measurements of angles can vary, depending upon which bone prominences are used for measuring, and that placing the legs in slightly different positions can affect the angles. Nevertheless, she clearly stated the 45 degree slope of the shoulder 'is only a myth' and that such 'a position would be a mechanical impossibility to the dog's function'. She provided what many feel is convincing evidence for her assertion. Mrs Elliott describes the correct angle of the shoulders as 30 degrees off a vertical plane, which of course means 60 degrees off the horizontal. This angle had previously been described by many as being too upright, resulting in the shoulder being considered faulty and inefficient in its functioning.

Previous writers had also stated that the angle between the shoulder blade and the upper arm (or humerus) should be about 90 degrees. Mrs Elliott's conclusion regarding the shoulder blade being more upright has an effect on the angle between the shoulder and the upper arm. I believe many breeders and judges would welcome further studies being made as Mrs Elliott's well researched evidence has created some confusion regarding what is the *correct* lay back of the shoulder blade.

We can still say, however, that shoulders must be of good length, laid back and inclined towards each other at the top. The shoulder blades almost come together at the withers, but do not touch.

The upper arm, which is the next bone down from the shoulder, is also vitally important and needs to be of good length and well laid back i.e. not too upright. If a dog has the correct length and angle of both shoulder and upper arm, it is likely to have well placed elbows that do not protrude, and the forelegs will be well under the body. This not only results in a good tight front, and usually straight forelegs, but also in optimum weight distribution.

Shoulders which are too straight can result in a dip behind the withers, thus spoiling the topline. This is because upright shoulders do not give the necessary support to the vertebral column. Wrongly angled shoulders and upper arm, and too short a forearm, can result in a stilted, shortened stride in front movement, even reaching a high stepping hackney action in the worst cases. Where there is slackness of the elbows, the dog when moving is likely to resort to pinning, or occasionally to throw its feet the other way i.e. outwards. When a dog is too short in the back this is often accompanied by upright shoulders, and occasionally by too much barrelling of the ribs which can push out the elbows.

The pastern is the lower part of the leg just above the foot (see drawing). It should be strong, straight and supple, thus facilitating a proud upright stance when motionless, but also assisting a positive driving movement. Pasterns act as a kind of shock absorber, cushioning the impact of each step. If the pastern is weak and bent, the dog is said 'to be down on its pasterns'.

The legs should be straight with the feet facing the front, and neither turned in nor out. The bone should be moderate – that is, not thin and spindly like a chicken, nor thick and heavy as in a Clumber Spaniel but a nicely rounded moderate bone that is appropriate to the Cavalier's size.

Front view showing
correct front

Front view showing out
at elbows

Front view showing
weak pasterns

Side view showing weak
pasterns

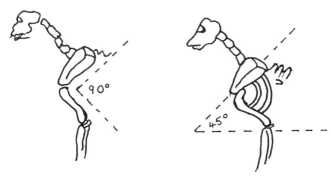

Previously regarded as correctly placed shoulders, this view is now challenged by Rachel Page Elliott

BODY: Short-coupled with good spring of rib. Level back.

Hughes' **Champion Loranka's Romancer**

I have already mentioned the importance of a correct topline. From the flat skull comes the graceful arched neck, which ideally then flows into a perfectly level back. The level back should be maintained when both standing and on the move; it should not dip or roach in any way. Nor should it slope from withers to the tail.

The length of the back should be well proportioned to the other parts of the body, particularly the neck, so that it all seems to fit together in a balanced way. Short-coupled refers only to the loin, that small part of the back between the ribs and the pelvis. The croup is that part of the spinal column from the last vertebra of the loin to the first of the tail. If the pelvis is at a correct angle of about 30 degrees this permits longer muscles from it to the stifle, and also allows the rear leg to swing well backwards, both of which assist in producing the required drive from behind. A bitch may often be forgiven if she is slightly longer bodied, for this is helpful when she is in whelp, since it allows more room for the puppies.

There needs to be a good spring of rib, but this does not mean a wide barrelled shape. Nor is slab-sided acceptable, as this reduces space for heart and lungs and also looks very unattractive. It is the happy medium which is required.

The American Standard gives further helpful information by stating: '... Back level, leading into strong muscular hindquarters. Slightly less body at the flank than at the last rib but with no tucked-up appearance.'

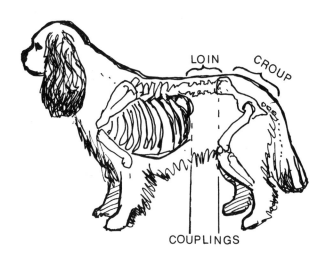

Loin, croup and short coupled

HINDQUARTERS: Legs with moderate bone; well turned stifle – no tendency to cow or sickle hocks.

The moderate bone called for is the happy medium between the too thin and spindly, and the too thick and heavy. Either of these extremes would look out of place on a Cavalier and would therefore be untypical. Once again we need to be thinking of balance and proportion, as related to the total Cavalier.

The bones and their alignment which make up the hindquarters can easily be seen in the drawings towards the end of this section. The pelvis is the uppermost bone in the hindquarters group. It needs to be broad and very slightly sloped. If it is narrow it may result in hind movement being rather close.

The stifle in the hindquarters is of similar importance as the shoulders in the forequarters. A well turned stifle, with well developed muscle on the thigh, greatly assists in producing the required strong driving rear movement. A nicely turned stifle also makes a useful contribution to the shape and attractiveness of the Cavalier, particularly in profile. Conversely, a straight stifle gives a rigid wooden appearance to the hindquarters, and this is often borne out by weak, short stepped movement which does not flow.

An important part of the stifle joint is the patella. An occasional problem arises in most small breeds, including Cavaliers, with what is described in various ways as slipping patella, patella luxation, slipping stifle or stifle dysplasia. W.A. Priester (1972) found that small breeds (under 9 kg adult weight) had a twelve times greater chance of encountering the problem than large dogs. The patella, or kneecap, is a small bone which runs in a groove and moves up and down as the leg is straightened or bent. Dislocation occurs when the patella slips out of the groove, often because the groove is abnormally shallow. Dislocation is painful to the dog. The dislocation can be corrected temporarily by manipulation but often recurs. A more permanent solution is possible by corrective surgery. The defect is hereditary. Therefore stock with this defect, or those suspected of carrying the gene, should not be used for breeding. As the defect usually appears at about ten months, i.e. before a dog reaches the age for breeding, there should be no problem in avoiding breeding from afflicted stock, be it dog or bitch. A straight stifle can be a contributory cause to a slipping patella.

HOCKS – Some disagreement arises over the correct terminology to use in describing that section of the rear leg which corresponds in humans to the ankle down to the heel. Many dog breeders use the word 'hock' to describe the whole section. However some, including Geoffrey Corish and Rachel Page Elliott, feel that 'hock' should only be used to describe the bony joint or protrusion, and that the length below should be described as the rear pastern. The Kennel Club, in its 'Glossary of Terms', relates the pastern to the forelegs only.

Having pointed out the differences over terminology I propose, with a little reluctance, to use the word 'hock' to describe not only the bony joint but also the section below, down to the heel. I am prompted to do so for two rather compelling reasons: (1) this is the most commonly accepted usage in Britain; and (2) the Breed Standard refers only to hocks, not hock joints and rear pasterns. (In fact the British Breed Standard for Cavaliers makes no mention of pasterns, front or rear.)

Hocks should be straight and short from hock joint to ground. It is often said that hocks should be 'well let down', and this term is actually used in the American Standard. When moving and viewed from behind, the dog's hocks should move straight and parallel to each other, with no tendency to cow or bow hocks. Cow hocked describes when the hock bony joints turn inwards towards each other with the feet turning outwards. Bow or sickle hocked is when there is an inability to extend the hock joint on the backward drive of the hind leg with a resultant shuffling motion, and the hock bony joints turn outwards away from each other with the feet turning inwards. A sickle hocked dog, as the description implies, usually stands with its hocks bent under it, rather than their being upright and vertical.

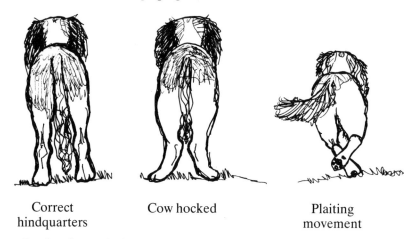

Correct hindquarters   Cow hocked   Plaiting movement

Lack of angulation at the stifle is often matched by a lack of appropriate angulation in the hock joint, and then movement suffers considerably from the combined faults and may result in 'plaiting' or 'knitting'.

There is an old saying that if they are made right, they will move right. The late Florence Nagle, who was an expert in breeding livestock as well as dogs, once said: 'I can get a head in one mating but hindquarters and fronts take generations – guard them with your life once you have them.'

International **Champion Faustine des Marliviers** owned by Danielle Marchand (France)

Several years ago the then President of the Cavalier King Charles Spaniel Club raised a specific matter which concerned her, i.e. some people keeping Cavaliers in cages, and asked 'I wonder if this is perhaps why we see so many bad hindquarters, bad movers and dogs down on their pasterns.' I cannot recall hearing of any responses to the President's expression of concern. I believe keeping any dogs in cages for much of their lives is wrong in principle and, thankfully, I believe it does not happen too often with Cavaliers. Confinement in cages may adversely affect movement, but there are many Cavaliers who do not spend much of their time in cages but who move badly, simply because they are made incorrectly.

FEET: Compact, cushioned and well feathered.

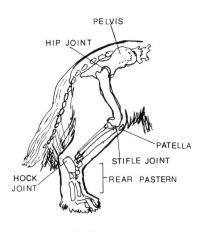

Hindquarters

Feet should be compact, rounded and neither catlike nor hare-footed. They should be well cushioned, which simply means they should have thick, springy pads. If a puppy has small, black pigmented areas on its pads it often means that, if a Blenheim, it will have good nose pigment and rich coat colouring in its adult life. The toes should be arched. Flat open feet can be hereditary, or caused by faulty care.

If nails get overlong they need to be clipped as walking on such nails can make the feet splay out, which is very difficult to correct. If most of a dog's exercise is done on a hard floor, this may well keep the nails rubbed down. However many experienced breeders believe that exercise runs should not be of concrete or paving slabs because, although easy to keep clean, they have two serious disadvantages. First, they encourage the feet to 'splay' out, and, second, as rain and urine tend to stand on concrete or slabs, even if on a slope, the feet of Cavaliers often develop a quite pronounced pink or fawn stain. This stain detracts from the appearance required in the showring, and once acquired it is very hard to eradicate. A much better base for the runs is ¾'' cleaned granite to a depth of 6''–8'', which ensures that moisture quickly drains off the surface, thus avoiding the staining. The small loose stones also help to keep the feet compact.

Excess hair between the pads should be clipped, as otherwise it becomes bulky and makes movement uncomfortable. This is particularly required when snow is on the ground because the dog can find it difficult trying to walk on four 'snowballs'. Feet and legs should be well feathered.

In some breeds judges pay some attention to feet, but this rarely seems to happen with Cavaliers.

TAIL: Length of tail in balance with body, well set on, carried happily but never much above the level of the back. Docking optional. If docked no more than one-third to be removed.

The tail should be a continuation of the spine, coming off level or slightly below the back. The angle at which the croup and pelvis

Meenan's Irish **Champion Sancem Emerald Lady**

are set will have an effect on the tail set. 'Well set on' simply means correct placement of tail on the body. Some dogs that carry their tails too high tend to have too straight stifles. The poor angulation of the hindquarters results in the tail being too highly set, and therefore carried 'gaily', i.e. too high.

The prevalence of gay tails concerns me greatly. I much prefer the clarity and preciseness of the American Standard on this matter. It simply states 'Set so as to be carried level with the back'. The English Standard, on the other hand, is woolly and vague. What does it mean when stating 'carried happily but never much above the level of the back'? Different people could argue that 20 degrees, 30 degrees or even 40 degrees above the back all conform to the Standard. Twenty-five years ago tails, with very few exceptions, were invariably swished absolutely level with the back, and how much nicer it looked than the present-day gay tails, flag-pole tails or even curled over tails. These tails spoil the topline, look awful in profile and revolting from the rear – the term 'monkey bummed' is often politely employed, with a rather cruder description used on occasions.

One judge recently expressed what many had been thinking

when she said 'I detest the choking and cowing that goes on to try and keep the tail low. Why don't you just breed for it? It is quicker and kinder in the long run!'

The problem is now so widespread that it is often necessary, when judging, to award prizes to dogs carrying their tails too high. If one fault judged on this issue and ruled out all the gay tails, there would be very few dogs left in some classes. The problem is also present overseas and is now one that needs urgent and close attention by breeders. It could also be very helpful if one breed club would undertake to research the problem.

These days there are a very small number of Cavaliers appearing in the show-ring with wry tails i.e. held more or less permanently over to one side. Lyon says this is because one of the two lateralis muscles which activate the top side of the tail is weak. He also says, more worryingly, that it is usually 'safe to conclude that muscles which are not functioning correctly at their terminals are not doing any better along the spinal column', and cautions to 'beware of any type tail that is not normally characteristic of the specific breed'.

Regarding the length of tail, the practice of docking up to one-third has been gradually less used over the years. Molly Marshall of the Kormar prefix advertised as long ago as 1955 her 'undocked' wholecolours. The probability is that in recent years

Gay tail   Low set croup and gay tail

Nervous – tail clamped   Correct tail carriage

only a very small proportion have been docked. Some would say it is outmoded. What this suggests is that some, possibly many, Cavaliers are now naturally producing 'correct' length tails in balance with the body, thus obviating the need for docking. Susan Burgess stated 'Crisdig tails certainly became shorter over the years.'

GAIT/MOVEMENT: Free moving and elegant in action, plenty of drive from behind. Fore and hind legs move parallel when viewed from in front and behind.

Lillian C. Raymond Mallock in her book *Toy Dogs*, published in 1915, wrote: 'The movement of Toy Spaniels in the show ring at the present time is notoriously bad.' Whilst judges still criticize the movement of Cavaliers from time to time, I believe our breed has made greater improvement in this respect, since separate registration in 1945, than have King Charles Spaniels. Nevertheless, we now need to try and further improve the movement of Cavaliers, so that we draw nearer the better moving breeds.

The Cavalier in motion should show a good length of stride and move with drive. Movement needs to be stylish and carried out in a smooth, flowing manner. It needs to be done economically with not too high a stride, instead reaching out and covering the ground well, and it should prove effortless to the dog.

When the dog is viewed moving away, the Standard requires that the hocks should move straight and parallel with each other and show plenty of drive and follow through to the rear. In profile the movement will show the length of stride, head carriage, neck and topline, tail carriage, overall balance, and whether the dog is 'free moving and elegant in action.' Any high stepping action, or pacing, will be easy to see. When the dog is approaching the judge, the Standard again requires that the legs should be straight and parallel, with no signs of waving elbows, pinning or paddling.

Movement in fact provides a graphic illustration of conformation. I find it surprising, therefore, that the otherwise fairly comprehensive American Standard says so little about movement.

In recent years a different view, supported by strong photographic evidence, has been expressed as to what constitutes correct movement. This is considered in the next chapter.

COAT: Long, silky, free from curl. Slight wave permissible. Plenty of feathering. Totally free from trimming.

Stanley's **Champion Genu 'n' Emerald of Astraddle**. (Breeder: Mrs J. Wealthall)

The Breed Standard requirements for coats are simply expressed and easily understood. The American Standard is a little more detailed but basically covers the same points. It does, however, state 'very soft to the touch', which most would infer from 'silky' in the English Standard.

Coats have undoubtedly improved. In the past there were more curly coats and these were often of a coarser texture than the required 'silky' feel. There also used to be much more colour 'ticking' or flecking in coats. This applied particularly to tricolours, but also to some Blenheims. Heavy ticking detracted from the appearance, and the present day clearer markings are much more pleasing to the eye. Also in the past muzzles were often spotted, sometimes quite heavily, but now they are usually quite clear, which complements the clarity of the body markings. But we must remember, as one prominent judge frequently reminds us, that a few spots on the muzzle are of little significance. I have in fact heard the purchaser of a pet puppy say, 'Oh I'll have the one with the beauty spots. Aren't they cute.'

The coat is an important feature of the breed. It should be richly coloured, fine, soft, straight and silky, and with profuse feathering which provides an attractive frill to the lower outlines. The chest has a frothy ruff and the legs, undercarriage and tail have their attractive hanging fringes. Additionally, the coat should be finished with a sheen to further enhance the visual impact. A well made typical, happy Cavalier, in full coat, is a picture to cherish.

There are four important factors which contribute to a really good coat:

1. BREEDING. Some lines are noted for their excellent long coats of correct texture. Joan Winters' Kentonvilles always seem to be well coated. It must be a built-in factor in her line.
2. CORRECT FEEDING. Well balanced meals containing all the necessary elements are essential. If a Cavalier is fed a diet deficient in certain essentials, then its coat will not be at its best.
3. REGULAR GROOMING. Daily grooming is advisable. This ensures the coat never gets into a bad state.
4. CONDITION. Assuming a dog does not have a skin disease, then its coat indicates its inner well being. A dog that is happy and is regularly exercised will be fit, content and alert, and this shows in its coat. On the other hand, a dog that is unfit, listless and bored because it receives very little attention or stimulation is very unlikely to have a good coat. Condition and coat go together.

Most coats do not develop fully until about eighteen months. Bitches tend to drop some coat at each oestrus or 'season', and when they have had a litter they lose nearly all their coat and usually do not regain full coat for about nine months. Dogs generally carry more coat than bitches. As a Cavalier reaches the veteran stage sometimes, but by no means always, the coat may become a little wavy.

Regarding trimming the Standard is quite explicit: 'Totally free from trimming'. The only trimming that should be done is underneath the foot between the pads, and this is for the comfort of the dog. In 1928 the committee when drawing up the Standard felt that 'as far as possible the dog should be guarded from fashion, and there was to be no trimming. A perfectly natural dog was desired.'

Colour

Whilst nicely broken markings contribute greatly to the picture presented by a tricolour or Blenheim, one has to appreciate that wholecolours, as their name implies, do not have the advantage of well broken markings with which to impress. Many judges, in fact, are not too concerned if a Blenheim or tricolour is rather heavily marked, giving greater consideration to such matters as type, conformation, balance and soundness. On the old Standard of Points only 5 out of 100 were allocated to colour.

Conversely, wholecolours (rubies and black and tans) should be wholecolours. I have heard this said repeatedly, and that any white markings should be penalized. But there is an opposing view that a few white hairs on the chest of a wholecolour is such a minor blemish that it should not be heavily penalized for it. One can say that wholecolours with such small white blemishes are now hardly ever seen at championship shows. This may be for one or more of three reasons:

1. Most wholecolours now come from long lines of solid wholecolour breeding, and therefore white patches appear much less frequently than previously when parti-colours were in the lines.
2. The quality of wholecolours has improved considerably in the last decade.
3. Judges do, in fact, penalize heavily any white patches.

The Standard merely says 'white marks undesirable'. It is important to remember that Blenheim and ruby puppies are born much lighter coloured than their eventual adult colour.

Most puppies have a fluffy teddy bear coat which is often shed at different ages – some at around three months, others at about the time they change their teeth, i.e. four to five months.

BLACK AND TAN: Raven black with tan markings above the eyes, on cheeks, inside ears, on chest and legs and underside of tail. Tan should be bright. White marks undesirable.

Whilst raven black is required, the breed has several, almost imperceptible, different shades of black. The black should be a dark blue-black and not a black tinged with brown. It is interesting that Mrs Lytton in her book published in 1911 said she had 'come across an authentic case of two blue and tan puppies bred from black and tan parents'. She also saw a dull blue and tan puppy. Although it did not live to maturity, she 'kept its skin as a curiosity'.

What varies rather more is the richness and brightness of the tan. Some are a yellowy gold and give an unattractive wishy-washy appearance. Where there is a rich deep and bright tan, it contrasts brilliantly with a sparkling black sheen and makes a pretty picture.

Porter's **Irish Champion Ringcreevy Ringlets**

RUBY: Whole coloured rich red. White markings undesirable.

As the only Cavalier with just one colour, rubies are at a

Inman's **Champion Chamanic Lucasta**

disadvantage visually to the other three colours. It is therefore important for the ruby to have the 'rich red' glowing colour called for in the Standard. Molly Marshall stated in 1962: 'The new born ruby (i.e. one or two days old) should look like a fresh peeled chestnut – smooth, glossy and rich red – no hint of gold.' If a ruby is out of coat it often looks lighter than its true colour, and therefore there are special reasons for not showing an out of coat ruby.

BLENHEIM: Rich chestnut markings well broken up, on pearly white ground. Markings evenly divided on head, leaving room between ears for much valued lozenge mark or spot (a unique characteristic of the breed).

Speedwell Massingham, when describing the colour of Ann's Son of 1927, said 'a lightly marked red-gold and silver Blenheim'. The colours of the Blenheim are today described as rich chestnut and pearly white. If one considers the colours of some pearls then the use of 'silver' to describe Ann's Son is more readily understandable. Today's use of 'pearly white' emphasizes the white should not be a staring, washing powder white. In those Cavaliers where the white really is pearly, one can see an occasional silvery glint, especially in bright sunshine.

Some years ago there was a rather vigorous argument as to what 'rich chestnut' colour actually meant. In the show ring were some of a very deep colour – some said mahogany, others said liver. Other dogs being shown were at the opposite extreme, very much lighter, and I heard them described as lemon-orange and yellow straw. Discussion then progressed as to what 'chestnut' actually referred to – was it a horse or a nut from a tree, and if a tree which type of chestnut tree? It was all very interesting for a while! The two extremes of colour now seem to have slipped away and everyone appears reasonably satisfied with the Blenheim colouring we have. The Cavalier King Charles Spaniel Club recently advised that the rich chestnut required is that of a horse, not that of a 'conker' from the chestnut tree.

The lozenge mark or spot is not vital in an individual Cavalier, but it is important that the breed tries hard to retain the lozenge. After all, it is unique, and therefore something to be cherished. Lytton in her book of 1911 said 'The spot should be cultivated in the Tricolour as well as in the red and white.'

TRICOLOUR: Black and white well spaced, broken up, with tan markings over eyes, cheeks, inside ears, inside legs and on underside of tail.

Mordecai's **Champion Millhill le Monde**

Before 1973 the section of the Standard relating to tricolours was worded as above but concluded with 'Black and White: Permissible but not desirable'. However, since 1973 black and whites have not been acceptable as a recognized colour.

I believe a tricolour is the most difficult colour to breed. To produce a high quality, typical Cavalier with the three colour markings in all the right places takes some doing. For the person who can produce an absolutely top quality, well bred, nicely broken tricolour dog of good temperament and health, there is a small fortune waiting in stud fees.

There is no dog that looks more attractive than a nicely broken tricolour with rich and bright tan in all the correct places. The colour combination of black and contrasting white, highlighted by small patches of tan, neatly placed, takes some beating. Even tricolour puppies in the nest, shortly after birth, when they have been licked dry by their mum, look fabulous. It is important that the tan be rich and bright, otherwise some of the colour combination is lost. Pale yellowy tan looks weak and insipid and spoils the picture.

I find when judging that there are now very few tricolours with tan on the inside of the legs as called for by the Standard, and this is largely ignored by most judges. What is often referred to by judges is the lack of tan under the tail. This is an important

Town's **Champion Barsac the Palio**

feature when viewing the tricolour moving away.

Ticking in a tricolour looks unattractive and fortunately is now rarely seen, whereas twenty years ago it was quite prevalent, with some tricolours being heavily flecked.

The colour section of the Standard concludes: 'Any other colour or combination of colours highly undesirable.'

SIZE: Weight – 5.4–8 kgs (12–18 lb). A small well-balanced dog well within these weights desirable.

When helping to form the Breed Standard in 1928, Amice Pitt and the other breed pioneers envisaged a glamorous, sound dog with moderate bone and weighing about 15–16 lb as the ideal size to aim for, i.e. a true toy spaniel.

But there have always been some difficulties in keeping Cavaliers within the Standard weights. This seems rather surprising when one looks back to the early history of the breed as Cavaliers descended from King Charles Spaniels, which are smaller than Cavaliers. Also Ann's Son, who was used extensively at stud in the late 1920s and early 1930s was said to weigh only 13 lb. Incidentally, the Standard minimum weight was 10 lb until 1968, when it was raised to 12 lb. Even so, one sees very few Cavaliers weighing between 12 and 14 lb.

From writings and photographs it seems that, in the early days, many Cavaliers were well over 18 lb. Why should this have been so? Was it because of the influence of the larger Marlborough Blenheim type, or possibly that other larger breeds were used in an effort to improve Cavalier stock? Such breeds would obviously introduce additional size (see Chapter 1).

Whatever the cause, size has been something of a problem throughout the history of Cavaliers and remains so today, but possibly to a lesser degree than previously. Nevertheless, it is apparent that a problem still remains when one considers the data from a weighing survey at three recent shows. A total of 296 Cavaliers were weighed, including 78 aged 6 to 12 months and 72 aged 12 to 18 months, making a total of 150 under 18 months. These have been omitted from the following figures because many aged from 6 to 18 months will still be growing or filling out. Therefore, for those aged 18 months and over the weights were:

Weight in Pounds – Ounces Ignored

	12	13	14	15	16	17	18	19	20	21	22	23	24	25	26	27	28	Total
Dogs				1	7	6	20	7	6	2	8	1	1	3	1			63
Bitches		1		5	16	15	19	10	5	3	4	2	1	1			1	83
Total		1		6	23	21	39	17	11	5	12	3	2	4	1		1	146

In summary, 22 out of 63 dogs (or 35%) were 19 lb and over while 17 out of 83 bitches (or 20%) were 19 lb and over. The 12 lb and 28 lb bitches were both veterans. The percentages of those above 18 lb show that we ought not to relax in our efforts to keep the Cavalier a true toy spaniel.

It is often said that, whilst being concerned about Cavaliers which are well above 18 lb, we should be equally concerned about weedy specimens which do not have sufficient substance or bone. This is obviously true, because a Cavalier must be typical of the breed. However, in my experience there are far fewer of the weedy types than the heavyweights. I believe we have to take care that attractive typical Cavaliers of a smaller type, weighing about 15 lb, are not frowned upon, simply because they are somewhat smaller than many in the show-ring. The truth is that 15 lb is mid-way in the Standard weights and is something we should all be aiming towards, rather than being content with heavyweights well above 18 lb. The Standard says '5.4–8 kgs (12–18 lbs). A small well balanced dog *well within these weights desirable.*' The American Standard states 13–18 lbs and also gives guidance as to height, stating 12–13 inches at the withers.

In an article in 1961 Amice Pitt mentioned 'the heaviest Cavalier on record being 40 lbs and the lightest 4 lb'. Have we at the present time any challengers to this Goliath and miniature? Hopefully not!

FAULTS: Any departure from the foregoing points should be considered a fault and the seriousness with which the fault should be regarded should be in exact proportion to its degree.

Every dog, even a champion, has faults. Of course a champion will meet the requirements of the Standard much more closely than a non-winner. But no dog will fulfil each and every requirement of the Standard, because the perfect dog has not yet been born.

The Standard itself is only a rather sketchy guide to the ideal Cavalier. It is not a precise, detailed blue print. It is therefore important for Cavalier enthusiasts to increase their knowledge, and thus be able to understand and interpret the Standard correctly. This book should be helpful in that respect.

As we know, there are four colours of Cavaliers, but the Standard makes no differentiation between them, except on the particular markings expected in each colour. In all other respects from head to tail, the expectations on the four colours are exactly the same.

In judging, the *overall* dog has to be considered, to see which one most nearly matches the Standard. Some faults will be of a more serious deviation from the Standard than others (for further information see Chapter 14).

NOTE: Male animals should have two apparently normal testicles fully descended into the scrotum.

This was readily accepted by most judges, as they believe that dogs awarded prizes in the show-ring should not only be those of merit, but also be able to take the breed forward by being able to reproduce.

The English Kennel Club has now decreed that neutered dogs and bitches can be shown, and judges are expected to treat them as equals to those who are 'entire'. Some top 'all rounders' who judge week in and week out admit to being perplexed about the situation. They feel that a long established principle about the aims of judging has been seriously breached. There are also side-effects which may give a neutered dog or bitch an advantage.

For instance in breeds needing to be long coated, such as Cavaliers, a spayed bitch often produces a very profuse coat merely because she has been spayed. If without being spayed she would never have produced such a profuse coat, then she has gained an unfair advantage through being spayed. Another issue raised regarding male dogs is that a monorchid (i.e. a dog with only one descended testicle) could be castrated and thus mask his monorchidism. Whilst we have to appreciate that the number of dogs involved is very small, nevertheless the 'all rounders' who have raised it believe it is an issue with serious implications. A suggested solution is that special classes be provided for neutered dogs, but this would hardly be satisfying to the exhibitor as more often than not there would be little if any competition.

Stevenson's **Champion & Irish Champion Ronnoc Rumba.** (Breeder: P. Connor)

The Kennel Club stand firm, however, and in the *Gazette* of June 1991 stated: 'Judges must be aware that neutering, particularly castration of dogs, is not a fault and should judge accordingly. Obviously it would be patently unfair if a responsible owner, not wishing to breed from their dog, were then penalized for acting within KC regulations in having the dog neutered.'

There is much more required in really knowing Cavaliers than being able to recite the Standard. To fully understand and appreciate the breed you need to be able, through increased knowledge and experience, to put flesh on the skeleton provided by the Standard. It is extremely satisfying gaining this knowledge.

We now move on to important considerations of a broader nature which re-inforce and build upon the Standard.

Early in 1995 substantial and controversial changes were imposed in the USA regarding responsibility for guiding the breed forward. As a result the breed may be facing a rather turbulent period.

3

Type, Conformation, Movement, Soundness and Balance

Type

What is type? Type can be said to be the combination of those points which make a dog like its own breed and no other. Perfection of type lies at the centre of the Standard, not at the extreme edges where exaggerations have been introduced in some breeds, but fortunately not in Cavaliers. A dog true to type has good overall quality.

Type is based substantially on the Breed Standard, but additionally it has some rather abstract and intangible qualities. For instance the standard requires a Cavalier to have large dark round eyes, not prominent, and spaced well apart. But additionally, if a Cavalier is to be typical, the eyes must have the soft, gentle, limpid look. The latter is not expressly stated, but it is known and accepted within the breed. Type is the same for all four colours of Cavaliers. If a dog is to be successful at shows it must, whatever its colour, be typical of the breed. Type is always present in abundance in the big winners.

With the Kennel Club Standard being only a guide and not precise in its description, there can be slight variations within the overall acceptable breed type. For instance in Cavaliers most experienced breeders will be able to recognize rather easily a certain head type from one kennel, and there are two kennels who keep different sizes of Cavaliers. Yet all three types are highly successful, and rightly so, for the quality of their stock is high. I am not describing three distinct types, only very slight variations within the Cavalier type. A breed that has two distinctly different types is the German Shepherd Dog and, not surprisingly, the breed seems to be in turmoil about the schism.

Assessment of type is an individual choice, just like an interpretation of the Breed Standard is individual. This is why judges' opinions vary slightly, but the outstanding dogs are usually there, or thereabouts, with all judges.

What constitutes type for Cavaliers? The head is always high on the list when determining type for any breed, and Cavaliers are no exception. The head must be almost flat with high set ears. Any semblance of a domed head and low set ears would indicate reversion to the King Charles Spaniel and therefore would be untypical.

A narrow head would also be untypical in that there would be insufficient width for the eyes to be widely spaced. But a too wide head that looks overdone and coarse would also be untypical. Cushioning under the eyes is required to contribute to the soft, gentle expression. Light eyes, bulging eyes, small eyes or almond shaped eyes would spoil the expression and be untypical.

Whilst head properties are important, breed type extends to the whole Cavalier. Perhaps two further extreme examples will suffice to complete the illustrations of type. The Standard calls for 'short coupled ... level back'. If a Cavalier was either long backed like a Dachshund or had an arched topline like a Bedlington, it would be untypical, however good its head might be. Similarly, if it wished to fight all the dogs in the ring that would also be untypical.

A Cavalier of true type is one that generally fits the breed expectations from head to toe, always bearing in mind that no dog is perfect.

Other matters which are closely linked to type will now be considered. They include conformation, movement, soundness and balance. All are vitally important. For instance a Cavalier may seemingly be teeming with breed type, but if it is unsound and moves very badly then its ability to take the breed forward is questionable.

Conformation, Movement, Soundness and Balance

A short introductory explanation of each word may be helpful.

Conformation – the form, structure and arrangement of the parts.

Movement – involves many parts of the body, and for movement to be correct the fore and hindquarters must work harmoniously together. The way a dog moves tells an experienced observer much about its conformation.

Soundness — sometimes used as an alternative to conformation; sometimes used to describe movement; but more often used to describe a combination of conformation, fitness and movement.

Balance — concerned with a harmonious relation of parts; whether symmetrical and well proportioned. Beauty of form.

Mosbron's **Norwegian Champion Sperringgardens Chavannes**. (Breeder: Nyby, Sweden)

Conformation

The Kennel Club glossary of canine terms states: 'Conformation – the form and structure, and arrangement of the parts.'

To have correct conformation, and thus be able to move as the Standard desires, a Cavalier needs to be made right. Its bones must be approximately of the correct size, correctly proportioned, correctly angled to each other, and correctly positioned within the body. This sounds logical, indeed obvious, and perhaps prompts the question 'What is the problem?' The problem is that a dog has more than 300 bones and to expect any dog to have them all absolutely correctly sized, proportioned, angled and positioned is expecting the unachievable, but we keep trying. Additionally there are the muscles, and many other vital parts, all making an important contribution to the well being and efficient functioning of the dog.

Before we can assess conformation it is necessary to have a reasonable understanding of the different parts, to know their individual functions and how they fit together. To understand fully can take years of experience and study. Obviously the first step is to read about the conformation of dogs. Then handle your own dogs and really feel the bone structure and different parts. Start off with something not too difficult such as neck, topline and stifle. Is the neck elegant or too short and stuffy; is the topline sufficiently level to balance a plate on it; is the stifle 'Well turned'?

Those parts will do for a start – get to know them well, before moving on to another part of the body. Work through the body systematically. Study the head carefully as it is such an important feature – the almost flat skull, the set of the ears, the depth of the stop, the length of the muzzle, the spacing of the eyes, etc. Do not hurry. Do a little at a time, and focus your reading to match your handling. If you have several Cavaliers, particularly of different ages, feel the same bones in each of the dogs and note any differences. Cavaliers will love being handled in this way, and the experience will stand them in good stead for the show-ring.

If you attend training classes the next step is to look at different breeds there and then try to get a turn at 'going over' the dogs. See how the individual breeds differ. For instance compare the hinquarters, particularly the turn of stifle on the Chow, the German Shepherd Dog and the Cavalier. Look at the exaggerated features of some breeds and compare to the naturalness of the Cavalier. If King Charles Spaniels attend the class compare their heads with the head of a Cavalier, and appreciate the differences that Cavalier breeders have been seeking to achieve, and 'fix', since separate registration was granted in 1945.

Your study of your own Cavaliers and their conformation will inform you as to what features they excel in, and others where they are not so strong. This should then prove invaluable to you in determining future breeding programmes, and thus assist you to produce improved stock. Do not be kennel blind and think all your dogs are perfect.

Movement

Movement is the critical test of conformation – they go together like fish and chips, or peaches and cream. Movement indicates whether all is well with conformation.

A Cavalier moving incorrectly is, nine times out of ten, due to poor conformation. By seeing a dog move, a judge is able to confirm what his hands told him as he 'went over' the dog, and what he saw when the dog was standing. A judge usually asks that a Cavalier be moved in a triangular route. Each 'leg' of the triangle gives the judge a different view of the dog, and provides specific information about conformation. When going away from the judge the dog shows whether the hocks are parallel or whether he is moving close behind, and whether there is the required 'plenty of drive from behind'. On the second leg of the triangle, when the dog is in profile, the judge can assess head carriage, neck and topline, overall balance, length of stride, and whether movement is 'free moving and elegant'. On the third leg, returning head on, the judge can consider the dog's front, whether the legs are moving parallel or there is pinning, and whether the elbows are flapping.

Movement can, in some instances, be improved by appropriate exercise i.e. a mixture of free running and controlled road work on a lead. This exercise tones up the muscles and puts them in firmer condition. Exercise may assist with such matters as moving close, protruding elbows and spread feet. But exercise can only make a slight improvement. If the basic conformation is wrong, the dog will never move correctly. We are back again to the old saying that 'if they are made right they will move right'.

Sansom's **Champion Bembridge Rainbow**. (Breeder: Peter Watkins)

Correct movement indicates a dog's conformation matches the Breed Standard very closely and that the dog is in good muscular condition.

It is necessary to be sure of what is correct movement because there are conflicting views. Let us first consider what three connected Breed Standards say:

1. English Breed Standard for CAVALIERS
   'GAIT/MOVEMENT. Free moving and elegant in action, plenty of drive from behind. Fore and hind legs move parallel when viewed from in front and behind.'
2. English Breed Standard for KING CHARLES SPANIELS
   Although Cavaliers were granted separate registration from King Charles Spaniels in 1945, it may be enlightening to compare the requirements regarding Cavalier movement with that required for King Charles Spaniels. The Standard for King Charles Spaniels states: *'GAIT/MOVEMENT. Free, active and elegant, driving from behind. Sound movement highly desirable.'* It will be noted that it does not expressly state that the fore and hind legs should move parallel.
3. The American Breed Standard for CAVALIERS does not have a separate section covering gait and movement. All that it states under General Appearance is: *'An active, graceful, well-balanced dog, very gay and free in action;'* and when referring to legs it lists as a fault *'stilted action'*. It makes no stipulation regarding parallel movement of the fore and hind legs.

Writers such as McDowell Lyon in *The Dog in Action* (1950) and Rachel Page Elliott in *The New Dogsteps* (1983) state that a normally built dog tends towards single tracking rather than moving with its legs parallel, particularly as its speed increases.

Lyon explains that when a dog is moving it never has all four feet on the ground simultaneously, therefore it does not receive full support at each corner. The faster it travels the less support it receives and the greater the need for the legs to converge in order to achieve better balance. When considering different speeds he states: 'In the walk, which has support on 3 corners, converging towards a center line is not pronounced; but take away one of these supports, as in the trot and pace, or 2 of them as in the gallop, and you have a different story. Speed means convergence ...'

Elliott puts it thus: '... slow motion photography has long since shown that normal leg movement inclines slightly inward, dependent – of course – on the type of dog and his rate of travel. Misunderstanding of this principle has brought unjust criticism of "moving too close" on many a dog that actually is moving well.'

Lyon and Elliott accept the qualification that wide, low-set dogs cannot be expected to single track because of the way they are built, and also because they are not expected to move at fast speeds. But that category apart, they are agreed that, in most dogs, as the speed of movement increases the convergence of both front and hind legs will become more pronounced and will eventually result in or approach single tracking i.e. all four feet being placed on one central line corresponding to the centre of the dog's body. Both Lyon and Elliott are also agreed that front and rear legs on the same side should follow the same line.

In the Cavalier world there are some supporters for this view of 'correct' movement. One person, whose views I generally respect, has given the matter considerable thought and states:

> Our breed standard is actually incorrect and does not allow for the laws of movement and gravity. The breed standard was drawn up at a time when little scientific work had been done on movement, and before the advent of convenient-to-use video and film cameras. What the breed standard should say is that front and back legs should move in the same plane. I think one of the reasons that Cavaliers have such bad movement is because people are trying to breed animals which move wrongly to fit the breed standard.

Supporters of this view therefore feel the breed standard should be amended.

I can recall that Elliott's book, and particularly the film and lectures, initially aroused a great deal of interest and supportive comment, but the proposals are now no longer centre stage. In fact some may suggest they have been side-lined or even conveniently forgotten. Perhaps what was being put forward was too innovative, too radical, perhaps even too revolutionary to be easily and readily accepted, despite the convincing photographic evidence. Whilst Elliott's submissions are not at the present time being actively canvassed by many persons in Britain, I believe the proposals have some quiet 'sleeping support' which could, perhaps, be easily re-awakened. But the degree of support is very difficult to quantify.

What criticism has been made of these proposals by Lyon and Elliott? One criticism came from the late Tom Horner, a very well respected and experienced judge who regularly judged at the very top level on a world-wide basis. He wrote in *Dog World*: 'What a lesson this breed provides for those armchair professors who are always telling us that it is correct for a dog's legs to converge in their front movement. Move these Beardies as fast as you like at the trot and they will prove the professors wrong by coming and going absolutely true at both ends.'

On another occasion Mr Horner wrote: 'At a run, any dog will tend to draw its legs towards the centre of its body, even the short legged ones, but at a trot (a steady trot, not an extended trot) a sound, well-made, fit dog should move parallel both in front and behind.'

I hope this statement of the differing views on desirable movement in Cavaliers will open the door to constructive discussion. Supporters of the Elliott and Lyon view need to convince the rest of us of the validity of their argument if any change in the breed standard is to be recommended. Any such change will not be undertaken lightly by breed clubs and will need to be proven as being necessary beyond any shadow of a doubt.

In the meantime it is clear that breeders, and certainly judges, have to act in accordance with what the Breed Standard *currently* states. Otherwise there would be absolute chaos. But I believe that at present there is probably a substantial majority who favour parallel movement as being the 'correct movement' for Cavaliers.

Soundness

I find this word is often used to describe slightly different things. For instance one definition I have heard is the soundest dog is the one that moves correctly with the least amount of effort.

The Kennel Club glossary describes soundness as 'the normal state of mental and physical well being. A term particularly applied to movement.' I have heard soundness used to describe good conformation, and on other occasions I know it has been used to describe correct movement. But I believe it is used most frequently to describe a dog with good conformation, one that is fit physically and mentally, and also moves correctly i.e. the three ingredients combined.

If you are ever in any doubt as to how it is being used then it is advisable to ask the speaker.

Balance

The Kennel Club glossary gives the following definition: 'A consistent whole; symmetrical, typically proportioned as a whole or as regards its separate parts; i.e. balance of head, balance of body or balance of head and body'.

Potter's **Champion Rheinvelt Red Hot**

This definition makes it clear that balance can apply to the total Cavalier or to separate parts e.g. a well balanced head. The important words are symmetrical and typically proportioned (we are back again to type). We are concerned with the harmonious relationship of parts and beauty of form.

In the Breed Standard for Cavaliers the word 'balance' is actually used in relationship to three features – general appearance, tail and size.

4

From Puppy to Champion

It can be helpful for breeders and judges who are building up their experience to be able to see how a young puppy progresses into adulthood. The following three photographs for each Cavalier show it as a young puppy, as a junior, and then when it has reached adulthood and become a champion.

The feature follows a similar pattern established by *Saluki Heritage* and *Dog World*.

The dogs featured are:

1. Ch. Craigowl Hoodwink, owned by Gordon and Norma Inglis.

Champion Craigowl Hoodwink

at five months   at ten months

at two years

2. Ch. Charlandra Dylan Thomas, owned by Ray and Marion Pearson and Helen Hamilton.

Champion Charlandra Dylan Thomas

at eight weeks

at twelve months

at two years

5

Establishing Your Own Successful Bloodline

It does not matter which breed, be it Cavaliers, Great Danes or Chihuahuas, most of the highly successful breeders all have one thing in common: they started off with well bred, high quality stock from a foremost kennel.

In Cavaliers this is certainly true. Just consider the following highly successful breeders. Mrs Burroughes' successful Vairire line was substantially based on Ttiweh stock from Amice Pitt. Mrs Susan Burgess's foundation bitch Ch. Vairire Charmaine of Crisdig came from Mrs Burroughes' kennel. The Crisdig kennel has subsequently produced twenty-six English champions. The sire of Ch. Alansmere Aquarius, Best in Show at Crufts in 1973, was Ch. Vairire Osiris. Mrs Molly Coaker built up her highly successful Homerbrent line from Crisdig breeding, resulting in many English champions for the Homerbrent, and associated Homaranne, lines. Continuing the movement forward to the present day there are now several well known successful kennels whose stock is substantially based on Homerbrent breeding. A great many similar examples can be quoted.

If you have been involved with Cavaliers for several years and have not yet made your mark, you need to give very serious thought as to whether you are ever likely to reach the top with the stock you now have. A remark was once made by Mrs Keswick of the Pargeter prefix that if you have not bred a champion within ten years you are probably never going to reach the top. Therefore if you have been in the breed for several years and your exhibits at championship shows are not meeting with the success you desire, you need to ask yourself whether you need to make a completely new start. For those just about to enter the world of breeding Cavaliers, and wishing to do so successfully, you have the opportunity to set a sound foundation from the very beginning.

For those who fall in either of the two categories the aim must be to obtain one, or even two, well bred, top quality adult bitches from a well respected breeder with long experience, one that wins consistently and, preferably, has bred several English champions, not just one which may have been a fortuitous fluke. This will not be easy; it may take time and therefore you will need patience.

Coaker's **Champion Homerbrent Tradition**

I suggest you approach the matter in the following way. First, study the photographic record book of champions and their pedigrees, and decide which kennel type or bloodline appeals to you most. Follow this up by visiting at least three championship shows to see the live examples of the various bloodlines. Then decide which type really appeals to you most and which you would be happy to base your kennel upon, and to live with, for the next twenty or thirty years. In that lengthy period you may eventually breed thirty, or even one hundred, litters. Therefore your choice of a foundation bitch is absolutely crucial. If at this stage you are still a little unsure regarding the bloodline you desire, give yourself further time – on no account rush your decision.

When you have made your decision, spend a further two or more shows studying very carefully the particular kennel's stock in the ring, and go round the benches looking at them whilst they are waiting to go in the show-ring. When you are absolutely sure of the type you would love to have, approach the breeder at an opportune time (not when she is preparing a dog for the ring). Tell the breeder how you have been looking at her stock, how much you admire them, and that you wish to obtain a foundation bitch of her breeding with which to start your kennel, or to make a fresh start with better stock, whichever is the case. Tell the breeder you are, preferably, seeking a three- or four-year-old soundly constructed bitch, with no major faults, that can spend the rest of her days with you, and possibly provide you with two litters. The breeder's immediate response is likely to be that she cannot help you. You therefore have to impress upon her how responsibly you are approaching the matter, that one of her bitches could have a first class loving home with you, and that you are prepared to wait as long as it takes. You must appreciate that the cost of such a bitch is likely to be substantially more than the cost of an eight-week-old puppy, and for that you may not be getting a championship show winner but, nevertheless, a well bred, sound, if rather plain, brood bitch. It may be quite difficult to obtain such a bitch, but that is the ideal way of setting up your kennel, and you should make every effort to start that way.

Do not consider taking a bitch on breeding terms. It is far better for you to purchase a bitch outright so that you can select and retain the best of any puppies rather than having the breeder cream off the best puppies, leaving you with the mediocre ones, despite all your hard work. Whilst the Kennel Club still permits the practice of bitches on breeding terms, it is nevertheless felt by many to be outmoded. It often leads to much frustration, conflict and dissatisfaction. For anyone trying to build up their own successful line, it should be avoided.

If you are successful in buying outright, ask the breeder's advice as to which stud dog to use with the bitch, and follow that advice completely. The breeder, after a lifetime's experience with her bloodlines, knows them far better than anyone else, and you must remember your future success depends on using those bloodlines appropriately. Find out as much as you can about your bitch's ancestors – what were their strengths and weaknesses. Ask the breeder, and indeed anyone else, whom you feel may be able to help you with information. Whilst there is never any certainty in breeding, the breeder knows best which lines usually link together successfully. The breeder will probably suggest line breeding i.e. mating the bitch to a reasonably close relative in order to preserve, and build upon, the strengths within the lines.

Selg's four **Swedish Champions. Bonnyville Trico Tricia** with her daughters: **Bonnyville Tri to Follow, Bonnyville Tri to Fancy** and **Bonnyville Tri to Favour**

If the bitch has sufficient puppies to allow you a good choice, you should aim to 'run on' the best two bitch puppies from the litter. Two are company for each other, and if you keep them until eight months you can then select the best, and let the other one go to a good home. If both still look to be promising at eight months you should consider keeping both. As they grow older you can be showing one, whilst the other takes time out of the show-ring for maternal duties. Ask the advice of the breeder of your original bitch about which puppies to keep. I suggest you forget about keeping a dog puppy for several years and concentrate on building up a strong bitch line. If you happen to breed a very promising dog puppy ask the breeder who sold you the bitch if she would like him. If he turns out to be a real show prospect she will probably get the best out of him in the show-ring, and any success can only reflect well upon you as the breeder of the puppy.

You now have your original bitch and one, or two, sound

typical daughters from her. These are to be the cornerstones of your future breeding programme. Continue to seek the advice of the original breeder as to which stud dogs to use with them. Your aim is to build up a consistent, soundly constructed, well balanced type that will be successful for you, and also be a credit to the breed. Do not consider using the latest champion stud dog without a great deal of thought as he may spoil the type you are seeking to establish, and his bloodlines may not link with those in your line. What you are seeking to produce is a *consistent type*, not a hotch-potch of breeding. Continue to line-breed with your bitches and concentrate firmly on building up the strong bitch line – never, never sell a highly promising bitch, whatever you are offered for her. You need your good bitches more than anyone else. At this stage keep the best bitch from each litter. After four litters you should then be acquiring much useful information about the lines you are building upon. By including your original foundation bitch you will have before you living examples of five successive litters, all bitches. From these you will be able to see which matings were most successful, but above all you should be able to see your own distinctive bloodline and type now taking shape. Continue to share discussions with the breeder who sold you your original bitch. She still has much to teach you, and will be interested in how your line is developing. Ask for her comments about any ideas or theories you may have about future breeding, and make a written note of any observations she makes. Such a note may prove invaluable in twelve or eighteen months' time.

At this stage, after several generations of breeding, if you find you have bred a very promising dog puppy you may wish to consider 'running him on' for possible showing, and future stud work. A dog really has to be outstanding if he is to be regularly used at stud. Therefore your assessment of a dog puppy has to be much more critical than for a bitch. To keep a dog you must have sufficient space to place him well away from the bitches when they are in season, or otherwise the dog may howl and become a nuisance.

By now you may be approaching the maximum number of Cavaliers you can keep. This is always a problem. You will have to be very selective, because it is easy to find the increasing number is getting out of hand. Therefore you need to determine a number which you will not go beyond. This will depend on the space and facilities you have; how many dogs you can afford to keep, taking account of food, vet bills, show entries, etc.; the terms of your breeder's licence; and the time you have available

Reed's charming litter of **Chantiz** tricolours

for the dogs. When you have decided upon your maximum number try to stay within it. It can be a little flexible in case you breed what looks to be an absolute cracker of a puppy.

Many of the highly successful kennels in all breeds keep their numbers to a reasonable level by allowing a brood bitch to go to a loving permanent home if they have a promising daughter from her. By so doing they are continually improving their breeding stock. You may now be able to assist someone who is in a similar position to that from which you started, someone who is looking for a good foundation bitch.

If you have kept to the principles outlined, and also had a little luck with your breeding, you will now be having success in the show-ring. More importantly, you will have established your own particular blood line, and be producing *consistently* a highly regarded, sound, balanced type. People will be recognizing your type and linking it to your affix. You have arrived in the breed! Congratulations!

But you still have much to learn, so keep your ears and eyes open and consider very carefully indeed your future breeding programmes. There are no easy short-cuts – success comes from dedication, observation and skill, based on sound knowledge. However, you are now in a strong position to build up further success because you have several generations of sound stock behind you. You also have intimate knowledge of your line and that is invaluable for future breeding. Do not introduce 'outside' lines to your stock without the very greatest thought, because you do not know what problems you may be bringing in. If you do use a dog whose breeding is not linked to your line, then when you subsequently mate any bitches resulting from such a mating you need to come back close in to your own line. Otherwise you risk losing the strengths of the line you have patiently built up, and instead end up with a hotch-potch of breeding. That, quite simply, would be stupid after all your efforts and show a complete lack of judgement. I well remember Susan Burgess saying many years ago that she kept fairly close in to her own Crisdig line, but occasionally went out for a 'dash' of Ttiweh or Pargeter breeding, but then returned to her own line.

Larsson's **International Swedish and Norwegian Champion Rodero's Abigail**

But what action can you take if you were unable to persuade the breeder to let you have an adult brood bitch? You should not desert the kennel whose type you admire. It may be that you have to ask for a bitch puppy and that you have to go on a waiting list for such a puppy. If so, be patient. An eight-week-old puppy is something of a risk because no one can guarantee how it will turn out when it grows up. You should ensure that its mouth is correct and hope that it remains so when its adult teeth come in at four to five months. Hopefully, it will not develop other major faults. If all remains well as it grows into a young adult, even if it is not a show specimen, then you can breed from her in due course. You should then follow precisely the advice given earlier. Seek the breeder's advice regarding the stud dog to use and follow that advice absolutely. If the stud dog lives 200 miles away you must go – it is no use considering an inferior dog, or one that does not match your bitch's line, simply because it means a shorter journey. You should always be aiming to use the best dog of the correct line so as to produce the best stock for your bloodline. If you really want success there can be no half measures.

When breeding, always have in your mind's eye the 'perfect' specimen, and aim always for perfection. If there is a Cavalier now, or from the past, which gets nearest to your ideal 'perfect' specimen, obtain a photograph and keep it in the front of your book of pedigrees so that it is there to remind you each time you are considering a future mating.

Breeding good stock is not easy. You will meet many disappointments, possibly even real heartache, when things go badly wrong. That is when dedication is needed to continue in the face of such setbacks. Breeding is both a challenge and an art. If the results with one litter are disappointing, try to do better with the next. Learn from your mistakes. Once you have several generations of a particular line, you have improved your chances of success, as you are building upon a known set of positives.

Careful record keeping, accompanied by a photographic picture gallery, is a must. You need to note the dominant features, good and bad, which each bitch and dog pass on to your stock. This information becomes invaluable for planning your future breeding programme.

Quality not quantity is the key to skilful breeding. You need also to develop that all important 'eye for a dog', to know which stock to keep and which to let go.

Unless you want your kennel to become overloaded with mediocre dogs you need to set a standard of quality which puppies must attain if you are to keep them. There are several ways of setting this 'standard of quality'. I will describe just two, as examples.

The method I have used is that I only keep a puppy if it has the potential to win, or at least be placed regularly at Championship Shows. This sets quite a simple benchmark of quality that I am seeking, and also keeps numbers down to reasonable levels.

There is a more sophisticated method of setting a desired standard of quality which I also find attractive. This method, whilst it is a little more complicated, is more thorough and,

Widdicombe's **Astralea Lady in Red**

importantly, is more revealing about particular strengths and weaknesses. Each important feature of a typical Cavalier is graded upon a numerical score of merit i.e. a possible score. Then each individual puppy, or adult, will be assessed and scored for each feature. The total score achieved will be simply converted to a percentage against the possible total score. It will then be possible, for example, to see that five puppies in a litter score 53%, 57%, 69%, 78%, and 83% respectively. If you intend to keep just one puppy it will normally be the one that scores 83%. However, occasionally it may be that the top scoring puppy may have one particular weakness that you are particularly concerned about (e.g. lightish eyes). You therefore decide to let that puppy go and instead keep the next highest scorer which has darker eyes.

With a scoring assessment as outlined you can see how a particular characteristic, be it light eyes, shoulder placement, movement, or whatever, scores in subsequent generations. You also have an informative written assessment of every puppy, and each litter you have bred, which subsequently you can refer back to. You can thus compare progeny scores for different parents. This is simply done by adding up the percentage scores for all the offspring, and dividing by the number of puppies, which will then provide an average score for the progeny. It is then easy to compare average progeny scores for your different breeding stock. This information will be helpful in determining future breeding programmes.

Let us consider an example.

CRIEDA TAMBOURINE   Ruby Dog.   Born 1-1-94

Sire.	CRIEDA BANJO	Black and Tan
Dam	CRIEDA MUSIC MAKER	Ruby
Litter details	2 Ruby dogs 2 Black and Tan bitches	

	Possible Score	Actual Score
Health and Breeding Potential	12	9
Temperament	12	10
Expression	10	7
Eyes	10	9
General Appearance and Balance	10	8
Movement	10	9
Shoulders and Upper Arm	10	8
Turn of Stifle	10	9
Body	8	5
Chest	8	6
Coat – texture and length	8	6
Colour and markings	8	4
Forelegs and elbows	8	5
Head and skull shape	8	6
Mouth	8	5
Neck	8	5
Nose Pigment	8	7
Hind legs	8	5
Size and weight	8	4
Tail set and carriage	8	4
Top line	8	5
Ears	7	5
Feet	5	3
Totals	200	144
Divide by two to give percentage	100%	72%

Note outstanding features – eyes, movement, stifles, nose pigment
Note more serious weaknesses – colouring weak and insipid
size – may finish up too big
tail set – too low

Champion Fontelania Capricious
(on the left)

**Champion Fontelania Burnt
Toast**

**Champion Fontelania Burnt
Honey**

**Champion Fontelania Silver
Memento**

The individual characteristics can of course be given a different weighting (i.e. score) according to your own preference. The range of possible scores may also be wider than the 12, 10, 8, 7 and 5 that I have used. You can also score more, or less, characteristics, depending upon how detailed you wish your assessment to be.

However, when you come to score individual dogs it is absolutely essential that in your assessment you are consistent year in and year out. Otherwise the exercise will lose much of its value. This method of assessment needs more effort than the first mentioned assessment of only keeping potential Championship

Show winners. It does, however, provide a more thorough and objective assessment which can be regularly referred to in the future and is therefore most useful.

It is a fitting conclusion to this chapter to congratulate Maurene and Jim Milton on having achieved, in 1994, the unique distinction of being 'the first' to have bred and owned champions in all four colours.

6

Breeders' Responsibilities and Code of Ethics

In the past the dog was referred to affectionately as 'man's best friend'. However the last few years have seen an undoubted increase in regulations and legislation regarding the keeping of dogs, and an anti-dog lobby has become stronger and more vociferous.

These developments should not have come as any great surprise, because in these days of greater attention to hygiene and associated health matters the attitudes and behaviour of some dog owners have been reprehensible. It is no use pretending that it is only a minority, made up of puppy farmers and those irresponsible owners who turn their dogs out on the streets all day. A much wider ownership needs to share the blame.

The Government has highlighted three areas of concern: (1) dog fouling of pavements, parks and playing fields; (2) strays, and the accidents and damage they cause; (3) the related problems of overbreeding and control of vicious dogs, some children having been seriously savaged and even killed by dogs.

It is often said that 'we' in the pedigree dog breeding and showing fraternity cannot be included in the ranks of such irresponsible owners, but does that bear scrutiny? What about:

1. Piles of dog faeces left at the approaches to shows.
2. Loudspeaker appeals regarding dogs left in cars, which become ovens, at dog shows on hot summer days.
3. Breeders who abuse their breeding bitches. Kennel Club information in 1989 showed that twenty-five Cavaliers had had ten or more litters (one poor Yorkshire Terrier had had fifteen litters). The Kennel Club has since decreed that no more than

six litters will be registered from any bitch, and that no litter can be registered after the bitch is eight years old.

4. Cavalier owners who continue to use breeding stock which they know have hereditary defects.

5. Cavalier stud dog owners who do not want to know when puppies sired by their dog show hereditary defects.

Thankfully, such irresponsible and uncaring breeders form only a small minority. Is it any wonder, however, that many Breed Clubs, including Cavalier Clubs both here and abroad, have deemed it necessary to include a Code of Ethics as a condition of membership? Such codes set out the standards expected of their members.

The code for the Cavalier King Charles Spaniel Club states:

CODE OF ETHICS

In accordance with Rule 2(a) of Constitution

Members of the Cavalier King Charles Spaniel Club are expected to:

1. Abide by the Rules of the Cavalier King Charles Spaniel Club and the Kennel Club.

2. Be familiar with the Breed Standard and not exhibit at shows Cavaliers which have been changed in appearance by artificial means, except for docking of tails and the removal of dew claws. NO artificial colouring of coat or pigment.

3. Keep accurate breeding records, registration papers and pedigrees.

4. Only use Cavaliers which are registered with the Kennel Club for breeding.

5. Maintain the best possible standards of canine health.

6. Furnish a record in respect of each puppy sold giving details of all inoculations and wormings, a pedigree, and Kennel Club registration or transfer documents, unless written agreement is made at the time of sale that papers are withheld, and/or conditions imposed.

7. Conduct themselves at all times in such a manner as to reflect credit on the ownership of Cavaliers in particular.

8. ALL surviving puppies to be registered at the Kennel Club by six months.

9. No puppies to be sold under eight weeks of age.

10. No puppies to be sold or advertised as show quality at less than five months of age.

11. All stock must be healthy at the time of sale and to have been checked for hereditary defects before sale.

12. Any puppy with a known hereditary fault should have a restricted registration certificate to prevent it being bred from.

13. All stock to be sold with a diet sheet.
14. No stock to be sold to a pet shop or puppy dealer.
15. Breeders are obliged to take responsibility for their stock if it proves unsuitable for its new home.
16. Stud dog owners must see the bitch's pedigree and registration certificate to check ownership, age, endorsements and should try to ascertain number of litters, number of pups and when she last had a litter.
17. Breeding terms only to be taken on with either a Kennel Club loan of Bitch Agreement or a written contract, and both parties must have a signed copy of said agreement and have full knowledge of what it entails.
18. No member should take on more dogs than they can care for and keep in a healthy environment.
19. DOGS TO BE USED AT STUD
    No dog with a known physical defect, which could be detrimental to the health and wellbeing of the puppy, to be used at stud.
    Any dog which is to be used at stud to be vaccinated, annually checked for good health and be in good condition at the time of every mating.
20. BITCHES TO BE USED FOR BREEDING
    No bitch with a known physical defect, which could be detrimental to the health and wellbeing of the puppy, to be used for breeding.
    No bitch to be mated so as to whelp before she is sixteen months old and then only if she is considered mature enough to raise a litter of puppies.
    No bitch to be mated so as to rear a litter after her eighth birthday (as K.C. Code).
    No bitch should normally rear a litter on consecutive seasons and in any case must have no more than two litters in any two years.
    No bitch to be allowed more than six litters in her lifetime. (See K.C. Code.)
    No bitch to be allowed more than two Caesarian sections, as this would indicate whelping difficulties.
    Any bitch which is to be used for breeding to be vaccinated, annually checked for good health, be free from any infection and be in good condition at the time of the mating.
21. OWNERS
    Owners of stud dogs must only allow their dogs to be used if they are confident that their stud dog meets the criteria stated and that the bitch to be mated meets the criteria specified for bitches.
    Owners of bitches must only mate them if they are confident that their bitch and the prospective stud dog meet the criteria stated above.
    Once a mating has taken place, the owners of the bitch have a responsibility for the good welfare of the puppies, and as such have an obligation to help the new owners if requested to do so. Stud dog owners also have a moral obligation for the welfare of the puppies.

22. BREEDING CONTROL PROGRAMMES

All breeders are expected to conform with any breeding control programme instituted in order to produce sound and typical stock. (See K.C. recommendation.)

It is to be hoped that ALL Cavalier breeders will take this Code of Ethics into their heart and resolve to do their utmost for our lovely breed.

Although the Kennel Club was intending to set up an approved breeders' register linked to compliance with a breed club's code of ethics, it recently stated that 'such a register is unlikely to be introduced in the foreseeable future'. It seems that the Kennel Club had been surprised by the abundance of material, including scientific evidence, that would have to be considered before any such scheme could be introduced. But new proposals mooted.

In these days when there is a greater inclination to sue through the courts, breeders need to ensure that stock they sell is suitable for the purpose for which it was bought. Show quality means one thing; sold as a pet means something else. But recent court cases have clearly indicated that all dogs need to be free from avoidable hereditary defects and to have the correct temperament, or otherwise a court action is likely to succeed. Such actions can be very costly to the breeder in terms of legal fees and damages; traumatic because of the worry; and very damaging to one's reputation because of the publicity. It therefore behoves all breeders to act responsibly and take every care.

Changing the subject slightly, I have always been a little concerned that, despite every care being taken, one of my Cavaliers might slip its lead, or do something unexpected, and cause an accident or injury to a third party. The thought of one of my dogs possibly causing a road accident with people injured, perhaps permanently disabled, hardly bears thinking about. Apart from the pain and distress caused, damages might be enormous, particularly in respect of a bread winner no longer able to work. I have therefore taken out a third party insurance policy to cover such eventualities. It is very reasonably priced, and whilst I hope I never have to use it, it provides peace of mind should anything untoward happen. The limit of indemnity is substantial and should cover all possible eventualities plus legal costs involved in the defence of a claim.

In March 1993 at Knutsford Crown Court, a farmer was ordered to pay £15,000 compensation, plus £7,583 costs, after his dogs had savaged a girl aged ten. Presumably the farmer's own legal costs would be additional to those amounts. In another case the Court of Appeal left the owner of a mongrel dog with a bill of around £10,000 following an incident when the dog knocked down and injured the owner of another dog. Third Party Insurance therefore seems worth considering.

Another form of insurance worth considering, particularly for Cavaliers, is that covering the cost of veterinary fees, or death from illness or accident (see the Swedish research results under Heart Valve Disease). Some 'health' policies also include third party liability.

7

Inherited Diseases and Conditions

Responsible Cavalier breeders should readily recognize the need to take every possible precaution against inherited diseases. Many of the Cavalier breed clubs in this country, and across the world, arrange screening clinics at shows with specialists in attendance to check eyes and hearts. These examinations are often free, or at a reduced charge.

The *Looking at the Breed* booklets produced by the English Cavalier King Charles Spaniel Club give much useful information about inherited diseases. Anyone who has not seen them should try to borrow copies.

I was Chairman of the Sub-Committee which produced the first three booklets, and the aim was to include reports by top specialists on the inherited diseases which provide some dangers to Cavaliers. The Club continues to provide helpful information through articles in the annual Magazine. This book can only touch briefly upon what is a wide ranging and complex subject.

By far the most important factor to remember is that, **wherever possible**, all breeding stock should be screened and declared free of any inherited disease *before* being used for breeding. It is no use breeding without screening tests having been taken, and then finding that affected progeny are spread far and wide and that they, in their turn, have been used for breeding and are causing further damage within the breed.

If you have your dogs checked, as advised, then you have done all that is possible. If problems are found you can ensure the dog or bitch is not bred from, thus avoiding future distress. Your conscience is clear because you will have taken the necessary precautions.

Ideally, what should happen regarding breeding is that when the owner of a stud dog receives an enquiry about its use, copies of the current clear screening certificates for heart and eyes and a copy of the hip scoring certificate should be made available to the bitch owner. If the stud dog owner is not forthcoming in this way the answer is simple – go elsewhere. There are other stud dogs available. I recently had a good experience in that I requested a copy of a stud dog's pedigree and by return of post I received not only the pedigree but also photocopies of recent heart and eye certificates, plus a satisfactory certificate regarding blood pressure. I was most impressed.

Bloomfield's **Rossbonny Good Tri of Oaklake.** (Breeder: Shail)

Similarly, bitch owners, without being asked, should provide the stud dog owner with copies of current clear screening certificates for the bitch. In some breeds many stud dog owners will not allow their dog to be used unless clear screening certificates are produced in respect of the bitch.

If such responsible attitudes were practised by all breeders, real progress would be quickly made in improving the health of Cavaliers and ensuring that the breed remains healthy. But, unfortunately, some breeders cannot be bothered to make the necessary effort.

Let us now briefly consider some inherited diseases and defects that affect Cavaliers.

Heart Valve Disease

Undoubtedly this is the major problem affecting Cavaliers. It can cause ill-health and early death in those seriously affected and it is, of course, very distressing both to the Cavalier and its owner. Bill Kendrick, President of the Cavalier King Charles Spaniel Club of Canada, expresses clearly the concern felt worldwide in his Presidential Message quoted in the Canadian Club's 1993 Year Book.

> It is gut-wrenching to all of us that at the same time we are establishing our breed in the show ring, we are faced with the devastating reality of heart disease. No one has been left untouched by it. It has caused many of our members to reassess their commitment to our beloved Breed. Should we continue to breed Cavaliers when we know we are producing dogs that are likely to die prematurely? This is a very difficult dilemma. It is a question that must be answered by each of us individually.
>
> As I step down as President ... one of the things that I am proudest of ... is that we have begun a project with Dr Michael O'Grady at the University of Guelph, that might eventually lead to answers to this problem. We should be under no illusions that this will result in a cure in the near future. But what we learn by having our dogs tested by Dr O'Grady, coupled with data being collected in Britain and the US, just might bring us closer to a solution. The only guarantee is that ignoring the problem will only make it worse for sure. I would hope that everyone who can will involve their dogs in this screening program.

What is the Disease?

In very simple terms it is caused by an early progressive degeneration (ageing) of the valves of the heart. As a result, blood leaks back from the main pumping chambers (ventricles) into the smaller receiving chambers (atria). The heart may cope with slight valve leakage for months, even years in some instances, but eventually the heart may not be able to compensate for the leakage, thus resulting in heart failure.

What are the Symptoms?

1. Often the earliest sign noticed by an observant owner is that the Cavalier becomes slower at exercise, sometimes accompanied by some breathlessness.
2. Breathlessness or coughing caused by fluid being squeezed into the lungs, or by the large left atrium pressing on the airways.

3. Swelling of the abdomen caused by fluid being squeezed into the liver and abdomen (usually late in the disease).
4. Losing weight, and sometimes a general weakness, or episodes of collapse with excitement.

It is worth emphasizing the difference between heart disease and heart failure. Heart disease may be innocuous in the early stages, but it often progressively worsens, leading to heart failure. It is advisable to ask for your Cavalier's heart to be checked at every visit to the vet.

Early Detection and Clinical Findings

A vet can discover the presence of heart disease before the owner of a Cavalier has noticed any symptoms. By listening with a stethoscope the vet can detect the presence of a heart murmur, which is the sound of turbulence in the blood flow, indicating leakage. In general the greater the turbulence, the louder the murmur. Therefore loud murmurs are usually associated with severe leakage. However, whilst the grade of the murmur usually reflects the severity of the disease, it does not always do so: very severe mitral regurgitation (e.g. after rupture of one of the chordae tendineae i.e. 'heart strings' as occurs quite often in mitral valve disease) can lead to a reduction in the murmur, as blood is flowing through such a large hole that the flow is no longer as turbulent as before.

Murmurs are usually graded on a scale of one to five or six, with one being the mildest and five or six the most severe.

Treatment

1. Do not allow your Cavalier to get overweight.
2. Reduce, but do not eliminate, exercise.
3. Restrict salt intake (vets can provide special diets).
4. Vets can prescribe diuretics to clear fluid from the lungs, chest and abdomen, and to prevent further fluid retention.
5. Vets can also prescribe drugs called vasodilators to improve the forward flow from the heart and reduce valve leakage.
6. Sometimes digitalis extract (e.g. digoxin) is used to slow and strengthen the heart beat.
7. Drugs such as bronchodilators (e.g. Millophyline, or aminophylline) can help to alleviate coughing when the dog has heart failure due to mitral valve disease.

Prevalence

Dr B.M. Cattanach, a geneticist, states: 'Because mitral valve disease (MVD) is widely distributed everyone who breeds Cavaliers faces the same problem. The disease will not be limited to a few kennels or bloodlines; all will be involved to some degree; all will be at risk. Reputations of kennels will not be tarnished by the disclosure of dogs with murmurs, indeed they will be respected.'

Only a few Cavaliers under the age of three have a murmur indicating the presence of the disease. But in research carried out by P.G.G. Darke, 59% of Cavaliers over the age of four were found to have murmurs. Therefore it seems that the murmurs, and the disease, often become apparent between the ages of three and four.

In Sweden it has been found that insurance claims for veterinary care, death or euthanasia relating to heart disease in Cavaliers are considerably higher than for other breeds. For instance for dogs less than ten years old, Cavalier claims are eight times more common than the average for all other insured breeds. If one considers claims for death in the seven to ten year age group, the frequency of claims is thirteen times higher in Cavaliers than the mean for all other insured breeds.

Is it Hereditary?

Whilst it is not yet strictly proven that the disease is inherited, it is strongly thought to be so. Dr B.M. Cattanach said in 1991 that, because of a number of reasons which he outlined, 'it may be reasonably inferred that the condition has some form of hereditary basis.'

In an article in the *Veterinary Record* of 12 December 1992, Swedish researchers Jens Häggström, K. Hansson, Clarence Kvart and L. Swenson stated: 'The premature form of the condition in the cavalier King Charles spaniel may be caused by a genetic disposition.' They went on to say:

> At present, it is not known how chronic valvular disease is inherited or how the genetic disposition for developing the disease has spread so widely in the breed, because it has not been possible to link any particular line of breeding with the disease. All the cavalier King Charles spaniels derive from a few foundation dogs in the 1920s and the disposition may originate from one or more of these dogs.

Current Research

Dr P.G.G. Darke, veterinary cardiologist, has been undertaking research into the condition for several years. He and Dr B.M. Cattanach advised the English Cavalier King Charles Spaniel Club on setting up research, with annual examinations and certification. Research is to follow from the certificates which contain the names of the dog's parents. Leaving aside the research advantages momentarily, the actual yearly examinations provide breeders with helpful information about the health of their breeding stock, and provide a certificate of freedom from murmurs when being used for breeding. The date of the onset of the disease, which is discovered through the first hearing of the murmur, is very important. The experts believe the earlier the onset, the more serious the condition is likely to be.

Swedish research has also been on-going for several years and is concerned with a number of different, but linked, studies. It has already provided useful information and, hopefully, Cavalier owners worldwide can look to the Swedish researchers for further assistance and guidance in the future.

I know also that Cavalier 'heart clinics' have been held in several countries. Therefore parallel research may be going on in different parts of the world. The earlier a genetic solution can be found, the better it will be for all Cavaliers.

When Cavalier Clubs are asking for the co-operation of their members in research, it is important that each Club treat its members as responsible partners and distribute information to them as regularly as possible. Otherwise co-operation will diminish.

Research can prove costly. In the Swedish research the largest Swedish animal insurance company gave financial support. I suggest this is a possibility worth pursuing in other countries.

Effective Breeding Practice

Cavaliers need to be tested annually. Ideally, only those who do not have murmurs should be used for breeding. Breeders should ask to see a *currently valid certificate* before deciding to use a stud dog.

The next best approach is to only use those who developed a murmur at a late age. Therefore when considering hearts it is advisable not to breed from very young stock, as the absence of a murmur in a two or three year old does not guarantee it will not soon suffer from heart disease. I suspect this advice to avoid breeding from young stock may be hard for some to accept. I recognize we are all keen to breed from our promising youngsters. However, think of the possible distress you may be bringing to yourself and your puppy customers, and the potential future suffering for any puppies that are produced from parents with defective hearts.

I also appreciate there is a dilemma in delaying a first litter from a bitch until she is probably past her ideal reproductive age for a first litter. With a stud dog it is probably simpler. If you consider an older dog you will then be able to ascertain when, if ever, he developed a murmur. A stud dog that develops a murmur before middle age has got to be considered a very doubtful proposition, however good he might be in other respects. Using an older dog also provides an additional bonus, as you can assess the quality of his progeny before deciding whether to use him.

Possible Ways Forward

Dr P.G.G. Darke in a personal communication states:

> ... I think that the breed should be trying to establish whether there are indeed lines with long-surviving dogs free from MVD, and we also need to be monitoring whether an attempt to give breeders the option of choosing dogs certified free from MVD is actually working – particularly to chase up those that withdraw their dogs from annual testing – and why (presumably because these dogs have developed a murmur). Furthermore, if we can establish a pool of dogs without much MVD, or with late development, to attempt to have these dogs adopted as relatively 'clean' breeding stock.

In any discussions amongst breeders the point is usually made that, whilst some Cavaliers with heart murmurs die at an early age, others with murmurs live to a good old age. Dr Darke in the same personal communication states that the Swedish research mentioned earlier 'effectively proves beyond doubt that MVD is progressive in Cavaliers as a whole (even if not so in certain individual dogs), and that it has a high prevalence in causing disease and death (at least amongst the insured Swedish dogs).'

Early Deaths

I find one of the most unhappy experiences is when a distressed, tearful person telephones to say their Cavalier has died of a heart attack at a young age, and then asks if I have any puppies, as they are seeking an immediate replacement. They are most upset at losing one so young. This happened again as I was writing this section. A family's black and tan had collapsed and died at the age of 2¾ years, which is extremely young. They would not allow the vet to conduct a post-mortem, but he said death was undoubtedly due to heart failure. The dog had one of the most popular bloodlines behind it. A short time later my wife, when exercising our Cavaliers, was stopped by a couple whose 4-year-old Cavalier had died of heart failure. They were still shattered even though it had happened several weeks earlier. Cavaliers should not be dying at such young ages.

I suggest that breeders of wholecolours need to be especially vigilant. In the last few years there has been an 'explosion' in the numbers of black and tans and rubies, and the stud dogs used have not been numerous because of the more limited gene pool of wholecolours. The result is that wholecolour pedigrees often show several instances of doubling up, and therefore if there are faults or problems (heart disease, eye disease, or whatever) they may well have been emphasized and compounded.

What is needed by breeders of all colours is information and positive guidance from Cavalier Breed Clubs based upon research. A very simple but most helpful beginning would be to publish (preferably in the yearbook) a list of all stud dogs, say six years and over, who are certified free from mitral valve disease. It would be even more helpful if the list was divided into sections – one section containing the names of six-year-olds; the next seven-year-olds, and so on. Those seeking a stud dog could consider whether to choose from the list, and this simple action might reduce the further spread of the disease in a swift and positive way.

When one hears of a number of young deaths in all four colours, and involving many blood lines, it is frustrating to hear some breeders pontificating that 'there is nothing wrong with my line – no need to have mine examined'. Situations can change drastically, as the following case will prove. One kennel that was known to produce very long-living Cavaliers then used a particular champion stud dog twice. The two litters that he sired are now dying, or are in the advanced stages of heart disease, at the ages of five to seven. A further worry, of course, is how long will *their* progeny live? This breeder is quite distressed at what has happened because of introducing the particular champion to her line. She states it is like sitting on a ticking time bomb, waiting for the dogs to be affected, and then watching them die at a young age. The champion concerned died at a young age, but during his lifetime he had been *very* widely used at stud. This case vividly illustrates to me the need to *see* a recent clear heart certificate before using any stud dog. Otherwise you may be letting yourself in for much heartache.

Mrs Bet Hargreaves, who collects Cavalier pedigrees as a hobby and is in communication with numerous pet owners, has been told by several people that, having lost their Cavalier at a young age through heart disease, they have decided not to have another Cavalier but to try a different breed. It is also known that a few vets are advising against Cavaliers as pets because of the heart problem. We therefore need to successfully tackle and eliminate mitral valve disease as quickly as possible, so that more pet owners do not become disenchanted with the breed, or are advised against it by vets.

Long Living Cavaliers

Mrs Hargreaves also invited Cavalier owners to inform her of those Cavaliers who lived to a good age. Mrs Hargreaves calls them 'golden oldies' i.e. twelve years and over. It is important to keep a balance between early deaths and those who live well into double figures, and it is a pleasure to record some of the 'golden oldies' that were reported to Mrs Hargreaves.

The oldest Cavalier reported is Kiki, said to have been put to sleep on 15 June 1993 at 19 years 5 months. Unfortunately, it has not been possible so far to verify her stated date of birth. Other long livers include:

15 Cavaliers that lived to 17 years
34 Cavaliers that lived to 16 years
100 Cavaliers that lived to 15 years
172 Cavaliers that lived to 14 years
183 Cavaliers that lived to 13 years
234 Cavaliers that lived to 12 years

Mrs Hargreaves has also compiled an interesting list showing litter brothers and sisters that lived to twelve years and beyond. For instance:

2 from one litter lived to 17 and 16 years
2 from one litter lived to 17 and 15 years
3 from one litter lived to 16, 15 and 15 years
3 from one litter all lived to 15 years

Also, one dog lived to be seventeen and one of his daughters lived to be fifteen.

Mrs Hargreaves has, in fact, details of thirty-six long living litters. Whilst one has to be extremely careful in interpreting this information, because Mrs Hargreaves does not have information about *total* litters, nevertheless it seems likely that there are bloodlines that fairly consistently provide golden oldies, and there are other lines that are less successful in this respect. But remember, from the earlier example, that the introduction of a dog with a serious hereditary fault to a long living line can damage and alter the situation drastically.

Incidentally, one champion from long ago not only lived to fifteen but is said to have sired a litter at that age. That certainly is enjoying life to the very end!

Eyes – Cataracts and Retinal Dysplasia

Concern in the past has been about cataracts which affect only a very small number of Cavaliers. There are two distinctly different forms. The first is congenital, i.e. present from birth, and it varies in its degree of severity. It is usually non-progressive, i.e. it remains static throughout life. The second form of hereditary cataract is not present at birth but occurs at around twelve months of age or sometimes a little later. It is progressive and all affected animals ultimately go blind.

Many breeders have been diligent in having their Cavaliers tested annually by veterinary ophthalmologists under the British Veterinary Association/Kennel Club (BVA/KC) Scheme. This has kept the number of Cavaliers with cataracts to very small numbers indeed. An occasional one is still discovered by the specialists but the action of breeders has been successful in keeping cataracts under control.

Veterinary ophthalmologists are now, however, becoming more concerned about retinal dysplasia, which also occurs in two forms:

1. **Total**. Puppies which have this condition are blind at birth. So far as is known, this condition, which is hereditary, does not affect Cavaliers.
2. **Multifocal retinal dysplasia**. This is the condition being found in Cavaliers. It is only very recently that veterinary ophthalmologists have become concerned about the condition in Cavaliers. Previously it was regarded as being so rarely found, and of such a minor degree, that it was said to be of

very little practical importance or significance in the breed. Recently, however, the incidence has increased, and rather more severe forms are being discovered in Cavaliers. Multifocal retinal dysplasia in its most severe form will impair vision. It is strongly thought to be hereditary but this has not yet been proved. It is difficult to be sure of the diagnosis or the severity of the condition in a young puppy. Some veterinary ophthalmologists suggest the severity of the condition can best be determined when the eye is fully grown at about nine months.

It seems to me that, as one form of cataract can develop at twelve months or a little later, there are strong advantages in having potential breeding stock checked by a veterinary ophthalmologist at fifteen months when a confident diagnosis should be able to be given about both cataracts and multifocal retinal dysplasia. Breeding stock should continue to be checked annually under the BVA/KC scheme for control of hereditary eye diseases until they reach the age of seven. In the light of current knowledge it would be highly irresponsible to breed from affected stock.

Hip Dysplasia

Dr M.B. Willis states 'Hip dysplasia is essentially a faulty fitting of the ball (femoral head) and socket (acetabulum) joint of the hip.'

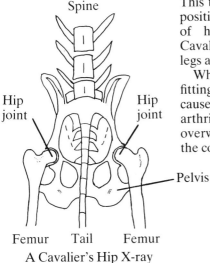

This tracing is intended only to show the position of the hip joints, not the degree of hip dysplasia. The anaesthetized Cavalier is lying on its back with its rear legs and tail stretched out behind.

When a dog has hip dysplasia the faulty fitting of the ball in the socket often causes inflammation, pain and eventual arthritis and even lameness. A dog that is overweight is likely to further aggravate the condition.

A Cavalier's Hip X-ray

For those who know little about the testing for hip dysplasia, it is done after the dog, or bitch, has reached the age of twelve months. The dog has to be tranquillized or anaesthetized so that its hips can be x-rayed in the correct position. Most vets prefer to have the dog anaesthetized whilst taking the x-rays, but there are some vets who, wherever possible, merely tranquillize the dog. You would need to discuss such matters with your vet.

The x-ray plates are then sent by your local vet to a specialist panel for scoring. The best score that can be obtained is 0–0 and the worst 53–53 (total 106). A dog only needs to be scored once in its lifetime. The current cost varies between vets but in general is about half the price of a stud fee.

Hip dysplasia is not a major problem in Cavaliers. It is difficult, however, to know its incidence and severity because so very few Cavaliers have been scored.

A few bad scores do come to light. The worst score recorded for a Cavalier is 91, and two others scored between 81 and 90. One dog that was exported had a score of 83. From personal communications I know of a few Cavalier puppies that had such bad hips that they needed operative treatment, but they were not scored, being under-age for the scheme. Also one yearling had extremely bad hips but the x-rays were not submitted for scoring. These examples, admittedly few, of bad hips which were not scored give a misleading picture regarding the average score for the breed. But Cavaliers are not alone in this respect and I suspect it applies in most, if not all, breeds. The cases I have quoted all had well known bloodlines in their pedigrees.

Whilst such cases are few it is nevertheless a little worrying, and I believe it is prudent to have prospective breeding stock of both sexes x-rayed and scored at twelve months. If an unsatisfactory score is received the decision can then be made not to breed from the dog or bitch in question, and no harm has been done to the breed, or to the breeder's reputation.

Dr Willis explains: 'All it needs for the hip status in the breed to worsen considerably is for breeders to use a few unscored sires who (unbeknown to breeders) happen to be bad in hip status ... Hopefully if more C.K.C.S. are sent in we can more accurately assess the situation and eventually produce progeny tests. At present most breeders are clearly turning a blind eye to the problem.'

There are about 14,000 Cavaliers registered each year with the Kennel Club and yet, after ten years of the new Hip Dysplasia Scoring Scheme, only 202 British Cavaliers have been scored. It really is a pitiful figure. Of those scored the scores range from 2 to 91, with an average score for the breed of 16.41.

Some breeders say they are not having their breeding stock scored because they do not wish to put their dog 'at risk' through having an anaesthetic. I have had my recent breeding stock scored and none of them came to any harm whatever. The risk is said to be very small indeed, and with good veterinary care, particularly in the recovery stage, the risk is said to be virtually negligible. As stated earlier, some vets are apparently willing to merely tranquillize the dog.

I feel that Cavalier breeders generally seem to regard hip dysplasia as having little importance or priority. This seems a pity when there is a good screening and scoring test available under the auspices of such responsible bodies as the British Veterinary Association and the Kennel Club. I feel we ought to be doing more, and a useful start would be if all regularly used stud dogs were scored.

Epilepsy

The term epilepsy is often used to cover fits in the widest sense, whatever the cause may be. The causes may be varied, including poisons; cardiac, renal and hepatitic disease; and, of course, hereditary epilepsy. The latter is what dog owners are mostly interested in. Hereditary epilepsy is sometimes called primary, or true, epilepsy.

Fits normally happen when a dog is relaxed. Therefore there is no need to stop exercise, as it is unlikely a fit will occur when your dog is out walking. Fits are convulsive seizures which are accompanied by a period of unconsciousness which may last for just a few seconds or several minutes. The dog's legs usually 'thresh' about and often there is frothing at the mouth. After a fit the dog may get up almost immediately, or lie exhausted for a little while. Sometimes the dog quickly seems to return to full normality, but others seem to be in a daze for a short period and bump into things before regaining full awareness and control.

To correctly diagnose the true cause of epilepsy is very difficult. It is particularly difficult to differentiate a case of epilepsy of inherited origin from one that is acquired. Therefore if your Cavalier starts to have fits you need to have the fullest information available for your vet. This would include time, place, what your Cavalier was doing immediately before starting the fit, what did the dog actually do in the fit and immediately after, how long did the fit last, had the dog previously had a serious knock or accident, been vomiting or had diarrhoea, etc. Such information will assist your vet in making a diagnosis, and also in assessing the best control methods. Medication is often required for life and dose rates are crucial.

It is possible that true or idiopathic epilepsy may occur in Cavaliers as an inherited condition, the onset of fits typically being 1½–4 years of age. Animals which suffer from epilepsy should not be bred from, and the owners of offspring of an animal which subsequently develops epilepsy should be informed of the condition and the possibility of its being inherited.

Conclusions regarding Hereditary Diseases

All breeds of dog suffer with some hereditary conditions, some more serious than others. The Cavalier is probably no worse than many breeds and may be better than some. We have, therefore, to keep these matters in proportion. This must not, however, lead Cavalier breeders to be indifferent or complacent.

Certainly the breed has a problem with heart disease and it needs all Cavalier Clubs, and Cavalier breeders, worldwide to conscientiously tackle the problem. Cavalier Clubs throughout the world need to keep other Cavalier Clubs informed about any research they are undertaking and to circulate progress reports. As previously mentioned, Sweden is undertaking very valuable ongoing research into heart disease (MVD), and all Cavaliers could benefit from regular information about the progress of that research.

Breed Clubs need also to appreciate that membership is expanding and changing all the time, with some dropping out and others joining. This poses a problem about informing newcomers of important matters and expectations, particularly about hereditary diseases, but it is something that needs to be faced.

Whilst mitral valve disease is our greatest problem, a continuing vigilance is required with hereditary eye conditions, hip dysplasia, slipping patellas and epilepsy. These are not widespread problems for the breed, but they could become so unless breeders screen their stock where possible and do not use for breeding any dog or bitch which poses a health risk.

Excellent screening checks are available for hearts, eyes and hip dysplasia, and if they are used conscientiously then stock showing any defect can be excluded from all future breeding. If all breeders do this, Cavaliers as a breed must have a healthier future.

What is needed above all else is that when hereditary problems are encountered by a breeder, responsible action is taken promptly. If others need to be informed then do so openly and frankly – you should be respected for it, and undoubtedly the breed will be better for it.

One would hope that such an approach would always be welcomed by all, but unfortunately this is not always so, as a recent example shows. A Cavalier breeder discovered her winning puppy had a serious defect. She informed those whom she felt ought to know, and conscientiously enlisted the aid of a specialist and a geneticist to look into the problem. It was expensive to her but she felt it was the right thing to do. However quite soon afterward she was informed by a friend in the breed that 'she was becoming unpopular because of pursuing the matter'. The breeder told me she felt extremely sad that some Cavalier breeders could take such a view.

8

General Health Considerations

You will soon get to know what is the normal state of health for your dog. If you suspect that he may be off colour or sickening for something it can be helpful to take his temperature. Put a clinical thermometer in his rectum, inserting it gently until it is about one-third of the way in, and hold it there for about 1½–2 minutes. The normal temperature varies slightly from animal to animal but is usually between 101°–102°F. If you are in any doubt about your dog's health, even if the temperature is normal, consult your vet.

Overall Health

In the first place, you should only purchase your Cavalier from a reputable breeder. Such a breeder should have taken all the necessary precautions to ensure his or her stock is fit and healthy. After all, their reputation depends upon it. Their aim is to breed good quality, healthy stock which are a pleasure to live with. They keep some of their puppies themselves and naturally want all their stock to be in the best possible health. Members of the Cavalier King Charles Spaniel Club are bound by the club's Code of Ethics regarding breeding healthy stock.

Never buy from a pet shop. Always go direct to the breeder so that you can see the mother of the litter and the breeder's other Cavaliers. You can see how they are kept, and can ask the breeder direct any questions you may wish to raise. If you are not fully satisfied, visit another breeder. In fact it may be helpful to visit, say, three breeders and then decide which stock you think might suit you best.

The same day you purchase the puppy, or the very next day, take the puppy to your vet for a thorough examination and possible inoculations. If your vet finds anything amiss, raise the matter *immediately* with the breeder. If you do this a reputable breeder should give you full satisfaction, including, if necessary, taking the puppy back and giving you a full refund of the purchase price.

I hear of far too many people who have bought a Cavalier from so called 'puppy farmers' or other disreputable dealers and have been 'landed' with a sick, ailing puppy that has cost them vast veterinary fees to get it into even reasonable health. The disreputable supplier often washes his hands completely of all responsibility, and it is difficult to make any progress with such people.

This book contains a list of Cavalier King Charles Spaniel Clubs (see Appendix). Select the one that covers the area in which you live and then contact the secretary. The secretary will be only too pleased to refer you to reputable breeders near to you. If you follow this advice you should start off, as far as is possible, with a healthy Cavalier.

Cavaliers are generally active, healthy and hardy little dogs, but like all animals they may occasionally be a little 'off-colour'. Let us now consider briefly some of the ailments that may arise with your Cavalier. Some of these matters you can deal with yourself, but if you are in any doubt you need to consult your vet. Remember your Cavalier is entirely dependent upon you to protect his health and deal sensibly with any problem that may arise.

You therefore need the co-operation of a conscientious vet, and you should aim to cultivate a relationship with a good vet in your locality. If you feel it is necessary to consult your vet go armed with definite information which can assist the vet to diagnose the problem and to prescribe appropriate treatment. Vague, woolly or panicky statements make diagnosis that much more difficult.

Protective Inoculations

A young puppy is very vulnerable to several serious diseases which can easily kill it. It is therefore essential that you do not let your youngster mix with other dogs, or go on land, or sniff lamp-posts, where these diseases may be lurking, until your puppy is protected by vaccination. The inoculations, usually two, are given between the ages of eight and twelve weeks. Some vaccines vary slightly and therefore you must heed your vet's advice in this respect.

The inoculations usually protect against distemper, hepatitis, leptospirosis, parainfluenza and parvo-virus. Dogs will generally need an annual booster, but not necessarily against all the above diseases each year. Be guided by your vet on this matter.

Diarrhoea

This can easily occur and usually does not mean anything serious is wrong, especially if your dog is otherwise bright and lively. Your Cavalier whilst out for a walk may have picked up some tasty but over-ripe morsel which has upset his tummy. A change of food, or too much food, can also cause diarrhoea. When a dog has diarrhoea it should not be given food for twenty-four hours, and then the food for its next two meals should not be too rich, say rice, chicken or fish. That usually does the trick and no further action is needed.

If the diarrhoea persists over several days, or if it contains blood, or if your Cavalier seems to be generally unwell, you should consult your vet.

Vomiting

This again often seems to be nature's way of cleansing, and usually is of little importance. Sometimes it is just frothy, and that usually quickly rectifies itself. If a dog vomits its dinner soon after eating, it usually means it has been greedy and gulped it down too quickly. A dog will often crop grass like a cow and then 'sick up' the undigested grass. This should cause no concern whatsoever as it often happens, and some 'old hands' say it is the dog's own way of clearing excessive acid in the stomach.

If your Cavalier is continually sick, and also seems unwell generally, you should consult your vet. Sickness and/or diarrhoea in puppies can be serious and veterinary advice should always be sought.

Cough

If your Cavalier develops a cough then seek veterinary advice immediately, because the cough may indicate the presence of a serious disease. It may be a symptom of a heart problem (mitral valve disease), or distemper, which thankfully is now much less prevalent than in years gone by.

It may also indicate kennel cough, which is highly contagious and can easily be contracted at shows, or from other kennels if your dog has been staying there whilst you have been on holiday.

If you have other dogs, then the one with kennel cough will need to be isolated. Kennel cough often lingers on, and sometimes does not readily respond to treatment. Your vet is the person to assist you, but if the treatment does not seem to be having much success, then some breeders say minced garlic is often quite helpful.

Any of these three problems – mitral valve disease, distemper or kennel cough – will need skilled veterinary treatment over quite a time.

Snorting

To the inexperienced Cavalier owner occasional snorting by his dog may be alarming, but it is nothing to worry about. The Cavalier lowers its head, appears to be gasping for breath, or possibly choking, and makes a loud snorting noise. All that is needed is for the owner to clamp the dog's mouth shut with his hand, and the dog's head to be lowered. The snorting then very quickly stops and the dog is then perfectly all right. One veterinary opinion about the condition is that it may be caused by a slightly soft palate which at times slightly restricts the breathing. My impression is that snorting is rather less prevalent now than it used to be.

Minor Cuts or Grazes

It is helpful to have a tin of antiseptic powder on standby. It is then a simple matter if your Cavalier does suffer a minor cut or graze to bathe it in a solution of salt water (one heaped teaspoon to half a pint of warm water), dry the cut carefully, and then sprinkle on the antiseptic powder. Regarding further applications of the powder just follow the manufacturer's instructions. It is usually a waste of time considering a bandage or plaster as your dog will have removed it before you have put away the first-aid box.

If the wound is deep or extensive you should seek your vet's advice as it may need stitching. Before treating any open wound, you should thoroughly wash your hands.

Interdigital Cysts

These occur between the toes and can be caused by grass seeds becoming embedded in the skin. Suggested treatment is to make a saturated solution of Epsom Salts i.e. dissolve the salts in a cup of hot water until no more salts will dissolve. The water should be hot enough so that you can keep your finger in it without being scalded. Put the dog's paw into this and keep it there for several minutes. Repeat every one to two hours until the cyst bursts. Then gently dry the area and apply antiseptic powder.

Strains

I believe many active dogs at sometime in their life strain a muscle or ligament. It is so easily done when running, jumping or playing. If the strain appears to be relatively minor the best treatment is rest for two or three days. Try to keep your Cavalier quiet, which I appreciate may not be easy. One of those wire cages, provided it is of adequate size to allow him to lie flat out, can be quite an effective aid in keeping him subdued and resting. If you do not have a cage rig up a temporary structure to confine him to a small corner of the kitchen.

It goes without saying that if your dog is obviously in much pain you must consult your vet as soon as possible. Similarly if the lameness is severe, or persists for more than a day without improvement, then consult your vet.

Allergies including Stings

Allergies can take many forms but the ones generally noticed by the owner show as skin rashes or raised plaque-like areas on the skin with the overlying hair standing up a bit. Other dogs sometimes develop red areas between the pads of the paws. Common causes of allergies are household chemicals, especially carpet cleaners and fresheners (both usually used because of the dog!); insect bites and stings; and contact with certain plants. Often the cause of the allergy is unknown.

Allergies are usually transient unless the source is still present for continual contact, e.g. carpet cleaner still in the carpet, but it is better to consult your vet if an allergy is suspected because an injection of anti-histamine or an anti-inflammatory agent will make the dog comfortable again very quickly.

Occasionally allergies can take a more serious form, especially stings in the mouth or throat when the swelling can cause obstruction of the airway. This demands immediate veterinary attention.

Sometimes an allergic reaction can cause a large local swelling and this can be alarming, especially if it involves the head – there have been cases of Cavaliers with heads swollen to resemble

Bulldogs – but again, prompt veterinary attention will soon put things right.

Eye Care

Cavaliers have large eyes which can have a tendency to water when it is dusty or windy. When the eyes are watering, clean them with damp cotton wool – a clean piece for each eye. Should the eyes become red or have 'matter' in them, consult your vet.

Some Cavaliers are prone to staining under the eyes. It may be due to a blocked tear duct. If the staining is persistent it is worth seeking the advice of a vet, particularly one who has a specialist qualification in veterinary ophthalmology. He will be able to tell you whether any treatment to correct the drainage from the eye is possible, or whether it is something you have to live with. If the latter is the case then you can clear the staining by wiping with witch hazel, or one of the proprietary products on sale at pet shops. The stain will of course need your on-going attention.

There are two congenital conditions, fairly rare in Cavaliers, which can cause irritation to the eyes. These are: (1) Entropion – a turning-in of the eyelids, causing the eyelashes to rub on the cornea; and (2) Distichiasis – extra eye lashes on the margin of the eyelid which turn inwards and irritate the eye.

An earlier section dealt with the serious hereditary eye conditions of cataracts and multifocal retinal dysplasia.

Ear Care

One of the attractive features of Cavaliers is their long silky ears but, like all spaniels, the long ear leathers and abundant hair can be a source of problems since the ear canal is not open to the air.

Ears should be groomed daily and the ear inspected to see that there is no excessive waxiness, reddening, discharge or bad smell. If any of these are present, or if your dog is scratching its ears a lot, consult your vet. Ears can become a problem if not treated promptly.

Your vet will probably give you drops or ointment to treat the ears and it is important you complete the treatment, even if the ears appear to be better. Your vet may also give you drops of a cleansing liquid to put in the ear every week to remove wax and dirt.

It is not a good idea to buy ear remedies in a pet shop as they may not be the right treatment. Never put powder of any kind in the ear as this can mix with the wax and become solid and difficult to remove from the ear canal.

In the summer and autumn it is possible for grass seeds or grain seeds to get into the ear canal and this can cause the dog a lot of pain and distress. If your dog starts scratching frantically at his ear, or shaking his head violently, and is in obvious pain, consult your vet immediately.

Deafness

In the past two years I have heard of a very small number of Cavaliers who are deaf, or partially deaf. When one keeps several dogs it can be difficult to detect deafness because the deaf dog comes to depend upon the other dogs to 'hear for it', or it will pick up visual signals or learn to follow the habits and routine of the household or kennels. Its deafness may therefore be concealed to a considerable extent.

Mrs Celia L. Cox is a veterinary surgeon who runs a referral service for dogs and cats with disorders of the ear, nose and throat. As part of that service she has established a Hearing Assessment Clinic which uses sophisticated tests, similar to those used in young children, to assess if dogs have a hearing loss. I am grateful to Mrs Cox for the following information.

How do you recognize a hearing loss?

Dogs with severe hearing loss do not respond to calling, are difficult to train, and ignore loud sounds like the doorbell. Some dogs have partial hearing loss which is very difficult for owners to detect, and the dogs are often mistakenly considered to be of low intelligence or stubborn, whereas in fact they cannot hear their owner's commands.

Recent tests on Cavaliers

Mrs Cox and Kevin Munro, an audiological scientist from the University of Southampton, recently assessed a group of nine *related* Cavaliers whose owners were concerned that the dogs might have a hearing loss because their dogs did not respond to commands. They compared the results of these to seven Cavaliers with normal hearing.

They used sophisticated objective techniques including the Auditory Brainstem Response test. The tests identified if the dogs had a hearing loss in one or both ears, the degree of deafness, and information about the cause of the disorder and, therefore, whether treatment was possible.

The results showed that eight out of the nine dogs whose owners were concerned *did* have a hearing loss in one or both ears. The hearing loss varied between mild and severe for each ear. In some cases the hearing loss was due to infection in the middle ear, while in other cases it was due to a disorder of the nerve supply to the brain or inner ear structures, which can be hereditary.

If closely related dogs have a hearing loss, there may be a possible genetic link. Then alterations to breeding programmes may be appropriate to reduce the incidence of pups born with partial or total deafness. The Auditory Brainstem Response test is a non-invasive objective method for accurately assessing hearing losses in dogs and has been used in a variety of different breeds.

Finally, it is worth noting that hearing loss may be present at birth, or it may be acquired in later life. Some types of deafness are hereditary. Dogs can be tested from the age of six weeks onwards so that where there is any cause for concern, puppies can be assessed prior to sale and any hearing loss identified. It has to be recognized that dogs that are deaf, particularly ebullient young-sters, may easily put themselves, and others, at serious risk when, for instance, they cannot hear traffic or the commands of their owner.

Fleas, lice and ticks

When grooming, check to see if your Cavalier has any of these unwanted visitors. If your dog starts to scratch frequently then a very close examination is indicated. He is probably scratching because of the irritation caused by one of the above mentioned parasites.

Fleas are a very common problem. They are so small they are not easy to see, but the tiny brownish-black specks of flea excretia are more easily noticed. Wall to wall carpeting and central heating have contributed to a constantly warm environment for fleas to develop in. Whilst adult fleas spend long periods on the host dog or cat, most of the flea life-cycle, including all the egg and larval stages, takes place in the pet's environment i.e. bedding, sleeping basket, or nearby carpets or upholstery. Therefore to achieve complete flea control not only has your Cavalier to be treated, but also its sleeping quarters and the immediate surrounding area. There are insecticidal shampoos, insecticidal powders, insecticidal collars and aerosol sprays available from pet shops and vets.

Lice often lay their whitish eggs (called nits) in little clusters.

They are frequently to be found in or around the ears and are quite easily seen. The adult louse is not too difficult to destroy but the eggs are very tenacious of life, and it often requires several treatments to completely eliminate them. The best form of treatment is an insecticidal bath, followed by two others at weekly intervals, in order to kill any newly hatched lice. Even after three treatments the closest possible examination is needed to ensure that all eggs have been destroyed; otherwise re-infestation will occur. Bedding and sleeping quarters also need to be thoroughly cleansed.

Ticks can be picked up easily from sheep or from walking in fields to which sheep have had access, or even when sheep have been nearby. Sometimes hedgehogs, rabbits or other small wild animals will transport ticks well away from sheep grazing fields. Ticks bury their head into the dog's skin whilst sucking the blood and all that is visible is the tick's body (like a bluish-grey pimple). Ticks do not give up easily and need to be removed in a particular way; otherwise the head is left inside and can cause infection. It is necessary to make a tick release its grip, and this can be done by dabbing with surgical spirit or paraffin. I have seen it recommended that touching the tick with a lighted cigarette makes it release its grip, but such a method may result in your Cavalier being burned. When the tick has been made to release its grip it can then be lifted off and destroyed.

Whilst hedgehogs can be very helpful in the garden, they are usually covered in parasites and will readily infect your dog. It is best, therefore, not to encourage their presence.

Skin Diseases

If you believe your Cavalier is suffering from a skin condition other than fleas, lice or ticks, you should immediately consult your vet. There are many different skin diseases including eczema, both wet and dry, ringworm, and several kinds of mange including cheyletiella or, as it is sometimes known, 'walking dandruff'. Skilled diagnosis is essential so that the appropriate treatment can be prescribed. Some diseases, such as ringworm, are contagious to humans – another reason why you may need your vet's advice.

There may also be contributory factors such as incorrect feeding, or poor kennel hygiene, which is causing or aggravating the skin condition. If these apply, your vet will be able to offer constructive suggestions for improving the situation. It can be said, however, that skin diseases in Cavaliers are very rarely heard of.

Worming

There are two main categories of worms, namely the roundworm and the tapeworm. There is also the less common hookworm. Mainly in tropical countries, but also in America, there is the dangerous heartworm which is spread by mosquitoes.

Roundworm (Toxocara canis)

This parasite has had such wild, often grossly irresponsible, publicity about the dangers it poses to children that it must be well known to all dog owners.

Roundworms are white, pointed at both ends, usually three to six inches long, and are often passed in puppies' faeces, coiled up like a spring or in a slightly less tight shape. Roundworms lie dormant in the adult bitch until the latter stages of pregnancy when they come to life, and some pass into the womb and across the placenta into the developing puppies. Therefore puppies at birth are already infected. Some worms continue to exist in the intestine of the bitch. It should be assumed that all newly born puppies and pregnant bitches, or bitches nursing puppies, have a problem with roundworm which needs to be treated. This applies whether you see any worms or not. It is likely the nursing bitch with young puppies keeps re-infecting herself through cleaning up the puppies' motions.

The symptoms in young puppies often include lack of condition, not thriving, pot-bellied, harsh 'staring' coat, being miserable and whining. Diarrhoea is often present. This can also be due to other causes, but with worms there is sometimes a slimy mucus in the motions. If a puppy is heavily infested it can be quite debilitating and result in anaemia. Badly infested puppies may vomit worms as well as passing them in motions.

When young puppies have been treated for worms, every effort should be made for the next twelve hours to prevent the dam cleaning up the motions as they will re-infect her. It is therefore advisable to dose puppies early in the morning so that you can keep an eye on them during the remainder of the day. It is, however, extremely difficult to prevent a bitch from cleaning up as most are very conscientious in this respect, and often start to clear up the motion as soon as it is being passed.

Roundworm can affect various parts of a dog's body, including not only the intestine but liver, lungs and the digestive system.

Disposal of affected faeces should be by burning or putting down the toilet. Do not bury faeces containing worms or their eggs or put them on the compost heap, as the eggs can survive for several years in soil.

Regarding treatment there are many worming products available – tablets, powders, and liquids. Be guided by your veterinary surgeon as to which kind of wormer to use and always follow the instructions carefully.

Dangers to Humans

It is a very serious matter if anyone, particularly a child, suffers through dogs.

The eggs of the roundworm, which are too small to be seen without magnification, are sticky and can attach themselves to the coat of puppies, their bedding, or to grass or soil. If a child then inadvertently picks up such eggs they may possibly get into his body by swallowing e.g. through licking his fingers. Occasionally some of the eggs may hatch, but most of the larvae will die. Any that do survive are likely to settle in body tissues and cause no harm. However, there is an extremely minute chance that one may travel to the child's eye and cause defective vision. The likelihood of this occurring has been estimated as no more than one in a million, and some say the estimate should be nearer two million. It is a great pity, therefore, that the more vociferous of the anti-dog lobby have exaggerated the risk out of all proportion, simply to discredit dogs. Children are at far greater risk from other matters in the environment than dogs. Nevertheless, dog owners must be entirely responsible with worming precautions so that no child is put at risk, however small that risk may be. Regular worming costs very little in time or expense, and there can be no excuse for anyone not ensuring that it is done responsibly.

Tapeworm

Tapeworms are less common but sometimes more damaging than roundworms. They can seriously affect a dog's general condition and it may become markedly anaemic. The symptoms are similar to those for the roundworm, but tapeworms can occur at any age, whereas roundworms are mostly active in the pregnant or nursing bitch and young puppies.

The tapeworm is flat like a piece of tape, but is divided into segments and is a greyish-white colour. It attaches itself to the wall of the small intestine and can grow to twenty inches in length, though all we see are small segments which have been excreted. Tapeworms develop these segments, with the new smaller ones forming at the head end. The segments steadily grow and mature, with those at the tail being the largest and containing the eggs. These end segments break off and are passed in the faeces and sometimes can be found sticking to the dog's coat around the anus or in the dog's bedding. The tapeworm eggs are similar to cucumber seeds, or when dried in the dog's coat are not unlike grains of rice.

Fleas and lice act as hosts for the tapeworm and it is therefore vital to rid the dog of them when treating for tapeworm. If you do not clear the fleas and lice, your dog will become re-infested as the fleas and lice will be carrying the infestation.

Treatment for Worms

The pregnant bitch should have been wormed on the first day of her season, and again at exactly five weeks into her pregnancy. When nursing her young puppies she should also be wormed when the puppies are wormed i.e. when they are three, five and seven weeks old. Thereafter she should be wormed at six-monthly intervals. The puppies, however, will need further worming treatment at four and six months, and then every six months. An adult Cavalier needs to be wormed every six months.

In some old dog books it was felt that one quarter of all dogs' ailments were caused, directly or indirectly, by the presence of worms, and it was recommended that an adult dog should be wormed four times a year. With present day treatments, vets seem to be generally agreed that six monthly worming is sufficient.

It has been recommended by some persons that regular doses of garlic act as a cure and a preventive in regard to worms. Others disagree very strongly. For example Olwen Gwynne Jones in *The Popular Guide to Puppy Rearing* says of garlic, 'I found it absolutely useless – indeed worse than useless.'

Anal (or scent) Glands

On either side of a dog's anus is a small gland. If your dog starts to drag his bottom on the floor (my family call it ski-ing), the very likely reason is that he is suffering irritation due to the anal, or scent, glands being full. These need to be emptied and this is a very simple job which most experienced breeders do themselves. When next you visit your vet ask him if he will show you how to do it. It is best to have a partner hold the dog's head, then for you to lift the dog's tail, feel the glands and squeeze inwards and upwards at the same time. A foul smelling dark brown liquid will squirt out and can travel a metre unless you have it covered with a piece of paper kitchen towel. With some dogs the 'liquid' may have become thicker like a fairly solid toothpaste. If the glands are not emptied regularly the contents may become firmer and in fact impacted, thus causing the dog serious discomfort. Also if the contents become infected a painful abscess may form and this needs veterinary treatment. If a dog is having serious problems with its anal sacs the vet may consider removing them.

I seek to express the contents from my dogs' anal sacs every two to three months in order to avoid any danger of them becoming impacted, or an abscess developing. If you do not wish to clear out the anal glands yourself ask your vet to do so each time you take your dog to him, or whenever your dog is regularly dragging its bottom on the floor.

It is said the anal glands are there to lubricate the anus each time a dog passes a motion. Some vets feel that with modern day feeding the motion is too soft to require lubricating, and therefore the glands have outlived their usefulness and therefore do not empty naturally. A diet containing more fibre may make the glands empty more regularly.

Emptying anal glands is one of the most frequent tasks undertaken by vets.

Poisons

Warfarin contained in rat poison, strychnine still used by some gamekeepers to kill vermin, and cyanide used to destroy wasp nests are obviously very dangerous poisons to be guarded against at all costs. But there are other dangerous poisons used in weedkillers e.g. sprays containing arsenic. Various sprays are used on roadside verges which some owners claim have made their dogs ill. Also, think about the products we use in our own gardens, for instance sodium chlorate to clear weeds from paths, and the lawn cocktail known as 'feed 'n weed and moss killer'. Or the quite deadly slug pellets. A puppy I bred and sold was at ten months seen to be eating in a garden where slug pellets had been scattered. It was immediately taken to the vet but was dead within the hour.

There are so many of these pesticides that we need therefore to be extremely careful in both our use and storage of them. When spraying, keep dogs away until the spray has dried, and then do not allow dogs to lick or sniff the treated plants. Also, when spraying, remove water and food dishes if there is the slightest chance that spray may drift on to them.

In addition there is a need for care with kitchen products e.g. detergents and disinfectants. Keep them secure, and remember most Cavaliers quickly learn how to 'nudge' open sliding or insecure doors.

The symptoms of poisoning include foaming at the mouth, vomiting, stumbling about and collapse. If you suspect your Cavalier has been poisoned, waste no time in taking the dog to your vet. If you suspect a particular poison, take the container as it may assist your vet to quickly determine the appropriate antidote.

Growths and Hernias

Obviously the position, size and malignancy or otherwise of a growth determines its seriousness. At one end of the scale may be a wart of little significance, whilst at the other end of the scale may be a cancerous tumour of the throat, necessitating euthanasia of the dog.

Author's **Champion Crieda Rosella** when she was twelve years old

Mammary tumours in older bitches are quite common. Ch. Crieda Rosella had such a tumour when aged about eight. Our vet removed all the teats down one side and Rosella took the operation in her stride. However when she was twelve a similar growth appeared on the other side. Our vet advised 'observation'. At twelve years eight months the growth began to expand rapidly and Rosella therefore had to have a further operation for its removal. Our vet took the opportunity to also remove several decaying teeth. Rosella made a good recovery. Some of the older Cavaliers are 'tough cookies'.

There are two forms of hernia found in the Cavalier. The first is an umbilical hernia which, as the name implies, is a small swelling on the navel. If I see a whelping bitch is having difficulty in severing the cord of newly born puppies I cut it with sterilized scissors. An umbilical hernia is of little significance and generally no action needs to be taken. It is the opinion of vets and geneticists that umbilical hernias are probably genetically controlled.

An inguinal hernia, located in the groin, is much less common than the umbilical one. Both sexes can have it, but it is more frequently present in bitches. It can be seen in puppies as young as six weeks. It is a small swelling which at times seems to vanish, and then re-appears. Vets have slightly differing opinions about it. Some say just watch it and usually no action will be required, as the small hole in the inguinal canal through which the slight swelling protrudes will usually heal-over by itself. Other vets say it is best to do a corrective operation at about six months and to spay at the same time. Most vets seem to be agreed that affected animals should not be bred from because of the possibility of inheritance, and in bitches there may also be a problem during pregnancy or whelping because of weakness in the inguinal area.

I have only known of one case of inguinal hernia. The bitch had had two previous litters and none of the ten puppies in those litters had an inguinal hernia. In the bitch's third litter of three puppies there was one difficult birth, and the pup had to be partly pulled out, and this was the puppy later found to have the inguinal hernia. The owner wondered whether the difficult birth might have caused or contributed to the formation of the hernia.

To sum up, there is no reason for concern with warts and small umbilical hernias, but all other swellings or growths need to be assessed by your vet.

False, Phantom or Pseudo Pregnancies

After the appropriate length of time following her 'season', occasionally an unmated bitch will begin to show some of the signs of being in whelp, e.g. making a nest, her abdomen beginning to enlarge, producing milk, panting, and carrying toys around. Some writers say they have even known bitches have contractions but I have never come across this myself.

The cause is unknown, although some suggest it may be caused by excessive hormonal action. With some bitches the problem becomes more severe at each subsequent season, but with others it becomes less. Helpful action that can be taken is to remove the toys she is mothering. Do not fuss over her because she is in this condition. Instead keep her active, take her for frequent walks. Also reduce slightly her food and water intake.

If these remedies are not successful then it may be necessary to consult your vet. He may consider a course of hormonal treatment, or sedatives to reduce the nervous stress. With severe false pregnancies some vets may recommend the bitch be spayed, as bitches that do not come on 'heat' do not have false pregnancies. But often there are side-effects to spaying e.g. obesity and excessive coat growth. Therefore the matter needs very careful thought.

Some vets say that as the problem is most common in maiden bitches, a cure can be effected by allowing her to have a litter. This seems to me to be an unsound reason for bringing further puppies into the world when there is already considerable overbreeding. In any case, it often does not work. Some bitches that have had one, or even more litters, are known to have had false pregnancies at subsequent seasons.

Oestrus Control

Sometimes when a bitch is due in season this can be inconvenient in that it seems likely to clash with an important event. Let me give you an example. Some years ago a friend had a young, top quality Cavalier bitch that was winning consistently at the highest level. He was greatly looking forward to breeding from her but first wanted to try and win with her at Crufts. Unfortunately it seemed likely she would be in season for Crufts, and therefore realistically he would be unable to show her. He consulted his vet who advised a product to postpone the bitch's season. The bitch was dosed accordingly. She appeared at Crufts but seemed lethargic, and was placed, but not in the first three. My friend was a little disappointed, but he looked forward to having puppies from her in due course.

But whereas her seasons had previously been very regular at six monthly intervals, her next season did not occur for fifteen months, and then did not seem to be a proper season. Over the next few years the owner reported that 'her seasons were all over the place'. She was mated at every opportunity but never produced any puppies, despite every possible attention, however costly, from vets. One might have difficulty in proving absolutely that her reproductive cycle was completely upset by giving the product to postpone her season, but my friend firmly believes that the product was to blame. The incident was enough to persuade me never to administer any such preparations to my bitches.

However, should it prove necessary to consider postponing a bitch's season you can of course discuss the matter of oestrus control with your vet. I am told there are now new products on the market which are much improved and cause fewer problems. These products, it is said, can also be used regularly to stop bitches coming into season and can be an alternative to spaying. Apparently there is now some evidence to show if bitches are given injections of some of these products before the first season and kept on them by injections twice yearly they are less likely to develop mammary tumours later in life. Despite the assurances I still prefer to avoid using them if at all possible.

Pyometra

This condition frequently comes to the attention of vets. Pyometra simply means pus in the womb. This results from the lining of the womb becoming diseased. The condition usually shows itself shortly after a bitch has been in season and is caused by an hormonal imbalance affecting the womb lining. The condition usually occurs in older bitches that have not had puppies.

There are two types of the condition – open pyometra, in which the neck of the womb is open and the pus (often foul smelling) is thus able to discharge through the vulva; and closed pyometra, in which the neck of the womb is closed and the pus cannot come away and builds up in the womb. As a result the bitch's abdomen becomes noticeably swollen. Open pyometra with its smelly vaginal discharge usually occurs as an extension of the discharge associated with being in season. It is therefore seen earlier than closed pyometra, which is usually noticed as a marked swelling of the abdomen six to eight weeks after the normal end of the season.

The first symptoms of both types are that the bitch seems unwell, she starts to drink excessively and then frequently urinates, and with some there may be raised temperature, but this is not always so. If swift action is not taken the bitch may become toxic (poisoned by the infection), vomit persistently, become seriously ill, and die.

Pyometra is therefore a condition which requires immediate veterinary attention. In an unusual case of a young bitch being affected, it may be possible to treat the infection with antibiotics because the degenerative change in the wall of the womb has not taken place. However with older bitches it is likely that the only realistic and successful treatment is surgical removal of the ovaries and womb, thus ending her breeding career.

Relationship with Vets

There is a need for owners, and certainly breeders, to establish a positive, understanding relationship with their vet. If this can be done the benefits are considerable, with a steadily increasing confidence in each other. Both parties then feel more at ease in the relationship and can express themselves more freely. They each have something to offer – the Cavalier breeder his experience from his many years with the breed, and the vet his training and skills. If both parties develop a respect for each other's contribution, the relationship becomes a partnership, which benefits the dogs considerably.

What can owners and breeders do to establish this positive relationship? I suggest the following may be helpful:

1. When visiting the vet have relevant objective information ready to share with him. Think about it before going to the surgery. If it helps, jot it down.
2. If you do not fully understand what the vet is saying, tell him, and ask him to explain it again in greater detail.
3. Be particularly sure of what the vet is saying about treatment. If in any doubt, outline your understanding to him and ask for confirmation that it is correct.
4. Be ready at any follow-up visit to report briefly and objectively on progress. Remember vets are busy people.
5. Do not be afraid, however, to make any observation which you feel is relevant.
6. Invite him to call unofficially if he would like a cup of tea and to talk about Cavaliers. Ask if he would be interested in seeing any research papers on the breed.

7. If you are not satisfied with a diagnosis or treatment, you can ask your vet to arrange a second opinion, and he is bound by his Code of Practice to do so.

Many breeders have an excellent relationship with their vet, but from comments in the weekly Dog Papers and at shows it seems that some breeders are losing confidence in them. Vets need to take notice of the expressions of concern and resolve to do something about it before matters deteriorate further.

It is to be hoped that where difficulties have arisen, these can be overcome. We need a good relationship with vets, and they certainly need us. Cavalier devotees that have a problem need to work conscientiously to improve matters, but if all your efforts fail, then change to another vet and start again.

9

Lifetime Service Chart

There are certain steps regarding a Cavalier's health which need to be taken regularly and should not be overlooked. A Lifetime Service Chart therefore follows. This is similar to a car service chart and sets out matters which need attention at certain ages. If the timetable is followed your Cavalier's health should benefit accordingly.

AGE	ACTION NEEDED
10 seconds	If my dam has not done so, clear foetal sac from my mouth so that I can breathe. Otherwise my service chart terminates now.
3 or 4 days	Have dew claws removed. Have puppies checked for any defects.
10 days	Clip puppies' nails with scissors, thus protecting dam when they feed from her.
3 weeks	Clip puppies' nails again. Worm puppies for first time.
4 weeks	Start to wean puppies.
4½ weeks	Clip puppies' nails again.
5 weeks	Worm puppies for second time.
6 weeks	Weaning of puppies should be complete.

7 weeks	Worm puppies for third time.
8 weeks	Have puppies checked before they go to their new homes. S2 of Code of Ethics states: 'All stock must be healthy at time of sale and to have been checked for hereditary defects before sale.'
2–3 months	Have vaccinations done.
4 months	Worm again.
6 months	Worm again.
12 months	Have future breeding stock x-rayed and scored for hip dysplasia under BVA/KC Scheme. Worm again.
15 months	Eye examination by veterinary ophthalmologist under BVA/KC Scheme. Heart examination and certificate. Booster vaccination. Have anal glands emptied.
18 months	Worm again.
2 years 3 months	For breeding stock, eye examination by veterinary ophthalmologist under BVA/KC Scheme. Heart examination and certificate. Booster vaccination. Worm again. Have anal glands emptied.
2 years 9 months	Worm again.
3 years 3 months	For breeding stock, eye examination by veterinary ophthalmologist under BVA/KC Scheme. Heart examination and certificate. Booster vaccination. Worm again. Have anal glands emptied.
3 years 9 months	Worm again.
4 years 3 months	For breeding stock, eye examination by veterinary ophthalmologist under BVA/KC Scheme. Heart

examination and certificate. Booster vaccination. Worm again. Have anal glands emptied.

5 years and annually thereafter	Continue with:

1. Eye examination by veterinary ophthalmologist under BVA/KC Scheme for breeding stock. This can be discontinued from the age of 7 years.
2. Heart examination and certificate.
3. Booster vaccination.

At every 6 months:
Worm again and empty anal glands.

At 7 years Consult your vet about dietary and health requirements for older dogs.

10

Genetics – Information to Improve Breeding

Genetics is the science of heredity, which means the transmission to offspring of the 'built-in' characteristics of previous generations. The genetic constitution of an embryo puppy is fixed at the time the egg in the dam is fertilized by the sperm from the stud dog. The genetic constitution of a puppy results from the sum of the parental contributions to it.

However, we must not forget that a Cavalier's make-up consists not only of inherited characteristics but also those that it has acquired from its environmental upbringing and experiences, particularly food, housing, exercise, socialization, stimulation, etc. A genetically sound dog can be ruined by unsatisfactory rearing. In other words, both nature and nurture make a contribution.

This chapter only deals with genetics. Environmental influences, such as the socialization of puppies, are dealt with in other sections of the book.

Successful breeding depends upon the careful choice, and matching, of quality breeding stock, so as to improve each successive generation. These principles have been acted upon over the centuries, long before Gregor Mendel produced his theories relating to the laws of heredity. However, we now have increased knowledge available to us. In order to breed intelligently and competently it is helpful for dog breeders to understand how traits or characteristics are transmitted from one generation to the next.

Genetics is an absorbing but complex subject, and to obtain a full grasp of its implications would take a long period of study and experience. The following is therefore merely a 'taster', aimed at

'Stop whispering!'
'But what do they mean by genetics?'
(Taylor's delightful trio of **Kemble puppies**)

establishing a simple knowledge base from which one can approach breeding in a more enlightened, creative and rewarding way.

Mendel

An Austrian monk, Gregor Mendel discovered the basic laws of biological inheritance in 1866 through his work with the common garden pea. Mendel discovered that certain particles (later called genes) are inherited in related pairs, with each parent contributing one gene to each pair. These pairs of genes control every characteristic in the genetic make-up of the organism, be it a pea or a dog. Mendel outlined the predictable, but different, roles undertaken by dominant and recessive genes. He also devised certain mating systems which have become classic tests of the mode of inheritance.

Although his work was published, little note was taken of it for many years. In fact it was 1900 before several prominent biologists then accepted: (a) its importance and (b) that it applied not only to vegetables but also to animals. Mendel has rightfully been described as the founder of genetics.

Let us consider now the current essentials of a subject that can make a useful contribution to the breeding of dogs.

Cells

A dog is made up of an immense number of cells. These cells are so minute that they can only be seen with the aid of a high-powered microscope. Each cell is encased by a membrane containing fluid, and in the centre is a nucleus enclosed within its own membrane. The outer fluid also contains other minute matters, but in this brief outline of genetics we need not concern ourselves with them. The nuclei contain the chromosomes and genes which control, and transmit, all hereditary factors from one generation to the next.

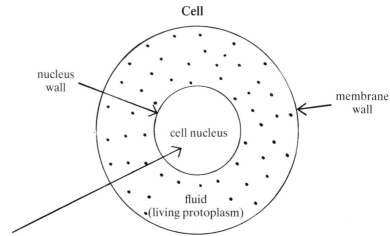

Cell

nucleus wall

membrane wall

cell nucleus

fluid (living protoplasm)

contains the chromosomes on which the genes are arranged like beads on a string

As the dog grows these cells divide and multiply, with each new cell normally being an exact replica of the one from which it was formed. The process is repeated over and over again and thus builds up tissue which eventually forms tissues and organs. This process of multiplying is called *mitosis*.

Chromosomes

Dogs have thirty-nine pairs of chromosomes in every body cell, whilst horses have thirty-two pairs, human beings twenty-three pairs, cats nineteen pairs and fruit flies only four pairs. It will be seen, therefore, that the dog has a large number of chromosomes compared with other mammals. Having this large number cannot, in itself, create inborn genetic variation, but where this variation is already present, the large number of chromosomes can encourage the widest possible exploitation.

Whilst the thirty-nine pairs of chromosomes look very similar, no two pairs are exactly alike. However one pair, the sex chromosomes, are significantly different to the other thirty-eight pairs. Each bitch has a pair of X chromosomes, whilst male dogs have one X chromosome and one Y chromosome. When a mating takes place the bitch can only provide an X sex chromosome in her eggs for X is all she has. The dog, however, will provide millions of sperms, half of which contain an X chromosome and half a Y chromosome.

Therefore the egg with the X chromosome will be fertilized by a sperm with either an X or Y chromosome. If an X sperm unites with an X egg, the puppy will be female, whereas if a Y sperm fertilizes an X egg the puppy will be male. It is pure chance which of the millions of sperms fertilize the few eggs produced by the Cavalier bitch. Therefore, whilst it is true to say the dog is responsible for determining the sex of the puppies, there is nevertheless a great element of chance as to which sperms, X or Y, actually reach the eggs first and complete the fertilization.

There is also a great deal of chance in that each sperm, and each egg, has thirty-nine single chromosomes, but it is pure chance as to which chromosomes are in each sperm and each egg. Therefore, however well planned the mating may be, a good slice of luck is needed to bring all the desired genes together.

At the time the mating takes place, if the dog and bitch each contributed their full thirty-nine pairs of chromosomes it would mean the resultant puppies would have seventy-eight pairs, and this would continue doubling with each subsequent generation. Nature skilfully solves the problem by reducing the chromosomes in the sex cells by half (one from each pair) before they meet and unite. The dog therefore contributes thirty-nine single chromosomes and the bitch does likewise, thus together reconstituting the required thirty-nine pairs.

Genes and Simple Inheritance

From chromosomes it is a natural step to genes. Each chromosome is composed of thousands of microscopic genes. A gene is the unit of inheritance and may vary for each innate characteristic. Each characteristic is dictated by a pair, or several pairs, of genes. No two dogs, not even litter siblings, are genetically identical.

Genes are made up of deoxyribonucleic acid (DNA) and you

will probably have heard about DNA identification ('genetic fingerprinting'). It is now regularly used to check involvement in major crimes such as murder and rape because each individual has a distinctive DNA profile.

The genes are strung out along the length of each pair of chromosomes like beads on a string, and the many genes are also in pairs. The genes which occupy the same position on each member of a pair of chromosomes will influence the same characteristic. If the pair of genes is alike for a particular characteristic (AA or aa), the dog is said to be *homozygous* for that attribute. Should the pair of genes for a characteristic be different (Aa), the dog is said to be *heterozygous* for that characteristic. When a dog is homozygous for a particular characteristic it will breed true on that point, but if heterozygous it will breed with a more variable result for the characteristic. A dog may be homozygous for one characteristic and heterozygous for another, and litter mates are not necessarily homozygous or heterozygous for the same characteristic. Frequent use of outcrosses in breeding will produce more heterozygous pairs of genes, and therefore provide more variability in the resulting progeny.

When the chromosomes, and thereby the genes, multiply they almost invariably produce self-copies which are perfect. However, on rare occasions the copy is not exact at gene level and this is known as *mutation*. It means that the mutant gene can act as an alternative in heredity, but this occurs so infrequently that we need not dwell on it in this brief outline.

Dominant and Recessive Genes

Dominant genes are represented by capital letters (*L*) and recessive genes by small letters (*l*), and each gene will determine a different characteristic. If at fertilization an egg receives a dominant gene from both parents, it is then *LL* and pure dominant for that characteristic. If, however, it receives a dominant gene *L* from one parent and a recessive gene *l* from the other parent, it will be *Ll*. The result will be that the characteristic of the dominant gene *L* will suppress the characteristic of the recessive gene *l* and the puppy gene will express the characteristic of the dominant gene. Although not showing in the puppy, the recessive gene *l* will remain 'hidden' and ever present. If the puppy is eventually mated to a partner also carrying the same recessive gene *l*, then by chance the offspring may have the paired recessive genes *ll*, and that characteristic will surface and express itself. A recessive gene may remain hidden for several generations until it is linked with its identical recessive gene, and then the characteristic will appear.

Other Hereditary Combinations

Sometimes biological inheritance takes on a rather more complicated form.

Polygenic Inheritance

Instead of a characteristic being inherited through the action of a single pair of genes, it may sometimes arise through the action of two, three or even more pairs acting in unison. Such genes are described as polygenes, and the attributes they control are known as polygenically inherited characters.

Polygenic characters are inherited in the same way as Mendelian characteristics, but as they are influenced by a larger number of minor genes (polygenes) it is not easy to identify the genotype (i.e. the dog's genetic make-up). Because polygenic characters are controlled by several and possibly many genes, there are likely to be several different degrees of any abnormality e.g. as with hip dysplasia.

Threshold Characters

This is when the cumulative build up of polygenes reaches a threshold developmental point, and then a particular jump in expression of a characteristic occurs. Before reaching the eventful threshold point which triggers the response, there may be no noticeable response, or alternatively there may be a lesser rather different expression. Geneticists believe that many cases of threshold inheritance are associated with anomalies.

The concept is a difficult one, and a particular problem is that with many threshold characteristics the trigger point (i.e. how many polygenes are required) is not known. It may be possible for geneticists to hazard an estimated threshold figure, but it would often be no more than a 'guesstimate'. For further information see Cryptorchidism later in this chapter.

Practical Use of Genetics

A knowledge of genetics has been used positively and successfully to combat a number of hereditary conditions in dogs. Some of these conditions have resulted in serious consequences e.g. progressive retinal atrophy (PRA), caused by a recessive gene, and resulting in total blindness in Setters. Geneticists are currently involved in seeking solutions to other hereditary conditions in a number of breeds.

The Cavalier King Charles Spaniel Club is fortunate to have been advised by the geneticist Dr B.M. Cattanach on the hereditary aspects of its research into heart disease (Mitral Valve Disease or MVD). From my own experience on the Cavalier Club committee I know that Dr Cattanach's guidance was most helpful in setting up the research on a sound basis. Without his help the Club may have drifted into inappropriate methods of data collection. He and Dr P.G.G. Darke, veterinary cardiologist, advised that establishing the date of onset of the mitral valve disease murmur should be a more reliable indicator than asking many different vets to grade the murmurs. The Cavalier Club will certainly need the assistance of both the cardiologist and the geneticist in assessing the information collected, and deciding how it can best be presented to members, so that they can use it to the maximum advantage in future breeding and thus benefit the breed.

I believe this work on specific Cavalier problems, with advice by geneticists and specialists in particular fields, is one of the most positive avenues open to Cavalier breed clubs worldwide. From my contacts in a number of countries it seems that there are specialists who are very willing to be involved in this way. I see a helpful, positive role for geneticists in such research projects. Perhaps in the past we have not given sufficient thought to the contribution that geneticists might make in these matters, especially in the setting up of projects.

Practical Application for Individual Breeders

When one moves on to consider the use made of genetics by individual breeders, it usually does not extend much beyond 'breeding like to like' from which we hope to produce a fairly consistent type. Therefore we seek, in a rather simple way, to strengthen the virtues in our bloodlines, reduce the weaknesses and avoid introducing serious faults. This approach has worked reasonably successfully for many breeders in different breeds. The successful breeders establish their own particular type, which is based at the centre of the Breed Standard requirements and not at the marginal edges. By sticking fairly close to their line, having a good knowledge of the strengths and weaknesses within it, and having a good eye for a dog, they gradually build on their strengths. They do so by aiming to make each youngster better quality than its forebears. Of course they have their disappointments, even an occasional disaster, but overall the steady successful growth continues and is cumulative.

However by using genetics in a simple but knowledgeable way, we may be able to further improve our breeding successes, and also avoid some of our disappointing litters. Genetics has already given us useful knowledge which we now take for granted e.g. in the colours we may expect from particular matings as genes determine colours. But so much more is governed, at least in part, by heredity, for example physical features including afflictions, size, behaviour, reproductive capacity, length of coat and susceptibility to various diseases.

Every time we breed a litter we are involved with genetics whether we appreciate it or not. Therefore a more knowledgeable and enlightened approach can only be helpful. I suggest that responsible, progressive Cavalier breeders need to consider how they can use the science of genetics to: (1) recurrently breed a large proportion of Cavaliers which are typical, have excellent temperament, resemble each other and *consistently* have the good qualities we are seeking; and (2) improve our stock and breed out, and avoid breeding in, undesirable hereditary characteristics or abnormalities. Methods of breeding such as in-breeding, line-breeding and outcrossing are obviously important in this respect and are covered in the next chapter.

But we can be more specific in seeking help from genetics. For instance if we have a particular problem in our bloodline, or believe there may be a problem lurking somewhere in the pedigree, we can check what hereditary factors are involved, and particularly what is the mode of inheritance. We shall then have additional information available, which may assist us to keep from making avoidable mistakes in our breeding programmes. We shall not always be able to obtain foolproof advice for each and every condition, because for some defects the mode of inheritance may be complex or unclear, but at least we ought to ascertain if simple genetic guidance is available. Lists of defects and genetic information about many defects are provided in *Practical Genetics for Dog Breeders* by Malcolm B. Willis, *Genetics for Dog Breeders* by Roy Robinson and *Dog Breeding* by Frank Jackson.

Let us consider as examples two defects which occur very occasionally in Cavaliers and where knowledge of the mode of inheritance can be helpful to breeders.

1. *Slipping Patella* – dislocation of the kneecap. Polygenic inheritance – threshold character.

2. *Cryptorchidism* – the failure of one (unilateral) or both (bilateral) testicles to descend into the scrotum. The bilateral cryptorchid is sterile, but the unilateral cryptorchid (often loosely but incorrectly called a monorchid) is able to reproduce. Genetically it is probable that this defect behaves as a threshold character. If you recall, this is when several polygenes, none of which are capable of producing the defect by themselves, do so by acting together. These polygenes usually have a low incidence, but can become more concentrated by chance in certain dogs, families or bloodlines. If a concentration does occur, particularly if it is in both parents, then their sons may well show the defect. It is unwise to breed from monorchid dogs. (I use the word monorchid because it is so widely used, and is in fact contained in the Kennel Club's Glossary of Canine Terms.) It is also inadvisable to breed from litter sisters to such dogs because, although they cannot show the defect, they can be carrying the polygenes for the condition.

An example of an abnormality caused by a dominant gene has not been given. This is because it is relatively easy to recognize those dogs that have the problem (it is there to be seen) and to exclude affected dogs from all breeding. Dominant defects only tend to survive when they are late in onset, and affected stock has already been used in breeding. An example would be a late developing cataract due to a dominant gene.

Knowing the mode of inheritance, as indicated in the examples, is helpful. If it is accompanied by a little basic knowledge of genetics, then one's chances of dealing with such problems are improved.

For those who have the inclination to seek a further understanding of the subject there are recently published books which are more 'readable' and which also concentrate on the *practical* application rather than the often complicated theoretical approaches. Genetics is, I suspect, for many people a subject which needs time and study rather than 'a quick read'. It is not the easiest subject to get to grips with, but it is certainly worth the effort in seeking to understand the basic principles. Such knowledge should help you to become a more skilful and competent breeder.

It would, however, be unrealistic at this stage to expect the science of genetics to provide all, or indeed most, of the answers. The subject, certainly in relation to dogs, has not yet reached that level of development or certainty, but there are undoubted benefits it can provide.

In some areas genetics is currently moving at a fairly fast pace. For instance, farmers can now choose the sex of their calves. In the human field experiments have started using gene therapy to treat serious inherited diseases like cystic fibrosis and muscular dystrophy. Just think of the possibilities that abound in the canine field. However, some people are concerned about where so-called 'genetic engineering' might eventually lead us. They say that such developments need very careful thought, as they raise important moral and ethical considerations.

11

Breeding – Mating, Pregnancy and Whelping

William's **Champion Johnasta Rudolf**

Management of a Stud Dog

Offering a dog at stud, and charging a fee for his services, is a responsibility that should not be undertaken lightly. The dog needs to be of good quality, fit and healthy, and should have had the appropriate breed screening tests. Above all else the dog must have a faultless temperament. An aggressive, noisy or nervous Cavalier should not be offered at stud as it can only damage the breed. The owner should be experienced in handling a stud dog, or have someone present who is well experienced. Some novices believe that all you have to do is to shut the dog and bitch in a shed and leave them to get on with it, whilst the owners go off for a coffee and a chat. The mating may take place satisfactorily in such circumstances, but there is a very good chance that it will not. The owners may be unsure whether or not a mating actually has occurred. There is also a possibility that the dog or bitch, or even both, may get seriously hurt.

In preparing a dog for stud work he should be kept well away from the kennel's own bitches that are in season or he will fret and lose condition. If he shows amorous instincts and mounts dogs, and also bitches that are not in season, he should not be scolded or you may dampen his ardour. For an actual mating he must not be allowed to get fat, should not be fed just prior to a mating, must be clean and well groomed and free from infection (always examine his sheath when grooming him). He should be happy at being handled, and be content that the bitch is held during the mating.

For the actual matings most breeders usually have a quiet room set aside where they can guarantee there will be no interruptions or distractions. The descriptive names given to these 'love rooms' is an education in itself! The floor should not be slippery, and it is helpful if it is carpeted, or at least has a rug covering one part. Just prior to bringing the dog and bitch together they should be given the opportunity of evacuating their bowels.

The bitch should be given adequate time to relax and become acclimatized to the particular room before the dog is brought in. Some stud dog owners ask to examine the bitch in order to ascertain if there are any obstructions, and whether the timing is right. The hand is scrubbed clean, the finger lightly greased with vaseline, and it is then gently inserted into the vagina in an upwards direction. This informs of any obstruction or tightness. The vulva itself should be swollen, the passage soft, pliable and open, and coated with a slippery vaginal secretion. If all is well, and the bitch is turning her tail to the side as you handle her, then the signs are that she is 'ready'. If the vaginal passage is tight and dry then it is probably too early or, more seriously, too late. But bitches vary considerably, and the actual size of the vulva can vary significantly.

When the dog and bitch first meet they should ideally both be on leads so that the introduction can be gradual. When they seem reasonably happy with each other they can be loosed off their leads but they must be watched very closely. If the dog rushes the bitch before she is ready she may not welcome his attentions, and if he persists she may attack him. I know of one champion who had his face badly ripped and it put him off stud work altogether for two years.

One hopes that they will be attracted to each other. If this is the case the bitch will usually flirt provocatively with the dog and they both will become sexually excited. When it looks as though they are ready to 'couple' the bitch should be held firmly by her collar, or around her shoulders, whilst the dog mounts her to perform the sexual act. The bitch needs to be held firmly because if the dog hurts her when penetrating she may pull away or attack him. When penetration takes place there is then a further important stage as the dog's bulbous urethra swells up inside the bitch and they become locked together or 'tied'. The bitch sometimes becomes frightened when this happens and may want to get the dog off her back. She needs to be held particularly firmly for this short period and talked to kindly. When she has coped with this stage both she and the dog become more settled.

It is wise to note the time that they become 'tied' and also when they disengage. At this time if you feel underneath the bitch you can feel the dog's penis locked inside her. The dog is likely to want 'to turn', either partly, i.e. drop his front legs over one side of the bitch, or fully, i.e. in addition to taking his front legs over he also lifts his back leg over so that the rear ends of the dog and bitch are now facing each other. They are of course still 'tied' together and will remain so for a period which may vary from ten minutes to about an hour. The longest tie with one of my dogs was in fact one hour and twenty-five minutes.

The bitch should be prevented from trying to pull away from the dog as this could cause injury to both of them. If they are fidgeting, you can hold them together by clasping the roots of the two tails in one hand, or if two persons are present – and this is always advisable – each can hold one dog. Both dogs and handlers need to be patient until the dog can disengage naturally. Often the dog and bitch lie down together until disengagement is possible. Handlers are warned that an hour on your knees holding two dogs steady can become pretty uncomfortable.

A few breeders undertake the matings on a large table, but this has its dangers and I prefer my dogs to be on terra firma. After the dog has withdrawn from the bitch his sheath should be sponged down with a mild antiseptic solution and inspected to see that all is well. He should not be returned immediately to the presence of other stud dogs or they may be resentful of his good fortune and start to fight him. Leave him quietly on his own for a few minutes.

On some occasions matings do not proceed quite as smoothly as one might hope. Some dogs, particularly a 'maiden' dog, may be shy and rather clueless about what he has to do. If he does not even appreciate he has to mount the bitch, then after a suitable period of foreplay lift him on the bitch and then see how he progresses. If little further progress is made put your hand under the bitch's undercarriage and hold the vulva steady and then encourage the dog further. It is best not to manually guide the dog's penis to actually enter the bitch as he may come to depend upon such assistance on future occasions.

A different type of problem is encountered with the highly sexed but inexperienced stud who mounts the bitch, begins thrusting and continues with it, even if his penis is not in the bitch's vulva. If he is not stopped he will ejaculate, with no benefit to the bitch. Often you can see his erect penis at the side of the bitch. He needs to be gently lifted off and encouraged to start again and aim better.

If a mating has not been successfully achieved after half an hour separate the dog and bitch, have a cup of tea and then try again. Often absence makes the heart grow fonder, or stimulates lust.

Some other problems that occasionally arise include the following:

1. The dog has difficulty in entering the bitch. A slight smear of vaseline on the vulva often assists.
2. A bitch may not yet be ovulating i.e. she has been brought too early. A vet can help to decide the correct day for mating. If a bitch has been brought too early it helps if you have accommodation to keep her for a few days.
3. If the dog and bitch are of different heights it can assist to have a telephone directory or a folded rug available in order to raise the small one up a little.
4. The bitch's owner occasionally proves to be a problem in that she gets anxious or upset and this is communicated to the bitch, which then becomes restless and unco-operative. In such circumstances it is best for the owner to leave, but to be called back in to witness the tie. In most cases, of course, the presence of the bitch's owner actually re-assures the bitch.
5. If the bitch is aggressive and likely to bite, put a muzzle on her or tie a bandage or stocking around her mouth.
6. If unsure of the 'right' day mate the bitch twice with an interval

of twenty-four or forty-eight hours between the matings. With maiden bitches it is sometimes felt that a second mating is advisable.

There need not be a tie for conception to take place but both owners usually feel more satisfied if there has been a tie. Very occasionally a short tie can take place even though the dog's swollen 'bulb' is just outside the bitch's vulva. Such ties, although unusual, often produce puppies because it means the dog has ejaculated successfully into the bitch.

Hull's lovely pair of matching champions: **Telvara Top Hat** (son) and **Telvara Kasanova** (father)

Upon completion of the mating the stud fee becomes due, but only accept a fee if you genuinely consider that a satisfactory mating has been completed. The fee is for the mating; it is not conditional upon puppies being produced. Many stud dog owners do say, however, that if no puppies are produced a further free mating, by the same dog, will be offered at the bitch's next season. If any offer is made it needs to be clearly stated, and defined, on the stud fee receipt. It is known that some bitch owners have asked if they can use another dog next time or, in one instance, if their friend's bitch can have the benefit of the free mating! The Kennel Club form needs to be completed and signed by the stud dog owner and handed, along with the receipt and pedigree, to the bitch's owner. Ask to be informed of the details of the litter.

If two or three bitches mated consecutively to a dog 'miss', i.e. do not have puppies, the stud dog needs to be tested by a vet. If the sperm count is low or the sperms are weak and non-vigorous, then action should be taken to rectify matters before the dog is used at stud again. A rest may be all that is required. With more persistent problems, hormone implants are said to be very successful. I admit to being a little unhappy about such treatments, especially on an on-going basis. My feeling is that if a stud dog cannot perform naturally through his own resources he should be withdrawn from stud duties.

Stud dog owners should appreciate that if no puppies result it is invariably the dog that is blamed! In fact in nine cases out of ten the fault lies with the bitch. Often she has not been brought for mating on the correct day and therefore has not produced eggs for fertilization.

A well bred, winning, prepotent stud dog is a very valuable commodity and needs every care and attention. The income produced by a successful stud dog can be very significant over several years. This is especially so in the case of a highly regarded champion. It is known that one extremely famous Golden Retriever sired no less than 294 litters. That was exceptional, but if a top Cavalier stud dog sires 100 litters, then 100 times the current stud fee is a substantial amount.

Many breeders recommend that a dog should first be used at stud between ten and twelve months or even earlier. I would hope that Cavalier owners would now see the wisdom of delaying a dog's introduction to stud work until he is at least fourteen months so that eye, hip and heart screening tests can be taken at about twelve months, and the results known before the dog is used at stud.

There is a lot of nonsense quoted that dogs will never perform at stud unless they are introduced to it well before reaching twelve months. I have two instances to disprove this completely. A dog I bred was used at stud for the first and only time at four years. Result: four puppies. Another dog I bred was used for the first time at nine and a half years because he had a clear heart. Result: five puppies. He was used once more at eleven years. Result: three puppies. No fuss, no palaver, both dogs joyously did the job when given the opportunity. Also, they did not develop any subsequent problems such as territory marking.

The question is often asked, 'How frequently should a stud dog be used?' After his first mating at fourteen months which, preferably, should be to an experienced, co-operative bitch, he could be used every two or three months until he is two years old. He should not be allowed too many bitches until he is two, as many a young dog has been spoilt by a greedy owner. From two onwards he can be gradually introduced to more frequent stud work, eventually reaching a peak of one, or even an occasional two, matings per week, if his services are so much in demand.

Your over-riding philosophy should be to not over-use your dog, and to keep him in tip-top condition. Use your discretion. If his condition or performance are suffering, he needs to be rested. Always feed him a top quality high protein diet and keep him well exercised. If you are showing him you will probably need to significantly reduce his stud work; otherwise, he may quickly lose his show condition.

A successful sire is a prepotent one who produces consistently good qualities in most of his progeny. You need, therefore, to let it be known that your dog is only at stud to approved bitches. Never allow him to be used with grossly inferior bitches, or with those who have a hotch-potch of a pedigree that lacks quality. It is very unlikely that, however commendable a dog may be, he can produce good quality progeny from such bitches, and when inferior progeny are produced it is always the dog's reputation that suffers! The bloodlines of the bitch should preferably be compatible with those of the dog. If you believe a bitch may have links, however tenuous, with serious hereditary diseases, avoid her like the plague.

Do not allow your dog to be used for close in-breeding, e.g. to his own daughters or sisters, and think very carefully of half-brother to half-sister, unless you or the bitch's owner are well versed in genetics and know precisely what is behind the pedigree lines for several generations. The risk to the breed can be very high with such close in-breeding in that any serious faults are doubled up and really brought to the fore. In the long term, the reputations of your dog and yourself will benefit from adopting such policies.

You need to keep a fairly detailed record of whether there were any problems at the time of the mating, and also what your dog produces. You will find this information is most useful in any dispute with a bitch's owner if puppies are not produced. Also it enables you to see, over a period of time, the number of puppies your dog sires, and with which lines he is most successful.

Once a stud dog has been retired from the show-ring he is out of the public eye and awareness. To maintain interest in using him you need periodically to remind breeders of his qualities, the successes of his progeny, and that he is still available.

S.16 of the Cavalier Club's Code of Ethics states: 'Stud dog owners must see the bitch's pedigree and registration certificate to check ownership, age, endorsements and should try to ascertain number of litters, number of pups and when she last had a litter.'

Choosing a Stud Dog

Surprisingly, the more one knows about any breed, Cavaliers included, the more difficult it becomes to choose a stud dog. Dog A might look a distinct possibility until we realize that he has a certain dreadful dog twice in his recent bloodlines. He is discarded. We then think Dog B might be a real possibility until we see that on his dam's side there are gay tails, and one bitch that is suspect for epilepsy. We rule him out.

When considering a stud dog for your bitch you need to start thinking months ahead so that you can seek information, sift through it, view progeny, etc., before arriving at your decision. No dog is perfect, and you have to select the one which is nearest to the ideal you are seeking. But aim high – use only a first class dog and never compromise on quality. Always seek to 'grade up' i.e. improve your stock with each generation.

But when thinking of breeding, the first decision you have to make is whether your bitch is good enough to breed from. If you have doubts, the answer is probably 'No'. If you do not have much experience on which to take an objective view, ask one of the top breeders for an honest appraisal. If you breed from an inferior bitch the likelihood is you will have inferior puppies. No dog can work miracles with a poor quality bitch. On the other hand your bitch does not need to be a world beater, but she does need to be typical, sound, match the Standard well and have a really good temperament. In other words, she needs to be above average and of good overall quality. If she is only mediocre then forget about breeding from her – just enjoy and cherish her as a pet. It is an old wives' tale that every bitch should have a litter because 'it is good for her'.

If you particularly want to breed, you need to obtain a better bitch (see Chapter 5). If you just want another puppy, then it will probably be cheaper, and certainly less worry and work, to buy one.

But let us assume you now have a well bred, good class bitch and that you are seeking a stud dog for her. How should you start? One simple way is to ask the breeder of your bitch to recommend a suitable dog. Or you can imitate a pattern of breeding which has previously proved to be successful, e.g. daughters of dog Joe, when mated to sons of dog Bill, have often produced top quality stock. If such a simple solution is not possible, there are three forms of breeding to consider.

Fox's **Champion Pamedna Dee Lite**

1. *In-breeding* i.e. mating very close relatives e.g. father to daughter, son to mother and brother to sister. It should not be considered unless you are very experienced and knowledgeable of the ancestors, as the dangers are considerable. Whilst it doubles up on strengths and type, it also doubles up on faults, some of which may be hidden, and these can come home to roost with a vengeance. The narrow gene pool may also become 'depressed' or 'fatigued'.

2. *Outcross* i.e. choosing a dog which has little, if any, similarity or compatibility with your bitch's pedigree. The usual result is a hotch-potch, with no consistency amongst the puppies, and very little chance of breeding a consistent type or quality in future generations. Also, you do not know what you are introducing to your line. The possibilities may be improved slightly if you are careful to select an outcross that is at least of a similar type to your bitch. When subsequently mating any progeny you need to move right back into the original line.

3. *Line Breeding* i.e. mating individuals which are related to a common ancestor, or strain, of outstanding quality and no major faults. The common ancestor is possibly in the second generation, or even further back, and therefore the link is not too close to be unhealthy or dangerous, but does tend to produce some consistency of type and improvement in quality. Examples of line breeding are grandson to granddam, grandsire to granddaughter and uncle to niece. Line breeding is the type favoured by most knowledgeable breeders.

To proceed further you need to assess your bitch against the Standard and list her strengths and weaknesses. For instance, she might have a particularly good head and topline but have poor pigment and rather straight stifles, or upright shoulders.

The next step is to carefully study her pedigree. You really need as much information as possible about her ancestors so that you know their virtues and faults. Also, and this is important, you need to know of any serious hereditary faults that may be lurking in the bloodlines. If there are such problems, you obviously need to avoid doubling up on those possibilities through the stud dog you choose. If problems do arise in a litter it is usually the dog that is blamed, but for a 'recessive' fault to appear it must be present in both dog and bitch. It is known that a recessive can skip several generations (eight have been known) and then rear its ugly head again.

No breeder will ever know everything that is behind every dog or bitch in a pedigree. That is quite an unrealistic expectation. However, it is wise to gather all possible information, even though it may not be an easy task. Some owners are courageous and bring an hereditary fault out into the open, whereas others mistakenly seek to conceal it. It is, of course, equally important for you to gather all possible information on the strengths of your bitch's ancestors, and then to build upon them.

So now we have reached the position where you have a good quality bitch and you have studied her pedigree. You know the bitch's own virtues and weaknesses, and what you must not double up on from her pedigree.

You now need, through line breeding principles, to focus on a successful prepotent dog, or bitch, in your bitch's pedigree. You then seek to breed your bitch back to that particular line. It may be through a particular dog in her pedigree, or to a son of an outstanding dog, or bitch, in her pedigree. You are aiming to bring that line to the forefront because you believe it to be a good line with many qualities. The dog chosen should not only complement your bitch's virtues but should also be particularly strong where she is weak.

If your bitch has one fairly major fault, do not go for a mediocre dog whose only strength is in the one point in which your bitch is weak. He may improve that one weakness but he will also bring all his mediocrity. The progeny from such a mating is likely to be below the standard of your bitch, whereas you are *always* seeking to make the next generation of better quality.

Not all top winners are suitable for all bitches. Therefore the latest big winning dog should not be considered unless he can fulfil the line breeding requirement and can complement her strengths and improve upon her weaknesses. No dog, not even a big winning champion, is perfect, and if one of his weaker points is the same as that of your bitch, it would be folly to consider mating them and thus doubling up on the weakness. Also, some very big show winners never produce any outstanding progeny, despite the many bitches they cover. A stud dog is only as good as his progeny. There are, therefore, advantages in considering older dogs as we can see some of their progeny in the show-ring.

Wouldn't it be wonderful if we could have a kind of time warp and be able to use dogs from the past which we know have been the truly prepotent sires in Cavalier history. These would include:

Champion Daywell Roger, who sired the winners of 73 Challenge Certificates

Champion Homaranne Caption, who sired the winners of 67 Challenge Certificates

Champion Aloysius of Sunninghill, who sired the winners of 44 Challenge Certificates

Champion Pargeter McBounce, who sired the winners of 39 Challenge Certificates

Champion Rosemullion of Ottermouth, who sired the winners of 38 Challenge Certificates

Minstrel Boy of Maxholt, who sired the winners of 35 Challenge Certificates

They were sires who really stamped their mark on the breed. Minstrel Boy just fell short of being made up to a champion, but he certainly did not fall short as a sire.

The three bitches who parented most Challenge Certificate winners never attained their championship titles. They were:

Dalginross Rosalind, dam of winners of 24 Challenge Certificates

Vairire Venetia of Crisdig, dam of winners of 23
 Challenge Certificates
Cassandra of Hillbarn, dam of winners of 20 Challenge
 Certificates

What a tremendous contribution these dogs and bitches made
to the breed, and there were others who almost matched these
achievements. This fascinating information, and much more, is
contained in Grahame Ford's excellent compilation, *Cavaliers at
UK Championship Shows 1946–1992*.

However, we have to come back to reality in the here and now.
Having provisionally selected the stud dog, I suggest you write to
the owner, stating that you think the dog might suit your bitch
and setting out your reasons for arriving at that conclusion.
Enclose a copy of your bitch's pedigree, together with copies of
heart, eye and, if available, hip certificate. Send a stamped
addressed envelope and ask for the observations of the stud dog
owner. Also, ask if you may have copies of the latest screening
certificates for the dog, and enquire of the stud fee. If all seems
satisfactory, then tentatively book the dog and state when your
bitch is due in season.

Tait's **Champion Downies Mary Poppins**

The Actual Mating

Just prior to your bitch coming into season you will probably notice that she is urinating more often than usual, and is also licking her vulva more regularly. On the very first day she shows colour (i.e. a dark red discharge of blood from the vulva) inform the stud dog owner and agree when you will be taking her. This may still have to be a little flexible because you need to take her when she is ovulating i.e. producing eggs for fertilization, and that may be a little uncertain. For the majority of bitches the correct day for mating is either the eleventh or twelfth, but some only conceive if they are mated on the fifth, twentieth, or some other specific day. You therefore need to be particularly observant in watching the signs. Many bitches show a deep coloured discharge until about the ninth or tenth day, and then the colour becomes much paler. A few bitches may bleed for the full twenty-one days, or, conversely, an occasional one may show no colour throughout the whole three weeks (often referred to as a white season). The vulva on some bitches swells to a very large size; others are not so big. The vulva at the ovulation period is usually at its largest, softest and most pliable. The bitch, when ready for mating, will often 'flag' her tail to the side, but other bitches do this throughout the full season. If you have more than one bitch, the one in season will often repeatedly mount the other bitches, or 'stand' for them to 'mate' her. If your bitch's ovulation days are different to the 'normal', your vet can assist in determining when she is ready to be mated. It is, of course, vital that she be mated on the correct day.

It is now assumed that you know the correct day for the mating and a time has been agreed. Whilst your bitch should not be bathed or even sponged down, because to do so would remove some of her interesting smells which should attract and excite the dog, she should nevertheless be clean and well groomed. She should be absolutely clear of any infections such as fleas or kennel cough. A stud dog owner will give you a 'roasting', and rightly so, if you take any infection into his kennel. Before the mating give your bitch the opportunity to empty her bowels. Ensure she has time to become acclimatized to the new surroundings before the dog is put to her. Hopefully she will then seductively flirt and encourage him and a satisfactory mating, complete with tie, will take place. When the tie occurs it is the bitch's vaginal muscles which 'lock-in' the dog's enlarged penis and 'bulb'.

But if the bitch makes it clear she has not the slightest intention of co-operating and turns really nasty towards the dog, you then have to make a decision. Do you call the whole thing off, or do you agree to her being muzzled and in effect forcibly mated? Or do you instead decide to leave her for a few days in case her awkwardness is because she is not ready and in the hope that she might be more amenable and co-operative when she *is* ready? Some bitches are mated even though they are not particularly co-operative and they subsequently bear and rear the puppies with no apparent problems. However when a bitch is fighting the mating all the way, some believe that she may suffer psychological damage if she is made to accept it. You know your bitch better than anyone else, and it is your responsibility whether or not to proceed.

After a satisfactory mating has taken place, ensure that until the end of her season no other dog has access to your bitch. Double conceptions are rare, but not completely unknown, and you would not be pleased with a litter of four puppies made up of two pure bred Cavaliers and two Cavalier/mongrel cross puppies.

Conception and Fertilization

Puppies are formed through the joining together of two sex cells, the egg from the bitch and the sperm from the dog. The fertilization occurs within the oviduct, a narrow tube of tissue down which the eggs travel after release from the bitch's ovary. The stud dog deposits enormous numbers of sperm in the vagina and these swim through the uterine fluid to meet the on-coming eggs. The sperm therefore need to be strong and active to reach their destination. Each egg needs only one sperm to fertilize it and it is pure chance which sperm fulfils the task. The egg is minute, spherical shaped, and full of nutriment to enable it to live from fertilization to implantation. The sperm is slightly larger, and shaped like a tadpole. Each egg and sperm has a nucleus containing the chromosomes which provide the genetic material to form the new life. When the two nuclei unite, the genetic blue-print of the foetus is then formed. Simultaneously the sex of the puppy is then determined.

The fertilized egg develops rapidly within the warm uterus. At about the nineteenth day the eggs implant themselves to the wall of the uterus. Growth occurs through the genes multiplying and forming new cells. This builds tissue, which eventually become organs. Growth continues, and approximately sixty-three days from mating and conception the puppies are born.

Gestation Period

Whilst the period of gestation (i.e. mating to birth) normally lasts sixty-three days, Cavaliers often have their puppies one or two days early. Misty, one of our bitches, whelped six puppies six days early, and Heidi had four puppies three days late. All the puppies were healthy and survived.

Inglis's **Rheinvelt Movie Star**. (Breeder: Potter)

Is your Bitch in Whelp?

This is an important question, and there are various helpful signs.

1. At about three weeks into the pregnancy some, but by no means all bitches, experience morning sickness and/or go off their food for a few days.
2. There are sometimes subtle behaviour changes, for instance the bitch seems to feel sorry for herself and wants more fussing.
3. One of the best signs that a bitch is pregnant is the presence of a very sticky clear vaginal discharge which sometimes starts as early as the thirty-second day after mating, sometimes later,

and continues until whelping. The amount of the discharge varies; some bitches have a lot and it can easily be seen as long strands coming from the vulva and usually, in a Cavalier, becoming stuck on the 'feathers' of the back legs. Others just have a little stickiness round the vulva itself. If there is a brown, green, or very fluid discharge, consult your vet immediately.

4. From about four weeks her nipples gradually become a stronger pink and more erect. At about six weeks she begins to fill out at the flanks and her body 'drops' slightly. Her appetite becomes stronger and she begins to look for more food.

5. At seven to eight weeks she may occasionally whip round and look quizzically at her rear end.

6. In the final week when the bitch is stretched out asleep, body ripples can be seen as the puppies move.

It is possible to have your bitch scanned to determine whether she is in whelp. It is also possible during the last few days to take her temperature twice a day, as a drop in temperature indicates whelping is near. I have never used either, believing them to be unnecessary.

Preparations for Whelping

There are a number of preparations you can make in advance of the whelping.

I suggest that if this is your first litter you should arrange to observe a friend's litter being born or, better still, have an experienced person with you during your bitch's whelping. It would be a pity to risk losing some of the puppies through your inexperience.

Cavaliers can cry out, and even scream very loudly, whilst giving birth to puppies. It is wise, therefore, to alert your immediate neighbours if you live in a flat, terraced, or semi-detached house. Otherwise, if the bitch whelps at 2 a.m., her screams during the dead of night might convince your neighbours that a murder is being committed. The last thing you want during a whelping is to have the Police thumping on your door!

Three weeks before the puppies are due I start to give the bitch extra food. I feed her a special high protein diet, and as the whelping date looms nearer she can virtually have all the food she wants. I continue with her exercise as long as she is enjoying it. I feel she does not need to be mollycoddled and treated as an invalid.

I like my bitches to have their litters in the kitchen. I bring her in at least two weeks before the whelping and we can then keep a close eye on her. Additionally, whatever the season, it is cosy and warm for her.

The whelping box becomes her sleeping quarters so that she can become used to it. It should be adequate for her to fully stretch out and then have room to spare. Some breeders prefer the box to have anti-crush rails but I have never found them necessary for Cavaliers.

It can be helpful to trim back any very long feathering at the bitch's rear so that puppies do not become entangled.

It is helpful to have several items of kit 'at the ready'. I suggest the following: round-nosed sterilized scissors, iodine or potassium permanganate crystals, cotton wool, Dettol, hot water bottle, electric warming pad, kitchen roll, rough towel for drying puppies, thermometer, kitchen scales, small cardboard box, notebook and pen, large plastic sack for soiled paper, mop and bucket for dribbles on the floor (the rug having been taken up), and a bottle of respiratory drops from your vet. Susan Burgess asks, 'What about some calming drops for the breeder?' In addition, I have a few rolls of white lining wallpaper as I prefer this to newspapers. With newspapers the ink gets on to the

Shearmon's **Champion Mossdown Cilla Black**

puppies and they always look grubby. The rolls of lining paper are quite cheap.

As the whelping becomes imminent you will also need a bowl, soap and the availability of warm water, a watch, and a warm milky drink with glucose that can be offered to the bitch between whelps.

G.W. Crighton (1968) pointed out in his article, 'Thermal Regulation of the New Born Dog', that many newly born puppies die from hypothermia. Puppies need to have an adequate supply of warmth for at least the first three weeks of their lives, and the first week is absolutely crucial. The mothering behaviour of the dam is a highly important factor in providing warmth. If the dam is a good mother she will lie close to her puppies for long periods and thus provide a high level of natural contact heat from her very warm mammary area i.e. teats and undercarriage, similar in some respects to a broody hen. Additionally, the puppies will receive contact heat from each other, provided it is not a very small litter. But the surrounding room temperature also needs to be comfortably warm.

Some vets and breeders believe that, following Crighton's pronouncement that many newly born puppies die from hypothermia, the pendulum then swung too far in the opposite direction. That is, too high levels of warmth were then provided which caused significant problems. Various types of lamps (especially infra-red) were placed over litters and the puppies often basked in temperatures well in excess of 80°F. As a result, the dam often could not stand the heat and moved out of the range of the lamp, and thus away from the puppies. The puppies therefore missed out on the close body contact and important 'bonding' relationship with their mum. The heating provided was also of a different nature to the direct body contact from the dam or siblings. It is felt by many that where additional heat is required it is far better to provide it by a low voltage heated pad providing contact heat from underneath, rather than using lamps which, in addition to providing a different form of heating, may also establish some swirling cool currents through convection.

To sum up: a comfortable but adequate degree of warmth needs to be provided. In the first week it should never be less than 70°F, possibly nearer 75°F. Such a level of warmth should be tolerable to the dam, and sufficient to the pups *when it is supplemented* by contact heat from mum, the other puppies, and possibly a heated pad. But observe the situation closely and react accordingly – if the dam is not a particularly good mother and spends much time away from the puppies, you will need to provide additional warmth to compensate for the loss of her body contact heat. Also watch the puppies. If they are adequately warm, and also well fed and healthy, they will lie contented and settled but be capable of strong movement and suckling. If they are miserable, noisy and continually on the move, then it is likely they are either cold, hungry or ill.

Some breeders now use enclosed (i.e. lidded) and insulated whelping boxes. These protect against draughts and are more efficient at retaining heat generated by the bitch and puppies within the box. Such boxes need to be so designed that the breeder can easily see what is happening in the box.

As the puppies grow older the temperature of their immediate environment can be gradually reduced. But always take great care: an adequate degree of warmth is vital to young puppies, especially to those just being born.

As the whelping approaches it is an exciting time, when the success or otherwise of your breeding plans and choice of stud dog will be revealed. You may therefore feel on an emotional 'high', but it is important that you keep calm and help your bitch to remain calm. If you panic, it will communicate to her, especially if it is her first litter.

It is probably unnecessary to say it but you need to remain with your bitch right through the whelping, however long it takes, day or night. All other commitments should have been shelved or delegated. I have an old arm chair which I take into the kitchen. I also take in a book, which I can glance at if nothing is happening, but most of the time I am looking over the top of the book, and thus keeping a watchful eye on the bitch.

Signs of Imminent Whelping

The signs of imminent whelping are:

1. Scratching up and ripping paper with her teeth. However this may not be a very reliable indicator as some bitches start two to three days in advance, whereas others will only start two hours before whelping.
2. A bitch may be sick just before starting to whelp, but not all bitches do this, so it may not be too reliable.
3. Restlessness, pacing about, being unable to settle, becoming a little agitated. This is a surer sign.
4. Panting – a firmer indication that things are beginning to happen.
5. Straining or contractions – this is the surest sign of all, and the first puppy should not be too far away.

It is advisable to make notes of the times and frequency of the above events in case you have to call in the vet. You will then be able to give him a factual summary, not mere guesses. This assists your vet to decide whether he needs to take action now, or whether he can allow a little more time for developments to take place naturally.

The Problem-free Birth

The bitch is now straining, which often shows itself by her pushing against the side of the box. She may give an occasional little yelp and keep trotting out of her box to you for re-assurance. All that is needed is a few words of encouragement. Do not make a big fuss, just allow her to get on with the whelping.

The 'water bag' will probably be the first thing you notice. When this arrives some novice breeders believe it is the first puppy, and they are troubled when the sac bursts and all that appears is a greeny-black or sometimes clear fluid. The water bag facilitates the egress of the puppies that are following, by preparing the way out.

Paloheimo's **International Champion Anncourt Parasol** (Finland)

The contractions continue and become more forceful. Eventually the first puppy arrives head first in its membrane sac, followed by the placenta or afterbirth, to which the puppy is attached by the umbilical cord. The placenta resembles a piece of raw liver. The bitch tears open the membrane sac, thus allowing the puppy to breathe. She will also bite through the umbilical cord and thus free the puppy from the placenta. She then licks the puppy dry and in so doing 'rough-houses' it around the box. Do not worry about this seemingly rough treatment as it stimulates the puppy into life, and you should soon hear it cry out, which is a good sign. In no time at all it makes its way to a teat and starts suckling. The bitch by this time will probably have eaten the afterbirth, which looks foul, but gives her nourishment. She will then lay quietly until the second puppy starts to arrive, and so the process is repeated with each puppy. As each puppy arrives note the time, colour, sex and weight.

Possible Problems

Normally there are ten minutes to an hour between puppies, occasionally a little longer. If the bitch has been straining for two hours without producing a puppy, or if there is a gap of three hours since the last pup was born without the bitch straining further, and you know that there are more puppies, telephone your vet.

A breech birth is when a puppy arrives rear end first instead of the normal head first. Usually this does not cause any concern as the dam delivers the puppy with no problems. Very occasionally when the rear end comes first, because it is narrower than the head it does not open the passage way sufficiently for the wider head to slip out. The bitch may overcome this by stronger contractions, but if the head becomes stuck you may be able to assist the bitch. Very gently put a clean finger in the opening around the puppy, and hold the protruding part of the puppy with the other hand, and as the bitch strains, work with her to try and ease out the puppy. Your finger, coated with Vaseline, is trying to expand the opening to give the head a little more room, and your other hand is pulling the puppy gently downwards, not vertical nor horizontal, but at an angle of 45°. The puppy sac is slippery and difficult to hold, and a piece of towelling often helps.

The need to act gently has to be your over-riding consideration. If the bitch becomes agitated, and starts to run around as some do, you need an assistant to hold her steady while you try your best to help her expel the puppy. If there is no progress, the bitch may eventually become tired with her exertions and 'give up'. This is known as 'uterine inertia' and some action needs to be taken by a vet to counteract the problem. If the sac bursts, and the head is still inside the bitch, the puppy will be unable to breathe and its chances of survival are not good.

We had a rather similar problem with a tricolour whose second puppy was enormous and became stuck. I tried to help her but made no progress. It was 1 a.m. but I contacted the vet and rushed her to his surgery with the puppy still half protruding. The vet tried to release the puppy, at first unsuccessfully. Eventually he did manage to do so, but the puppy was dead. We took the bitch home and shortly afterwards she had two normal-sized puppies without any problems.

Sometimes when the puppy has arrived the bitch, particularly a maiden, looks bewildered and makes no effort to sever the cord or tear open the sac so that the puppy can breathe. These are simple jobs and need to be done quickly. Rip open the sac with your fingers and wipe away the mucus from the puppy's mouth, and cut the cord with sterilized scissors about one inch from the navel.

If the puppy is blue and gasping for breath, or is apparently lifeless, it is likely to have mucus in the lungs. This needs swift, vigorous action or you will lose the puppy. Hold it vertically, with the head facing downwards, and rub it roughly with a dry towel in front of a very warm fire. If it is still gasping it needs the mucus dislodging. Hold the puppy firmly, extend your arm level with your shoulder and bring it swiftly to the vertical. Do this three or four times and sometimes you can see blobs of mucus shoot out. Continue towelling the vertically held pup in front of the heat. It is a wonderful feeling when the puppy starts to breathe normally. Do not give up on the puppy, even a seemingly lifeless one, for at least twenty minutes, possibly half an hour. When it is breathing normally, put it back with the dam, and see that it gets on to a teat and starts to feed. Vets can supply a product to help deal with such respiratory problems. You just put a couple of drops on the puppy's tongue with a dropper.

If a puppy needs this kind of attention, and simultaneously the bitch is having the next puppy, it is obvious that another person needs to be standing by ready to assist.

Occasionally a bitch will try to sever the umbilical cord but seems unable to bite through it, and the cord is being pulled and tugged. (This is more likely to occur if the bitch does not have a scissor bite.) This tugging may result in an umbilical hernia, which is a small hard swelling on the navel, although it has to be said that some vets doubt this, believing instead that a hernia will not occur unless there is a pre-disposed weakness already present, which is probably genetic in origin. If the bitch cannot sever the cord, assist her by cutting the cord about 1″ from the navel. If it bleeds just dab the end with either iodine or potassium permanganate. Do not leave the cord longer than one inch as I find some bitches obviously feel it is then too long, and start biting and pulling at it. The bit of cord eventually withers away.

There are differing views about what to do with the puppies that have already arrived whilst the bitch is in the process of having another one. Some say leave them with the dam during the whole whelping. Others, and I am one of them, prefer to remove the puppies into a small cardboard box containing an electrically warmed covered pad, or hot water bottle. They are then out of the bitch's way as she struggles to expel the latest puppy. She often moves about the box, and if it is not an easy birth she could easily tread on one of the puppies. Also, with the arrival of the latest puppy the whelping box paper becomes wet and messy, which is hardly helpful to the puppies already there. Puppies left in the whelping box whilst the bitch is giving birth to the next puppy can easily become chilled, as during this period they are not having body contact with their mum. I only leave the puppies with the bitch during subsequent births if she becomes really anxious when I try to remove them. That has never been a major problem in my experience. As soon as the latest puppy has arrived, the wettest paper is swiftly removed, replaced by clean lining paper, and the puppies put back with the dam. They are, therefore, only away from the dam for a short period at each birth.

Owner's Role at the Whelping

The owner's role during a whelping is merely to observe and leave it to the bitch if she is coping well. It is only when problems arise as outlined that the owner, or indeed the vet, becomes directly involved.

The owner should, however:

1. Record the time of each birth and weigh the puppy.
2. Try to keep the whelping box reasonably clean without upsetting the bitch.
3. Offer the bitch a drink of warm milk and glucose during a lengthy whelping.
4. Ensure that each puppy feeds from a teat very soon after birth.

An occasional puppy takes a little time to understand how to feed, and you may need to keep pushing him back on to a teat. Once they have got the idea they guzzle away noisily and contentedly. Just watch them push against the dam with their paws when only a few minutes old!

For each puppy there should be an afterbirth. You are advised to see that all are accounted for and one does not remain inside the bitch. However during a whelping matters can become a little hectic, and I have to confess that very occasionally I could not guarantee that all placentas were accounted for. Luckily, I have never yet experienced any problems from this source. After the bitch has eaten two placentas I tend to take the remainder away, unless she seems ravenous for them. They are said to be good for the bitch's milk production.

The Bitch and Her Young Puppies

Barwell's **Charlottetown The Mary Rose** with her puppies

When all the puppies have arrived, the bitch will settle contentedly with them and usually is not interested in anything else. Whilst trying not to disturb her, clean up the box as best you can by replacing most, if not all, of the soiled paper. The whelping box should contain an electrically warmed covered pad. It cannot be stressed enough that the temperature for the puppies must be fully adequate as otherwise they may die from hypothermia (for further details see earlier section in this chapter).

As soon as the bitch will allow you to do so, give her rear end a sponge down with warm water and thoroughly dry her. Then put in the box a synthetic sheepskin dog blanket. I find the puppies settle contentedly on such a blanket.

You will find it difficult at first to persuade the dam to leave her puppies, even momentarily, and go outside to relieve herself. Do not worry, as she will go when she feels she absolutely must. For the first two or three days keep the bitch absolutely quiet and do not allow visitors.

Your bitch may not fancy her usual food for the first forty-eight hours but will usually partake of baby milk foods and a little fish, chicken or scrambled egg. Others, however, tuck-in to their normal food straight away. At this stage some bitches will not leave the puppies to feed, but if the food dish is put in the puppies' box she may eat there.

I believe the first three days are the most critical period for the survival of puppies. If in fact you can get them through to ten days, I believe they have a good chance of holding on to life. Weigh each puppy daily for the first ten days; if they are steadily gaining weight that is a healthy sign. Thereafter I weigh them each week until eight weeks. I keep these records permanently, as I find they are useful in comparing the progress of any subsequent litters the bitch may have. It is fascinating also to compare the weights of different young litters and then see how they compare in size when they have reached adulthood.

I ask the vet to call the day after the puppies are born. He checks them to see there are no defects like cleft palate, and also checks the bitch. He usually gives her an injection to clear away any debris. On one such examination my vet found, by feeling, a dead puppy still within Sarah, a tricolour. Operative treatment showed the puppy had started to decompose and could well have proved very serious to Sarah if the problem had not been discovered. Since then I have never regretted paying for such examinations. For a few days after whelping, the bitch may have a slight dark discharge. This is normally nothing to worry about and soon clears up.

When the puppies are four days old the vet visits again to remove the dew claws. Some breeders do this themselves. When the puppies are ten days, three weeks and four and a half weeks old, the breeder should trim their nails with small scissors;

otherwise they will make the dam's undercarriage quite sore when the puppies are feeding.

As the puppies grow, particularly if it is a large litter, they make heavy demands upon the bitch. Remember she was also feeding them through the gestation period. It is essential therefore to keep feeding her adequate amounts of a top quality high protein diet. Watch out for any signs of eclampsia in the bitch.

Eclampsia (or Milk Fever)

In thirty years' experience I have never had a bitch with eclampsia, but one hears of an occasional case. When it does occur it needs immediate action because the nursing bitch's life is in danger. No vet will refuse immediate treatment whether it be mid-day or mid-night.

Eclampsia most often occurs when the puppies are about three weeks old, but it can happen at any time during the suckling period. I have read that, very rarely, it can occur during pregnancy, but I have never known such a case. The symptoms are that the dam starts panting and becomes dazed and groggy, eventually falling to the ground and trembling violently as if in a fit. The cause is a deficiency of calcium as a result of the dam supplying the puppies during the gestation period and since birth. The puppies need ample supplies of calcium for development of teeth and bones, and therefore make heavy demands upon their mum. If, due to a large litter, incorrect feeding, or whatever reason, the demands are beyond the bitch's capabilities, then eclampsia is the result. The bitch needs an immediate injection of calcium, and recovery is often spectacularly quick and complete. I did, however, hear of one bitch who never seemed fully fit thereafter and she died at a relatively early age.

After eclampsia it often helps to ration the milk the bitch gives to the puppies, certainly for a day or two. If they are old enough, start to wean them, and thus reduce the demands upon the dam. In an emergency, puppies as young as two and a half weeks can be encouraged to lap.

Remember that a pregnant or nursing bitch needs adequate supplies of a top quality high protein food to help her meet the very heavy demands made by her puppies. Nothing should be skimped – she needs the best. To guard against eclampsia many breeders give their bitch supplementary calcium tablets during pregnancy and lactation. If, however, you are feeding a 'complete' food devised specially for pregnant or lactating bitches, then supplements should not be required.

Puppies need to be wormed at three, five and seven weeks of age.

I start to wean my puppies at four weeks and aim that it be completed by five and a half weeks or six weeks at the latest. Do it gradually so that it is not traumatic to them or the dam. If she continues to produce milk you can obtain tablets from your vet to stop the production.

Puppies are often said to be the biggest time wasters in the world. On reflection, it is not time wasted but time well spent. You are enjoying their presence, they are benefiting from your attention, their growth and development are fascinating (they are funnier than any set of clowns) and they are the end result of plans that you long deliberated over. Introduce them gradually to everyday noises such as the sounds of the kitchen and domestic appliances, including a radio; handle them and fuss over them, and generally give them a good positive introduction to the big world opening up before them.

Lamont's **Irish Champion Moorfields Merci**

Helpful Tips

1. A split pedigree book is a most useful tool when formulating breeding programmes.

2. Try to be comparative in assessing a stud dog's performance. A popular dog may have sired one hundred litters and have had ten of his progeny achieve some success in the show-ring. A less used dog may only have sired six litters but have had five offspring achieve success. Obviously the latter has a better success ratio. Some big winning champions never produce anything of worth.

3. Your bitch needs to be wormed on the first day of her season, and five weeks into her pregnancy.

4. Your bitch should not be mated too young – eighteen months is plenty early enough. If she is immature, better to leave it until she is two. The longer you wait the more satisfactory it is for obtaining clear heart certificates. Her eyes should also have been tested and clear at twelve months, and it is prudent to know she has a low hip score.

5. When using a stud dog always pay the fee rather than promise a puppy. If there is only one puppy you have nothing. Or if the dam has three dogs but only one bitch, and you have promised the stud dog owner a bitch and want a bitch yourself, you are again left unsatisfied. It is far better for you to have the full choice; then, if there are surplus puppies, the stud dog owner can purchase one, possibly at a reduced fee.

6. The bitch basically determines the size of the litter through the number of eggs she produces for fertilization. The dog invariably produces an abundance of sperm, which determines the sex of each puppy.

7. Keep detailed records and photos of litters so that you can eventually look back and compare quality. It will assist your future breeding plans.

8. If you find you have inadvertently introduced a serious hereditary fault or disease, be prepared to scrap that particular line completely and start afresh.

9. Vet all puppy purchasers carefully. You should be seeking a loving, permanent home for every puppy. Too many Cavaliers end up in the hands of rescue schemes.

10. When puppies have been Kennel Club registered, enter their names in an A–Z index book so that, inadvertently, you do not try to use the same name again several years later.

12

Caring for Cavaliers

Pat Winters and family with their Cavaliers (Virginia, USA)

Most dogs of any breed steal your heart, but owners of Cavaliers seem to be particularly proud of their dogs and develop a deep affection for them.

This chapter outlines the day to day care that is needed to keep your Cavalier fit and happy, and the simple training that produces an affectionate, companionable dog.

The Family Pet

Why have Cavaliers become so popular as a family pet? Perhaps it is because they are:

1. so agreeable to live with
2. affectionate – a real companion dog
3. active and lively
4. attractive in all four colour combinations
5. so happy, with a soft gentle expression and wagging tail
6. a nice size for today's smaller houses and gardens
7. small dogs, thereby making the cost of feeding reasonable
8. dogs that require no trimming
9. dogs that live happily with other dogs and cats.

Why did you choose a Cavalier? Did the above reasons influence you, or were there other qualities which attracted you to the breed?

What does the family pet Cavalier need? Above all else he requires a loving, caring home. Preferably the Cavalier should have some company during the day, and not be shut up on his own from 7.30 a.m. to 5.30 p.m. whilst everyone is at work. Solitary confinement is not appropriate for a Cavalier. He may tolerate it, but it is not much of a life for him and he may well become bored and listless. Your Cavalier also needs consistency of approach – for instance if one family member encourages him on the chairs but someone else shouts at him when he does so, the dog becomes confused and does not know what he should be doing. He needs his own draught-proof box and blanket. He should have regular meals. I prefer to feed at breakfast and tea times, but I know others who give just one feed daily. Fresh water should always be available. Your Cavalier also needs daily exercise, preferably mixed, with some on the lead and some running free. All that is needed otherwise is a sensible, practical approach regarding inoculations, grooming, lead and car training, etc.

Buying and Training a Pet Puppy

Cavaliers make delightful family pets. An early decision you will need to make is whether to have a dog or a bitch. With the breed being so very loving, there is little difference in the degree of affection they will provide. A bitch will usually be in season twice a year, each season (or 'heat') lasting three weeks. For those six weeks she may be discharging slightly, but most bitches keep themselves scrupulously clean. You have to ensure that dogs do not have access to her during this time.

When you have decided upon a dog or a bitch I suggest you proceed in the following way.

1. Select the nearest Cavalier Club from the list in the appendix.
2. Telephone the secretary and ask for details of several breeders who have puppies.
3. Visit three of the breeders before you finalize your choice.
4. Look particularly for healthy puppies kept in clean surroundings by obviously caring breeders. In choosing a puppy look for one with an almost flat head, large round dark eyes and nice proportions, one who walks with style and, above all, who has a happy, confident temperament.

   Ask to see the parents, but appreciate that the breeder may not own the sire of the litter. Also ask what screening tests the parents have had for heart, eyes and possibly hips, and ask to see copies of their most recent clear certificates.
5. If you purchase a puppy you should receive a receipt, the Kennel Club Registration Certificate, a pedigree, a diet sheet and a statement of general advice.
6. As soon as you get your puppy home, or the very next day, ask your vet to give the puppy a thorough examination. If there is anything that concerns him about your puppy, raise it with the breeder *immediately*. If the vet gives it a clean bill of health, ask him about vaccinations.

Now enjoy your Cavalier. But be careful in two respects. First, your garden needs to be escape-proof, or he may wriggle through on to the road with tragic consequences. Second, you do not wish him to 'pick up' any serious infection, so keep him on your own premises, away from other dogs, until he has had his vaccinations and a further ten days have passed.

Aim from the start to build up a close, loving relationship because this is what Cavaliers thrive on. Their capacity for giving affection and companionship is boundless. Their faithfulness is

Koster's **Harana Horace**

complete, and they become a full member of the family, loving all and being loved by all.

Make the training of your puppy 'fun' and not harsh. When he has done well praise him and pat him. If he does something naughty let him realize by your tone of voice that you do not approve. If he persists, raise your voice a little and divert his attention to a permissible activity. Cavaliers have a strong wish to please and are therefore relatively easy to train. Make training sessions short and enjoyable. Play games with him – he will love them.

Let him meet your visitors. But as soon as possible train him to go into his box on command, and stay there, until you tell him he can come out. He then does not become a nuisance to visitors, because not all people love dogs.

Cavaliers soon learn toilet training. At eight weeks, during the day they need to be put outside as soon as they awake (each and every time), after each meal, and at about 1½ hourly intervals in between. When they relieve themselves outside praise them, and they soon learn what is expected.

Car training is important as a dog that is sick in the car is not a pleasant experience for anyone. I suggest you sit with the puppy in the car two or three times without moving the car. Then each time you drive to the nearby shops take the puppy with you. Give him experience of several short trips before you introduce him to longer ones. In fact, most Cavaliers are excellent travellers.

Train your dog to lie quietly in one place throughout any journey. Do not allow him to do acrobatic routines across the seat, on to the rear shelf and then back again. Such antics are distracting and therefore dangerous. Undoubtedly one of the safest, and most comfortable ways of travelling for all, is for the dog to have its own comfortable place in a wire folding cage containing his blanket. He is then not a nuisance climbing over the occupants; he is protected if there is sudden braking or an accident; and he loves his own special position. I have a hatchback which allows a decent sized cage, and my Cavaliers just cannot wait to settle in there. Some pet owners may feel that putting a dog in a wire travelling cage is 'not right', possibly even mildly cruel, but I can assure them it is not. It is safe and more relaxing for the dog, and it is a happy way of travelling for all.

As soon as your puppy has completed its vaccinations then it is very important to press on with its socialization. First of all you need to train it to walk quietly by your side on the lead without pulling. Do ten minutes daily in your garden first, and then when he is fairly proficient continue the training on a quiet road. When you are satisfied that he is ready, take him out to experience 'life'. Let him meet all and sundry, people, dogs and animals of all sorts, and encounter the noise, bustle and air turbulence caused by traffic, especially large lorries. Keep encouraging him so that he confidently takes it all in his stride. His walks should only be very short at three months, gradually increasing as he gets a little older, but never take a puppy under nine months for long walks or strenuous exercise, as he will tire quickly and bones and joints can become stressed.

When you have trained him to come back to you on command, let him off the lead in appropriate safe spaces and allow him to go up to other dogs and say 'hello'. This further develops his confidence. Too many owners pick up their young dogs when they see another dog approaching and this often causes all kinds of problems. Obviously be sensible, but do not mollycoddle him. He does not need it – he should be absolutely fearless, friendly, non-aggressive and with no tendency to nervousness. An adult Cavalier needs a brisk walk for about twenty to thirty minutes each day and, if possible, some free running exercise.

I find that when my Cavaliers get wet and dirty during exercising, an easy and successful way of cleaning them is to wipe them down with a chamois leather soaked in warm water and squeezed fairly dry, and then finish off with a brisk rub down with a dry towel. The dogs enjoy it and it takes so little time.

The anti-dog brigade is very vociferous at the present time, but, this apart, all dog owners should act responsibly. If your dog makes a mess always clean it up wherever it happens. It is easily done with a plastic bag and piece of kitchen roll or a proper scoop. If your Cavalier is noisy and starts to yap continuously, then stop him. He should not do this.

Tappenden's **Loranka's Dreamboy of Vival.** (Breeder: Hughes)

Choosing a Puppy for Showing

No one can guarantee a nice puppy of eight weeks will become a show winner as so much can go wrong. Taking an eight-week-old with a view to showing is, therefore, a gamble. The most that experienced breeders will say at eight weeks is 'that one seems to show some promise; I will run it on and hope that all goes well.'

Just occasionally however, perhaps once in a lifetime for a small breeder or once every ten years for the large breeder, they may produce a puppy so outstanding that it is possible at a young age to say 'that one has every chance eventually of taking top honours, unless something seriously goes wrong' (e.g. its mouth goes undershot).

When Messrs Hall and Evans allowed me to have Alansmere Rosetta at ten weeks John Evans said 'I believe you will get her made up.' Sure enough, before she was two she was a champion, and she also won the Challenge Certificate at Crufts. Another example is that I had 'saved' the name Crieda Lucida (it means the most brilliant star in a constellation) for several years, waiting for a really outstanding puppy. When we bred such a puppy we gave it this name and at only her seventh show she became a champion. But such puppies are very much the exception – when it happens it is a dream come true!

When seeking a puppy with show potential, what does one look for? My priorities would be a puppy of good overall quality with no serious fault, and then I would look particularly for:

1. an attractive head with large, dark round eyes;
2. correct scissor 'bite' and reasonable length of muzzle;
3. good forequarters and well laid shoulders;
4. elegant neck, head held high and level topline;
5. correct hindquarters with good turn of stifle;
6. parallel movement (it is possible at eight weeks to assess movement);
7. harmony in overall balance and proportion;
8. happy, confident temperament;
9. correct and symmetrical markings within reason;
10. above all, an indefinable something extra – be it class, style, brilliance or showmanship. Put it all together and call it 'star quality', that extra which will take it to the top.

If your present interest is showing, but is likely to extend into breeding, you should obviously think of seeking a bitch. One with the above qualities should offer considerable potential for breeding.

Adult Dogs and the 'Oldies'

What about the caring of adults and the 'oldies'? These are the backbone of the kennel in that they comprise the current show dogs, the breeding bitches and stud dogs, whilst the 'oldies' provide the golden memories of previous great wins. It is a lovely combination of the past and present. From this platform it is a simple step to dream of the future, especially when one can see the young hopefuls in the puppy run.

I know several breeders who once they have made the decision to 'run on' a puppy at eight weeks then 'forget' about it until it reaches six months. The reason for this is that from two to six months it goes through several stages when it can look 'good', 'plain', 'brilliant', 'awful' or 'I am not quite sure'. Far better to leave the assessment until six months when the puppy is at a more settled stage and has a little more maturity. I can remember Molly Coaker saying how she decided to run on Caption, and several friends made remarks such as 'you are not still keeping him are you?' or 'I should let him go.' Molly said she felt he had 'something' which compelled her to keep him, and how right she was when one looks at his subsequent great record.

Condition

The condition of your dogs is important and is dependent on many factors. I have dealt separately with breeding, feeding, grooming, health considerations and vaccinations. But other essentials are exercise, good housing and stimulation through companionship and training.

If the dogs are kept in kennels, the kennels should be of good quality so that they are completely rain and windproof. I prefer the small individual units rather than the long, large, corridor type which can be very noisy and must be a nightmare for the possibility of infection spreading like wildfire. Whatever kennels you choose select those that you can stand up in, or otherwise you will continually feel like the hunchback of Notre Dame. Each kennel, housing two to four Cavaliers, should have its own decent sized run, and there are advantages, if space allows, of having an additional large grass run in which the Cavaliers can occasionally let off steam by having a real charge around. In each run put a wooden raft or pallet, as the dogs love to lie on these when the normal run surface is too hot or cold. Strong chain link fencing on concrete posts is needed for security and long life, as concrete posts last much longer than wooden ones. Plant a small colourful tree in each run, which will eventually provide shade and make the runs look more attractive. Put a chain link 'cylinder' around the trunk to protect it from the dogs.

When considering 'condition' it is important not to breed too frequently from bitches. Give them ample time to recover from having a litter and you will then find that future puppies are stronger and get off to a better start in life. Many breeders feel that four litters is sufficient for any bitch.

I believe Cavaliers enjoy family life in the house more than a life in kennels; they are family dogs. But there is a limit to how many one can keep in the house. They do settle very well to kennel life, although I try to bring my small group into the house, in rotation, for short periods. They love it when it is their turn.

My puppies are born in the kitchen and spend their early life there. One problem we regularly encountered was that they would keep chewing the wallpaper. No sooner did I replace a strip than they ripped it again. Eventually I fitted clear perspex sheets over the lower wallpaper sections. They are secured with chromium mirror screws so that the perspex panels can be easily removed when the kitchen needs re-decorating. It seems to have solved the problem.

To help with training there are ring-craft and obedience classes in most areas. These can be useful if the Cavalier owner lacks knowledge or confidence in training. But really, with a few minutes' training each day at home a Cavalier can be taught all the essentials.

Older Dogs

Older Cavaliers tend to rest more the older they become. They need to be separated from the younger, more playful dogs who can easily knock them about in their more boisterous moods. Older dogs appreciate warmth and thick sleeping blankets. They may also need their food to be moistened. Make sure they do not get fat as nothing looks worse, and it is not good for their health. Their daily walks will probably need to be gradually shortened, but do not deprive them of these outings, as they help to keep them alert and active. Their hearing often suffers a little as they age.

The best situation for your oldies, if possible, is to let them live out their lives with the family in the house. They are no trouble if they have been house trained earlier, and they appreciate the home comforts and extra attention. But when their health seriously deteriorates and they are suffering pain, do not shirk from making the very difficult, but sometimes necessary, decision to have them put to sleep. I was once persuaded by a vet to prolong my Monty's life, then aged twelve, for six weeks by various injections and treatments, and I vowed then I would never, ever do it again. The poor dog had no quality of life for those six weeks, he was barely alive, he really did not know us, he was very ill, had great difficulty in eating and had no enjoyment whatsoever. When the time comes my dogs now die with dignity. I am convinced that, however painful the decision may be, when the time comes, it has to be made. In fact we owe it to them after their lifetime of faithfulness to us.

Feeding

I am a traditionalist from Yorkshire and so far as my own food goes, whilst I will readily try most dishes whatever their country of origin, I still retain a great fondness for traditional English dishes.

With dog foods I was also a strong traditionalist. Years ago I bought ox-heads from the abattoir and laboriously cut off the meat – about 9 lb or 4 kg from each head. I also bought the large 'green' unbleached tripes and cut them up in small strips. Then I would boil them up in a large electric boiler and the smell, particularly from the tripe, was awful. It was fed, with a good quality biscuit meal, and the dogs loved it. I also fed 'supplement' tablets daily to ensure the dogs had all the necessary vitamins and minerals etc.

It then became impossible to buy ox-heads, as I was told they were all sold on a contract basis to the beefburger makers. Difficulties also arose in purchasing the fresh large tripes. Therefore about four years ago I spoke to several breeders and received good reports about 'complete' foods. For four years my Cavaliers have been fed on these foods and I am impressed. My son, who works and trials gundogs, has also been impressed with the zest and stamina his Labradors show on complete foods.

We wean both our Cavalier and Labrador puppies straight on to a complete food, and they thrive really well. All my dogs whatever their age, are on it, including Champion Crieda Rosella, aged thirteen. With the complete foods there are various grades, and protein levels, to suit dogs of different ages and with differing needs. For instance the elderly have a lower protein level, whereas the puppies, pregnant or lactating bitches, or highly active working dogs need a high protein product. The complete foods are said to contain everything a dog needs and do not need to be supplemented in any way. Palatability is high, in fact the dogs seem to really enjoy them. The amounts to be fed are quoted on the packs. I give two meals per day.

The cost is generally quite reasonable, although there are two particular brands which I feel are outrageously priced. I have used one of these and it does not provide any additional benefits to the more reasonably priced ones. Therefore it was dropped from my shopping list. I know there are some traditionalists who will not consider the complete foods. I needed a lot of persuading but I am now convinced of their merit. They are also better for preserving teeth than sloppy foods.

Whilst on the topic of feeding I wish to offer suggestions

regarding poor feeders, which I know can be a very great problem. In fact when you have one it can almost drive you to distraction. Often a young Cavalier, particularly when being fed a variety of foods, will suddenly decide it will not eat one. It may be tinned food. You therefore decide to try it with fish, which it eats greedily, and then after a few days it decides it does not like fish. So you start to give it chicken, and after a few days the pattern is repeated, and so it goes on with mince, eggs or whatever. Eventually one resorts to hand feeding just to get some food into the dog. Once you set out on this very worrying path you are in a no-win position, because your dog has got you over the proverbial barrel. The dog is controlling you.

In my view there is only one successful solution, and it needs the owner to be absolutely firm and not give way. The first step is to decide the *one food* that your dog is to receive in the future. It may be tinned food and biscuit, or a complete food, or whatever else you decide upon. The second step is not to feed the dog *anything* for twenty-four hours. The third step is to offer the dog a *half portion* at its next meal time. If it is not eaten within fifteen minutes, pick it up. At the next meal time offer it a half portion again – I shall be surprised if it is left again. But if so, pick it up again, and there is a good chance it will eat the next time it is offered. There must, of course, be absolutely no tit bits offered between meals, and you must stand absolutely firm on the tactics. I have never found it to fail yet, and the most important aspect is that the dog becomes a good eater thereafter. Once it starts eating give it slightly more until it reaches the full amount allowed.

If such tactics become necessary a complete food has the advantage in that it is the same each time. Therefore the dog cannot leave one food in anticipation of obtaining something it believes might be tastier, as with different flavours of tinned food.

Grooming

Regular grooming, daily if possible, is advisable for Cavaliers. If this is not done a Cavalier's coat can quickly become unkempt and knotted. If this occurs then it is not an enjoyable experience for the dog when the 'day of reckoning' arrives, with a long painful session of tugging and pulling. If knots are present gently ease them apart with your fingers, and then comb through sensitively. A final brushing with a soft bristle brush will bring out the sheen, especially if it is done daily. I question the advisability of the harsh wire brushes and rakes for the soft, silky Cavalier coat. Pay particular attention to the rear edge of the ears as knots often appear there. Also comb the feathering on the rear legs and tail – you may find your Cavalier sits down when you attempt to comb this region but persevere.

Care of Teeth

When a puppy changes its teeth at four to five months its mouth is sore. The youngster sometimes goes off its food for a short time as it is painful to eat. Also it sometimes feels a little sorry for itself, and welcomes a little extra attention and fussing.

When the teeth are in the process of changing, occasionally the four long canine baby teeth are obstinate and refuse to drop out. If they seem to be preventing the new teeth from coming in naturally, you need to consult your vet as there is a possibility the new teeth may be forced out of line, or have to grow at an incorrect angle. If this happens it will reduce your dog's chances in the show-ring. It is a relatively simple matter for your vet to remove the baby teeth, should it prove necessary.

Once the permanent teeth have appeared they need to be cleaned regularly – preferably daily, but at least once a week, in order to prevent decay, painful gum infections and bad breath. You can use moistened salt, moistened bicarbonate of soda, or a half and half mixture of the two. But do not use moistened salt on the teeth of a dog that has heart trouble. As alternatives there are variously flavoured toothpastes for dogs at the pet shops, though some of these are ridiculously expensive.

If, despite your efforts, your dog's teeth become heavily encrusted with tartar there are two possible lines of action. You can either very, very carefully scrape it off with a de-scaling tool. You must not cut the gum and should appreciate that the dog is usually very restless and not happy to receive the treatment. Attempt it a little at a time, not all in one go. If you cannot manage it, then ask your vet to do it. He will probably anaesthetize your dog so that he does not have problems with it being restless.

Wipe around the mouth, especially the bottom lip, several times a week with damp cotton wool to prevent the lips becoming smelly and developing sores from dried stale saliva.

Nails and Dew Claws

If your Cavalier receives most of its exercise on hard pavements or concrete runs it is likely that its nails will be kept short. They need however to be checked regularly and if they become too long they must be clipped.

Dew claws are the ones on the inside of the leg just above the paw. Most Cavalier breeders have them removed when the puppy is a few days old but some leave them on. If your Cavalier has dew claws they should be checked regularly to make sure they have not curled over and are not cutting into the skin or pad.

13

Shows and Exhibiting

The following simple table shows how the number of Challenge Certificates (CCs) on offer to Cavaliers have risen over the years. Alongside I have included the number of Cavaliers registered with the Kennel Club for the same years.

Year	Sets of CCs on offer	KC Registrations
1946	1	134
1948	10	183
1951	17	310
1962	20	1,595
1973	30	5,071
1980	33	8,898
1991	37	15,514
1992	37	13,918
1993	36	13,705

It is said that figures can be made to prove anything, but it certainly appears that there are now many more Cavaliers available to compete for each set of Challenge Certificates. We also know from the entries at championship shows that there are in fact more Cavaliers actually competing for each set of Challenge Certificates than was the case say ten, twenty and forty years ago.

It is interesting that at all Championship Shows, totalling 1,168, from 1946–93, Blenheims won two-thirds of the Challenge Certificates awarded to both dogs and bitches (source Grahame Ford).

Whilst show entries seem to have dropped slightly very recently, nevertheless it is surprising that they remain as high as

Schofield's **Canadian and Bermudan Champion Beaverdams Five Card Stud** handled by Elaine Whitney

they are when one considers the tremendous increase in the cost of entries over the past few years. Another surprise is how the cost of entries varies so considerably between similar championship shows. Driving to shows is also now a very costly item that has to be taken into consideration. But the cost of showing in the United Kingdom pales into insignificance when compared with the USA where, because of the distances involved, journeys often have to be undertaken by air and prove very expensive indeed, especially when the cost of overnight accommodation is included. To reduce the costs of attending each show in the USA and some other countries, two championship shows are sometimes held at one venue over a weekend. The exhibitor therefore pays one travel bill but has the opportunity of two shows.

Shows now form a vast commercial network. How has this come about? The first multiple breed dog show is believed to have taken place on 28 June 1859 at Newcastle-upon-Tyne. The first Crufts Show was held in London at the Royal Aquarium in 1886 and Charles Cruft continued to organize this annual event until he died in 1938. During the Second World War his widow asked the Kennel Club to take over responsibility for the show as she could no longer carry on. The Kennel Club accepted and has since been responsible for organizing this highly prestigious show. It is wonderful how the Crufts Show still retains its charisma and attraction. Exhibitors talk all year of how many of their Cavaliers have qualified. The Cavalier world almost went 'bananas' when Alansmere Aquarius had his superb Best in Show win in 1973. In 1977 it was almost a canine national tragedy when Champion Blairsville Royal Seal, a Yorkie who had won 'everything' before Crufts and was widely expected to win Best in Show, did not even win the Challenge Certificate in his breed.

To qualify for Crufts it is required that there be the same placings in every breed. Although this may sound equitable, it is manifestly unfair. In some breeds, because of the extremely low number of entries, it is supremely easy to qualify, whereas in those breeds, like Cavaliers, with massive entries it is extremely difficult. The following illustrates my point. In Puppy Classes at championship shows with Challenge Certificates the first and second qualify for Crufts. At a recent South Wales Championship Show the American judge for one of the Terrier Breeds reported: 'Puppy Dog (3 entries) 1st ANON's G. Celtic Star – to be brutally honest he should be taken home and loved. 2nd. ANON's G. Hercules, the same as first.' Both these dogs qualified for Crufts despite the judge's low opinion of them. The owner's name has been disguised to avoid embarrassment. Both dogs came from the same kennel.

In 1992 the Kennel Club appointed a sub-committee under the chairmanship of Mr W. Bryden to look into every aspect of shows and exhibiting. As a result of the report submitted by that committee the Kennel Club, in May 1993, produced a 'Discussion Document on the Exhibition of Dogs'. All parties were invited to submit written comments to the Kennel Club and almost 700 submissions were received. The Kennel Club has now introduced a package of important changes which affect judges and shows. It also states that consideration is still being given to other matters, and therefore further policy changes seem likely.

Exhibiting at Shows

Those who win *regularly* at shows have five things in common:

1. They breed from quality stock.
2. They have an 'eye for a dog' and select puppies who usually fulfil their potential.
3. They show high class dogs.
4. They only show dogs that are ready i.e. the dogs are trained, fit and in sparkling condition and good coat.

Rix, Berry and Lymer's **Champion Lymrey Top of the Pops**, the breed record holder for number of bitch Challenge Certificates won. On 23 July 1994 she broke the previous record of fifteen Challenge Certificates held since 1970 by Alansmere McGoogans **Maggie May. Top of the Pops** has since won further Challenge Certificates and by October 1994 had reached a magnificent total of nineteen.

5. They are very good handlers and show their dogs to the maximum advantage.

Others should not begrudge these exhibitors their successes but resolve to try and develop similar qualities in themselves and their dogs.

For a dog to be shown to its maximum advantage, much preparatory work has to be done, long before the day of the show. Going right back, its breeding had to be planned correctly, and its rearing skilfully done. Its training for the show-ring has needed thought and careful attention. No two dogs are the same, and the handler's approach has to be matched to the individual needs of the dog. Some dogs are natural showers, others are more scatterbrained and some are wilful or stubborn, whilst some are bored out of their minds with it. The handler will need to use all his skills to bring out the best in such a variety of Cavaliers.

Training needs to begin at an early age and always needs to be based on the encouragement, praise and 'reward' system. The aim is to preserve the gay, friendly disposition of Cavaliers, not to subdue them, or make them stand like statues. What we want to see is the Cavalier's 'joy of living', the alert expression and wagging tail.

Handling calls for many skills which need to be finely tuned. Handling at its best has been described as an art. The young dog's confidence and understanding need to be built up so that the Cavalier and his handler should eventually be working successfully together as a team. For this to happen there needs to be a strong bond of affection linking them, and from this bond develops close understanding and fine teamwork. With such a relationship and training, performance in the show-ring is at a high level. A dog must enjoy showing if it is to perform at its best. The handler must therefore give this 'high enjoyment level' a top priority if he is to get the best possible performance from his dog. It is especially important to make the first show particularly enjoyable for the dog.

Prior to the first appearance at a show, much effort will be needed in training the youngster to stand appropriately on the table. The puppy needs to accept a stranger opening his lips and looking at his teeth – this certainly causes some problems to a number of young Cavaliers. He needs to be trained to walk closely at heel for the triangle, similarly for the 'straight up and down', and then to 'stand', showing himself off, whilst the judge walks around him in a fairly tight circle. When the judge has seen all the dogs and is ready to make his placings, the handler needs

Boardman's **Volney Shenanigan**. Promising young dog and winner of
the Cavalier Club Puppy Tray for most points at shows in 1993

to be able to get the very best out of his dog at that precise
moment. Thirty seconds earlier, or thirty seconds later, is no
good – the opportunity to impress has been missed. To bring the
best out of his dog at that moment the handler may have a
particular word or sound, or a tit bit, with which to attract the
dog's attention. Whatever it is, it should galvanize the dog into
the appropriate response. When the pressure is really on, the
handler has to be concentrating really hard and bring the best out
of his dog.

Attendance at a ring-craft training class may help a little – it
certainly accustoms the dog to being with other dogs that it has
not seen before. But undoubtedly the main part of the training
should be done at home, just five or ten minutes daily.

The Cavalier should be able to perform its manoeuvres whilst
being shown on a loose lead. Cavaliers are not expected to be
'strung up' like Terriers. I know that some handlers do string up
their Cavaliers in order to get the head high, but it should be
possible to train for this without the tight lead. A dog that is

strung up tightly can have its movement adversely affected – it cannot be 'free moving and elegant in action' as the Standard requires.

Some Cavaliers become distracted, some even 'spooked', if there is an unusual noise e.g. a chair is knocked over, a child screams, the heating system roars in, the tent starts flapping or a jet plane screeches overhead. The handler should try to prepare his dog for many sounds that might confront him, so that he remains unflappable, in fact quite 'bomb proof'.

Tit bits should be used sparingly. It is irritating to judges, when trying to look at a dog's teeth, to find either they are flecked with recent bits of liver, cheese or chocolate, or even worse the dog is still chewing a large tit bit. It would be far better for the exhibitor to win the dog's attention and response by the promise of a tit bit, but one which is not actually given until after the dog has been seen by the judge. The best solution of all, however, is if tit bits can be dispensed with altogether and the appropriate responses are stimulated by words of encouragement, and possibly a little fuss later when the dog is not under scrutiny. Some Cavaliers do get so hyped up, indeed fixated by, the continual feeding of tit bits that their attention is solely on the tit bits rather than the showing. The result is that some show poorly, despite, or because of, the tit bits.

Another important skill required of the handler relates to the actual appearance of the dog. The coat should be spotless, finely groomed and shining with condition. Under the eyes should not be tear stained, and the hair under the body and on the legs and feet must not be urine stained or otherwise stained.

A good dog that is very well presented looks far more attractive than an equally good dog which is grubby. Presentation varies considerably. There are some who are real experts at it while there are others who have made very little effort, but the majority of exhibitors lie at various levels between the two extremes. When bathing your dog prior to the show use a good quality shampoo, if necessary shampooing twice, and then rinse thoroughly. If you believe the coat may not be quite at its best, then use a conditioner and again rinse well. Some exhibitors give a final rinse with their own 'magic solution'. This sometimes contains a small amount of one or more of the following: beer, vinegar, egg, glycerine and herbs. When using such a rinse be careful of your dog's eyes. When drying ensure you direct the warm, not hot, air down the natural lie of the coat and that you brush and comb in the same direction. This helps to keep the coat straight and not tousled or 'springy'. When you arrive at the show make sure you do not allow your dog to become dirty in getting from the car park to the venue, otherwise all your earlier efforts have been wasted.

When moving your dog for the judge, try to keep its gait flowing, especially on the corners of the triangle. Remember also it is the dog that the judge wants to see, and therefore do not put yourself between your dog and the judge. When judging in America I noticed that at the beginning and at each corner of the triangle manoeuvre some handlers did a twirl, which for a moment put the dog behind the handler's legs. I discussed this with one or two exhibitors after judging was completed and was told that is how they had been taught. I still believe the twirl is unnecessary and unhelpful. I have not seen anything similar when judging in other countries. I believe the exhibitor should *never* be between the dog and the judge, as this blocks the judge's view of the dog. The American handler George G. Alston in his book *The Winning Edge* takes a similar view: 'Most important do not get in the way of the judge seeing your dog. Always keep the dog between you and the judge.'

W. Hilberts-Goodman's
**Dutch Champion Royal
Companion Going for Gold**

Many exhibitors do not appreciate just how little time a judge can spend on each dog, and therefore how vital it is to get your Cavalier performing at its very best for the short time it is under scrutiny. Let us consider a typical example. Judging begins at 10.00 a.m. and ends at 4.00 p.m. with one hour for lunch – therefore five hours, or 300 minutes, judging time. Allow a modest thirty minutes for stewards to assemble ten classes and for the judge to write his notes on the first two placed dogs in each class. That leaves 270 minutes to judge 200 dogs – approximately $1\frac{1}{3}$ minutes per dog! It is not a lot of time, and you need to have your dog performing well, indeed at his best, whenever the judge is looking at him. Keep your eye on the judge and respond immediately he shows any interest in your dog. When the judge is considering his placings your dog's response in that very brief period can mean the difference between first and second place, particularly if the two dogs under consideration are evenly matched. The quality of your dog's response will depend upon you displaying its good points to the maximum advantage, whilst seeking to minimize its weaknesses.

If you have a dog with a suspect top line, and rather straight stifles, you need to ensure the stance it takes does not emphasize these weaknesses. In fact you need to produce a stance that minimizes them. In your training at home it can be helpful to practise in front of a large full length mirror, or alternatively to have an experienced handler observing and pointing out any shortcomings. Better still, ask a friend to take a video of you handling. You can then play it back as often as necessary to iron out any faulty handling techniques.

A few handlers use their feet to try and push their dog's legs into position, and one lady deliberately treads on her dog's toes to make it push its feet back. I think the latter is deplorable, and all are examples of poor handling. The dogs become anxious and their stance is often very poor.

If your dog has a 'best' side try to present that side to the judge, especially when placings are being decided. One or two judges may ask you to place your dog the 'correct' way, i.e. the same direction as the others, but most judges are prepared to see the dog as you stand it. In that one or two minutes when the judge is deciding the five placings, your dog's better balanced side may just earn it a higher placing.

One of the most important factors of all is for both dog and handler to be relaxed. Take the opportunity to relax yourself, and your dog, when not being scrutinized. With the big entries in most Cavalier classes there is ample time for relaxation. You can be sure that if tension is present the performance will suffer. If the handler is worried, the tension will be communicated to the dog, who will also become anxious. This is bad enough for that one show, but if the dog logs it in his memory that shows are stress-provoking, then his future performances will also be adversely affected. At Crufts one of the main reasons for visits to the Vet Centre is stress-related problems in dogs. The vets feel that these are mostly caused by dogs and/or their owners getting het-up at showing. Stress will subdue the spontaneity and gaiety expected in the Cavalier.

An immature puppy's confidence and natural development is not assisted by being carted all over the country at six or seven months, often being away from home for twelve, or even fifteen hours at a time. Such journeys and experiences can be stressful for a very young puppy. It is far better to keep it at home until it is slightly more mature or, if you must show it at a tender age, take it only to local shows. It is known that some very promising puppies, in a number of breeds, have had their show careers blighted by too early and repeated exposure. They were immature and unable to cope with it, and it has affected them on a long-term basis.

The handler needs to think also of his, or her, own appearance. Dress and footwear need to be practical, comfortable and smart. The handler's appearance should complement that of the dog. Even though it is the dog that is being judged, handler and dog are a team. I feel a scruffy handler lets down the dog, whereas a smartly dressed handler can enhance the overall team appearance and performance. With handling being so important, and competition in Cavaliers being so strong, it is surprising that we do not see professional handlers competing in the breed. In America professional handlers are, in fact, excluded by the show rules of the American Cavalier King Charles Spaniel Club, unless they are handling their own dog.

A word about sportsmanship. Showing dogs is a hobby and it should give a great deal of pleasure to all who participate. Anyone can be gracious when winning, but accepting defeat in a gracious manner says a lot that is complimentary about a person. The exhibitor who screws up the card, or tuts loudly in disgust at a second or third placing, shows vividly how ungracious he or she is. Such actions taint the atmosphere of the show and reduce the enjoyment level for many who witness it. I feel it is deplorable. May I suggest that it would increase the warmth of the ringside atmosphere, and thus contribute to everyone's enjoyment, if the ringside spectators were to applaud the placings in each and every class. We go to shows for pleasure – let us make the enjoyment level as high as possible.

Whilst mentioning enjoyment, did you hear of the husband and wife who made the journey of 150 miles to Blackpool Championship Show, and, after unloading all their equipment and Cavaliers, found they had arrived on the wrong day – Cavaliers had been judged the previous day. It is said their comments to each other blistered the paintwork on Blackpool Tower a mile away. No names; my lips are sealed. I value my life too much!

14

To Progress as a Judge

Author judging in the USA with top-winning bitch Sturman's **Champion Grantilley Secret Love at Ambleside.** (Breeder: Bidgood)

It is a great responsibility to undertake a judging appointment and should not be taken on without a great deal of thought. You need to be sure you are ready, through experience, training and study. You will want to do it well, and, above all, not make a fool of yourself or let down the exhibitors.

Gaining the Necessary Experience

There are several ways in which you can obtain the necessary experience and knowledge to qualify you as a judge. They include the following:

1. The most helpful way is to have had several years in Cavaliers trying to breed good dogs and, hopefully, having had some success. During this experience you should have assessed your own dogs, recognized their strengths and weaknesses, and at least thought of breeding plans to correct those weaknesses. You will have exhibited at shows and seen dogs there that have been good, bad and indifferent. You will have discussed with others the merits of certain dogs. You will no doubt have discussed previous judges – what you liked about their style, their final line up, and what you did not approve of, for instance being rough in handling the dogs, particularly the puppies. All these matters will have formed a bank of experience that is locked away in your mind and is being added to as your experience grows. This is all practical experience which is so valuable.

2. Another very useful practical experience is to have assisted at shows as a steward. You will then have been directly involved in organizing the ring in accordance with the judge's instructions. You will no doubt have heard asides from exhibitors as to what they found pleasing, and not so pleasing. You will have witnessed the style, the competence, perhaps the dithering, of a variety of judges. But above all you will have seen good dogs placed above inferior dogs. Stewarding is a most valuable experience.

3. There are a number of positive helpful learning experiences which can be grouped together as theoretical, they include:

   (a) Studying and knowing the Breed Standard. You have to appreciate, however, that the Standard is only a guide, and is brief at that. You need to know how to interpret the Standard and what constitutes its greater depth and meaning. An earlier chapter of this book covers the Standard in detail, and together with the chapter on type, conformation, movement, soundness and balance should prove most helpful to aspiring judges. The Cavalier Club booklet, 'Interpretation of the Breed Standard', is also a useful, brief resumé which should prove of assistance.

   (b) Some Cavalier Clubs organize judging seminars. These can be helpful as long as you do not expect too much from them. They can only cover so much in a day. They also have a particular problem with the students having so many different levels of experience, and therefore having different expectations. These sessions usually combine theoretical teaching with practical 'hands-on' experience. The Kennel Club intends to enquire, through its judges' questionnaire, about attendance at breed instructional seminars.

(c) There is a correspondence course which, if successfully completed, leads to the award of the Judging Diploma. This is the college's own diploma and does not carry any official recognition or qualification. The students of the course that I have spoken to say it is hard work, but worthwhile.

4. You need to combine practice and theory. Know what the Standard requires and relate it to your dogs, and to others when you have the opportunity. 'Look' under the skin – the dog has important moving parts there. Feel the turn of the stifle, the various bones, the set of the tail. Is the neck elegant or stuffy? Count the teeth, assess the eye colour. Is there cushioning under the eyes, and what about the balance of the head, or the overall proportions of the dog? Then watch dogs move – are the front legs straight and not out at the elbows, and is there 'drive from behind'? What does 'drive from behind', and the other terms, actually mean – again, the earlier chapters should assist you. Do not *ever* give up trying to learn in this way – you *never* stop learning. I have heard it said so many times, 'After thirty years in Cavaliers I am still learning', or even, 'After twenty years, the more I know makes me appreciate just how little I know.'

To climb the judging ladder you will need considerable experience at many shows. If members of the Cavalier hierarchy have been impressed with your judging you may eventually be invited to judge a breed club limited, or open, show. When that happens it usually means you are knocking at the door of the big time. It may not be too long before you are invited to judge a championship show and award challenge certificates. To do so you need to be approved by the Kennel Club and you will be required to complete a questionnaire detailing all your judging experience, show by show. You must therefore keep accurate detailed records. Keep a list in the following form:

Date of Acceptance	Date of Show	Show	Type	No. of Classes	No. of Dogs Actually Judged	Comments

If you put the columns lengthwise across the page you will have a little more room.

Pam Thornhill judging in Sweden with her best breeding group: Länsberg Larson's four **Swedish Champions: Rodero's Abigail, Heavenly, Flashdance and Hackensack**

Guide to Judges

The Kennel Club has produced a five-page booklet which explains what is expected from a judge at shows of all levels. Part One states:

1. **Obligations of a Judge**. The essential ingredients of competent judging are:
   (a) **Breed Knowledge** – The most important single aspect of judging is knowledge of the breed to be judged and its Standard. Judges must know the Standard of the breed, fully understand its implications and be able to apply this knowledge. They should also be able to recognise breed type and have a basic knowledge of canine anatomy.
   (b) **Integrity** – Judges must be honest and impartial, judging the dogs on merit.
   (c) **Temperament and Stamina** – They should have a suitable temperament to judge and sufficient stamina for what can be a physically demanding task.
   (d) **Procedures** – Judges should develop a sound and methodical ring procedure while conforming to Kennel Club Show Regulations. They should know the latter in relation to judging and be sufficiently well-organised to put the desired ring procedure into practice.

The Qualities Required in a Judge

Judging at the highest level is not easy. The qualities needed include:

1. An 'eye for a dog'. That almost indefinable ability to recognize quality, balance and style, etc., in a dog. Being competent to sort the wheat from the chaff.
2. Knowing the Kennel Club Standard inside out and being able to interpret it with skill, precision and balance.
3. Having considerable powers of observation, concentration and memory to be able to cope with 200 dogs.
4. A high level of integrity. Being honest, impartial and judging the dogs on merit. Friendships, enmity and reputations of breeder, exhibitor or dog are completely irrelevant – it is simply your opinion of the dogs that 'fit' the Standard closest on that day. Do not complicate it for yourself by even thinking about other factors.
5. A good degree of organization so that his judging, and the ring generally, proceed in an organized way. The judge is in charge; it is his responsibility that things go smoothly.
6. A reasonable degree of fitness and stamina. To judge a large entry at a championship show he may be on his feet continuously for seven hours, apart from a short lunch break.
7. Ability to cope with the isolation and loneliness of being in the centre of the ring, under close scrutiny, with no help in making decisions.
8. Confidence and decisiveness. But a judge must also be relaxed in manner, so that he helps stewards and exhibitors to relax and enjoy their day. His style, dress and general presentation all make an impact.
9. Ability to take criticism. Judges seem to be receiving more and more 'flak' these days, perhaps a reflection of the more questioning and aggressive society in which we now live.
10. Recognition of the considerable responsibility for the future well being of the breed. Judges need to accept that those dogs they 'put up' will be seen as approved, and that type, and the breeding, will be copied. Therefore their decisions have to be based on a very sound knowledge base.

Finally, a very important quality is to recognize when judging is getting beyond you, and to say enough is enough. A few years ago I witnessed a very sad event, where the elderly lady judge became overwhelmed and confused. Exhibitors heard her repeated comments of 'Oh dear, Oh dear', 'there are too many', etc. Her so called 'final placings' were endlessly shifted about like musical chairs. I am sure she only completed her judging through the assistance of her close friend, a championship show judge, who was stewarding. The judge concerned had previously been a highly respected figure and judge, and that day was a tragedy. Some laughed and made jokes about it, but those who previously had seen her judge competently were very saddened. Perhaps this is one of the problems associated with being invited to judge three years in advance – if elderly, one's faculties may deteriorate considerably between accepting and fulfilling the appointment.

Criticisms of Judges

Many judges have been criticized for not having sufficient knowledge of the breeds they judge. It is alleged that there are 'rings' of show secretaries who hand-out judging appointments to each other on the basis of: 'You let me do Spotted Dick Water Heelers at your show, and you can judge Cavaliers at mine.' It is further said that many have no real interest in the breed, but want the experience in order to be able to 'give tickets' eventually, and thus add another notch to their judging belt. In other words it is furthering their ego trip, and possibly taking them nearer group judging appointments.

This may well happen in some breeds, but is it widespread in Cavaliers? Certainly there have been strong criticisms of a few championship show judges officiating with Cavaliers recently, but I would find it difficult to say that, categorically, it is happening on a wide scale in Cavaliers.

When criticisms are made of judges they are often wild, not based on fact and therefore unfair. I find that, when exhibiting, if my dog is of a high standard I usually get placed. If and when I take a dog that is below top quality I do not get a card, which is what I expected. My biggest wins have always been when I was showing very good dogs. Usually I did not know the judges. I had never spoken to many of them; to others I may just have said 'Good Morning'. There was no favouritism. The broad point I am making is that an experienced, realistic exhibitor usually knows whether his dog deserves a card. If an exhibitor knows in his heart the dog is really not top quality, then it is illogical to criticize a judge who does not place it.

An important factor is, of course, the judge's interpretation of 'merit' as related to the Breed Standard. It is individual – no two judges see things precisely the same, and that is what makes exhibiting so interesting. If it was all done by computer, the same dogs would win every time, and dog showing would rapidly die.

My experience leads me to believe that the vast majority of judges are honest and impartial and try to select the best dogs as they see them. You may not agree with their decisions but you have been looking only at the outside, the superficials of the dog, and from a distance. The judge has had the advantage of looking right into the dog, e.g. feeling the angle of the shoulder, inspecting the bite, etc., and he has been very close to the dog to see depth of eye colour, etc. He has also seen at close quarters the lack of merit in other dogs in the class which may not have been so obvious to ringsiders. At one championship show I had before me a bitch that had done a lot of winning. She looked glamorous on the table and had a lovely head, but when going over her I was not impressed with her hindquarters. When she moved my suspicions were confirmed – she plaited her hind legs. She was not placed despite being beautiful in many respects. I felt she was unsound.

If a judge has done her best, and has not been interested in who was holding the leads, then I would not want to criticize. Remember, there is always another day and another judge. I keep a file of all judges' critiques, which I check before entering. If I find a judge is keen on a particular fault, then if my dog has a tendency towards that fault I do not enter. I thus save my money and my time.

What the Judge is Looking for

The judge's task can be simply defined as to judge the dogs according to the Breed Standard and place them in order of merit. There are, however, twenty-two sections of the Cavalier Standard and the judge is required to consider them all in assessing the total dog.

The basic make and shape of the Cavalier has to be right. The judge is not only concerned with superficial glamour; that counts of course, but there are other fundamental matters such as conformation, type, soundness, and balance that need to be given a high priority.

The judge is looking for quality Cavaliers that fit the Standard well and will take the breed forward positively when used for breeding. It is a heavy responsibility.

Three generations of winning dogs in New Zealand:

Grand Champion Homerbrent Cardinham. Sire of 31 New Zealand Champions and several in Australia. (Breeder: Coaker)

His son **Grand Champion Glen Gariff Carnaby**. Sire of several champions

Carnaby's son the promising youngster **Glengariff Poldhu**

These dogs belong to Anne and Ian Dobie. It is a magnificent achievement to become a grand champion as it requires fifty Challenge Certificates plus three Best in Show at All Breed Championship level

Your First Judging Appointment

You should not solicit judging appointments. Wait until you are asked, because this means that someone has recommended you, feeling that you are ready to undertake the task. When the invitation arrives, consider it very carefully, and honestly assess whether you feel you are ready. If so, then indicate your willingness. You should have the offer confirmed in writing, and you should write confirming your acceptance. Once you have accepted, you are committed; it is a contract. Keep a copy of all correspondence and start a 'judging file'. Just prior to the show you will often receive a note, or a schedule, setting out the number of entries you have received.

When the day arrives you need to be at the show at least thirty minutes before your judging is due to begin. Report to the secretary, who will give you your judging book, badge, etc. Meet your stewards and make your way to the ring. Inspect the ring for any hazards, e.g. glass or nails, and check where you want the table sited to achieve the best light. Advise your stewards where you want the dogs that have 'previously been seen' to stand, etc. When judging time arrives, start promptly. Another judge may follow on in your ring when you have finished.

It is worth repeating that exhibitors have entered under you, and have paid to do so, because they want your opinion. Forget about friendships and past reputations of dogs or exhibitors. You have simply to choose which are the best dogs on the day.

I find it helpful at the start of each class to send all the dogs around the ring. It gets the dogs warmed up and relaxed, but it also gives me the opportunity of having a 'first look' at them. Even at this stage I usually see a few dogs that 'take my eye', and look likely to be strong contenders. Allow the first exhibitor sufficient time to set up her dog on the table. Sometimes a judge eager to get on with it descends on the first exhibitor before she is ready, and this can make a novice exhibitor quite flustered.

Be courteous and pleasant to exhibitors, and handle the dogs carefully and gently. I ask the age of each dog in every class. I do so for two main reasons. If I have an eleven-month-old puppy in Limit Class I want to know, and then I ask myself why the puppy is not competing in the Puppy Class. Is it because it is so big and coarse that it would look out of place against its contemporaries, and this is the reason it is in Limit, competing against older adult dogs? The second reason is that the simple question establishes a connection, however small, between judge and exhibitor, and often the few words exchanged help to relax both exhibitor and dog.

Give each dog an equal opportunity to show its merit. If one dog is obviously of poor quality you still have to examine it and give it the same opportunity to move. You need to concentrate fully, and be seen to be paying attention to the dogs. If you allow your gaze to wander about the venue when a dog is moving, the ringside spectators will notice and criticize you for it.

Feel the dogs in the way that you believe is necessary to check their conformation. Ask for the dogs to be moved in any way you prefer, but most judges believe the triangle has much to offer, as each of the three legs of the triangle provides important information about the functioning of different parts of the dog. When you are contemplating your final placings it is helpful to stand well back from the dogs and see them in profile. That enables you to consider the total dog, and to assess how well proportioned it is. When you have placed the dogs you will need to make notes to enable you to complete your critique.

The main requirement of judging is to assess the overall merit of dogs against each other, i.e. the total dog. No dog is perfect, and therefore one has to consider what particular weighting one gives to a fault in dog A as against another fault, or faults, in dog B. What also enters into the comparison is how serious is a particular fault – is it slight, moderate or severe? Let us consider an example. In one class there is an outstanding dog with just one fault, but it is of a serious degree – say poor hindquarters or quite light eyes. The other dogs in the class cannot match the overall quality of the first mentioned; in fact they are all rather moderate, but with no serious faults. What does the judge do? Many would say you have to assess the degree of damage that might be done to the breed if the serious fault dog was made the winner, and as a result was widely used at stud. Poor hindquarters and light eyes are both very difficult to breed out. But the other dogs are only moderate, and do not have a lot to offer to the breed. Which would you choose, remembering always you should not 'fault judge', but must consider the total dog?

The Kennel Club gives explicit guidance regarding one particular fault. The Guide to Judges S.5(g) states: 'Judges should dismiss from a class any dog which is of savage or vicious disposition.' The Kennel Club has also made an important statement regarding another matter, that 'Judges must be aware that neutering, particularly castration of dogs, is not a fault and should judge accordingly.' (See end of Chapter 2 for further details.)

With a large entry such as at a championship show, it often assists a judge to make a tentative timetable. You will know what your total entry is, and it is fairly easy to estimate that by 11.30 a.m. you want to have completed, say, Junior Class; at lunch break, Graduate; at 3.00 p.m., Mid Limit; and at about 4.00 p.m. be ready to consider unbeaten dogs for the Challenge Certificate (CC). The actual times and classes are immaterial, as long as you have the tentative timetable in mind. Otherwise what happens occasionally is that a judge takes too much time over the early classes, and then has to speed up considerably in the afternoon, which is unfair to the exhibitors in the later classes. It is the later classes which usually provide the CC and Reserve CC winners.

During your judging ensure you note down accurately the numbers of the placed dogs, and ask your steward to check them before the slips are taken to the secretary. Too often one reads in the Breed Notes that Dog X, and not Dog Y, was third in a particular class. This correction occurs after a mistake has been made by the judge in his paperwork.

After handing out the Challenge Certificate, it is wise to deliberately pause for a moment, and decide whether you want the second to the CC winner brought in to challenge for the reserve CC. Remember that both your CC and Reserve CC winners must, in your opinion, be worthy of the title Champion.

After completing your judging notify the Secretary, and check that all your judging slips etc. have been received and are in

Egan's **Australian and New Zealand Champion Homerbrent Cartoon**. The top-winning Cavalier of all time in Australia. (Breeder: Coaker)

order. Then relax – all you have to do now is write your critique!

I have deliberately left to the end of this section an innocent sounding but tricky and demanding matter which sometimes occurs early in your judging career. Occasionally when a Club Secretary telephones, and you agree to judge a few classes of Cavaliers, she may say, almost as an afterthought, 'Would you also mind doing a few classes of Any Variety Toy? They are pretty simple.' The inclination is to feel rather pleased about this additional offer, and to accept without giving the matter any real thought. But beware, as there are twenty-two different breeds in the Toy Group. To do justice to possible entries you need to know twenty-two Breed Standards, and a fair amount about each breed. There is a very great deal of preparation needed before one should accept such classes.

The Judge's Critique

One matter which is frequently complained about in the weekly dog newspapers is the lack of consideration shown by judges who do not write a critique for publication. Some complainants say that if a person accepts a judging appointment it should be compulsory for a critique to be written. The Kennel Club merely says 'it is expected, although not mandatory' that a critique will be provided.

Writing a critique gives a judge the opportunity to show that he cares for the breed and is interested in its future. In his preliminary comments he should aim to provide a few general observations *based on the entry* as to how he believes the breed is progressing, what are its strengths, and those matters which need the attention of breeders. Such general comments by cham-pionship show judges were most helpful when I was writing the Cavalier Club's 'Looking at the Breed' booklets.

As far back as 1976 Amice Pitt, then President of the Cavalier Club, wrote in the yearbook: 'I would also like to thank the judges for their outspoken comments on the dogs shown under them; the remarks of one judge do not cause much comment, but the drawing of attention to prevailing faults by many well-known judges does bring out the weaknesses in our breed, and shows where breeders' efforts must be directed.'

A critique needs to be written as soon as possible after the show whilst it is still fresh in the memory. Discussion often takes place as to how honest and critical a judge should be, or can be, when the next week she is back amongst the exhibitors. The report needs to give a balanced, objective view bringing out the qualities, as well as any serious faults. I believe the critique should be sensitively and tactfully written – to severely criticize a winner begs the question why did the judge place it first if it has all those faults? It must also be remembered yet again, that no dog is perfect, and furthermore not too much can be expected of the placed dogs in a Novice class of four entries at a Limited or Open Show. Writing a critique may seem a chore, but it enables the judge to explain the placings she made.

Judging Overseas

As you would expect, judging overseas varies according to each country. For instance in Sweden each dog has to be graded and only 'first grade' dogs compete for the placings. Additionally, the judge has to dictate a report on every dog during the class, and a copy is given to the exhibitor there and then.

In America, at the Cavaliers of the North East Show I was required to make a written report on the first four in each class. In Australia, at the Cavalier Club of New South Wales show I was required to report on the first five in each class. In New Zealand, at the Tiki and Canterbury Cavalier Club shows there were Nursery Classes for very young puppies (and delightful they were). But at both the New Zealand shows I was only expected to provide a written report on the first three in each class.

It is the different expectations at overseas shows which help to make them so interesting. The demands made upon a judge officiating overseas mean, however, that he or she should have a good level of experience and self confidence, and preferably have judged at least several championship shows in the United Kingdom before contemplating going abroad to judge.

Having accepted a judging appointment overseas one needs to obtain a copy of that country's Standard for the breed, and their show rules. It could also be helpful to talk with someone who has recently judged in that country. The conversation should, of course, only be about show regulations and expectations of the judge. There should be no conversation about individual dogs or kennels, nor should a future judge be tempted to look at video recordings of previous shows. One must not only be impartial; one must also be seen to be impartial.

Overseas Judges Judging in the United Kingdom

In the past, Cavaliers in the United Kingdom have been judged only very occasionally by overseas judges. The few judges who officiated were mostly all rounders, but with an occasional specialist Cavalier judge like Jeanie and Dennis Montford, and Mollie Grocott, who I regard as a Cavalier specialist despite her considerable expertise and love for Griffons.

Montford's **Australian Champion Elvenhome Buckthorn**. Top-winning Australian bred Cavalier.

However more recently we have been pleased to welcome a few more specialist breed judges from various countries including America, Finland, Holland, Australia and New Zealand. I for one very much welcome their contribution. I believe this cross-fertilisation can only be helpful to Cavaliers, both here and in the judge's own country. We can benefit from their observations and constructive criticism, and when they return home they will be able to compare Cavaliers in their own country with those in the United Kingdom.

It may be that in the future it could be to our advantage to import a few outstanding, and healthy, Cavaliers from abroad to strengthen our own stock. When I judged in New Zealand I was told that two promising puppies were shortly to be exported to Canada. Therefore enthusiasts overseas are not just seeking Cavaliers from Britain. On my judging trips abroad I have seen a number of Cavaliers that I would have been very happy to have brought back home.

15

Purchasing a Cavalier from a UK Breeder

For our overseas friends who wish to purchase a Cavalier from the United Kingdom there are advantages if you can visit Britain, go round the kennels that interest you, and choose your own stock from that which is available. You will then have the opportunity to speak to several breeders, which may help you considerably in making your choice. You could also attend two or three championship shows which would give you a 'snap shot' of the current crop of show Cavaliers.

If a visit to this country is not possible you need to contact a breeder that you know exports good quality Cavaliers, preferably of the type that particularly appeals to you. Avoid contacting any breeders who only seem to export mediocre stock, because that will not satisfy you.

Ideally there are advantages in purchasing, if possible, a Cavalier aged about fifteen months. By then you should be able to ascertain if it has been shown and with what success. It should be approaching mature adulthood and should hardly change any further. Importantly, it should have had health screening checks at twelve months, e.g. clear eye and heart certificates, and possibly have been hip scored. The heart certificate at this young age will not guarantee freedom from future mitral valve disease but it is at least a step in the right direction. Obviously to purchase one of this age and quality you will have to pay a higher price, but it is likely to be more satisfying in the long term.

The following export pedigrees for Cavaliers were issued by the Kennel Club in 1992 and 1993.

	1992	1993
Australia	3	6
Belgium	3	3
Canada	7	2
Denmark		2
Finland	6	7
France	54	22
Germany	9	14
Greece		1
Italy	6	3
Japan		4
Kenya		1
Lebanon		1
Luxembourg		1
Netherlands	7	5
New Zealand	2	
Norway	6	3
Saudi Arabia		1
Slovenia		2
Spain	2	1
Sweden	16	16
Switzerland	6	2
United States of America	70	51
TOTALS	197	148

I am a little surprised at some of the countries listed for 1993
Cavalier exports.

16

Breed Record Breakers

1. **Amice Pitt's Ttiwehs**

    Her Ttiweh prefix the most successful of all in producing twenty-seven English Champions. Also Mrs Pitt was founder of the breed and held high office in the Cavalier King Charles Spaniel Club for fifty years.

2. **Alansmere Aquarius**

    Best in Show Crufts 1973. The only Cavalier, indeed the only toy dog, ever to have won this Supreme Award.

3. **Ch. Homaranne Caption**

    Top Stud Dog. Sire of sixteen English Champions. He also won thirteen Challenge Certificates and three Toy Groups.

4. **Ch. Spring Tide at Alansmere**

    Breed Record Holder for winning most Challenge Certificates.

Most Successful Cavalier Affixes – Champions Bred.

Ttiweh – 27 Champions – Breeder Amice Pitt

Mrs Pitt died in 1978, but her affix still holds the record for the number of Champions bred. The Crisdigs of Susan Burgess are only one behind, and the Homerbrents of Molly Coaker are very close and still producing champions. Even if Mrs Pitt's record is eventually overhauled, as seems possible, it has been a magnificent achievement. It says a very great deal for Mrs Pitt's skill in selecting animals for breeding, because she had to try and

Mrs Pitt with several of her Cavaliers

revive an almost extinct breed. Some thought it had gone for ever.

From a very young age Amice Pitt was closely connected with dogs. She was born 5 July 1897 to Sir Everett and Lady Millais. Her father, a son of John Millais, the well known pre-Raphaelite painter, was a dedicated dog enthusiast. In 1874 he introduced the Basset Hound to this country and studied dog breeding very seriously. He wrote the highly regarded book *The Theory and Practice of Breeding to Type*. Unfortunately he died when Amice was quite young, but she always attributed her appreciation of line breeding to his work. The family was also involved with horses and Amice was a fine rider. Her interest and knowledge of breeding animals, therefore, was not only confined to Cavaliers but covered several breeds of dog and was also more broadly directed toward other animals. In addition, she liked salmon fishing. She was a talented and dedicated pianist who intended to pursue a classical musical career by training at a conservatoire in Germany, but the outbreak of war in 1914 put a stop to that. This strong artistic talent influenced her approach to breeding dogs – not only was she seeking soundness but also beauty and naturalness. She had an accomplished and knowledgeable eye for a dog and was constantly seeking to breed better dogs. She was always a realist and constantly stressed there were no easy short cuts. In 1972 she wrote, 'The Show side never interested me in the same way as trying to breed first class stock, sound in temperament and of good conformation. Of course I like winning, so does everybody, but I would rather have bred the winner than have scooped up the cups!'

She said her first love in dogs was Chows, and later she also had Pugs. However, in 1927 Amice's mother, Lady Millais, owned a Blenheim King Charles Spaniel, and Amice's attention was drawn to the special classes being sponsored at Crufts for the earlier type of long nosed, flat skulled toy spaniel, then almost extinct. She entered her mother's bitch, Waif Julia, and won the class.

The following year, 1928, the Cavalier King Charles Spaniel Club was set up with Mrs Pitt as secretary and leading light. Then followed a remarkable half century of dedication to Cavaliers, ending with her death in 1978 at the age of eighty-one. A few months prior to her death she acted as referee at the Club Golden Jubilee Show. She has been described as 'the creator' of the breed and 'Mother Cavalier'. Old yearbooks and articles describe her as being at the helm, working indefatigably for the breed, and there was quite a lot of opposition to the breed in the early days. She was a strong character, not afraid to voice her opinions, and many of today's highly respected and experienced breeders sought to follow her teachings. For instance Gertrude Biddle wrote in *Canadian Cavalier Quotes*, 1985: 'In my early days Susan Burgess said her great aim was to breed Cavaliers which would meet Mrs Pitt's approval and I have tried to follow her advice.' Also in another *Canadian Cavalier Quotes* of 1985 Lady Forwood wrote: 'I learnt from a hard school – from our greatest Cavalier personage, Mrs Amice Pitt.'

Christopher of Ttiweh seems to have been the first Cavalier registered with the Ttiweh prefix in July 1928. The foundation sire to the kennel was Peter of Ttiweh whose own sire was the famous Ann's Son.

Then followed a steady flow of Ttiweh successes, amounting to

27 champions and 143 CCs from 40 Cavaliers. Trilby of Ttiweh is the youngest Cavalier champion of all time at 11 months 26 days.

Champion Trilby of Ttiweh born 1950

It has to be said that, since 1971, by Kennel Club rules it has not been possible for a dog to become a Champion unless at least one of its three CCs was won when the dog was over one year old. Trilby won her crown in 1951. The many Ttiweh champions, and others who did not make their title, have contributed much to the successful development of the breed. It was a large kennel with sixty to eighty dogs at times, consisting mainly of Cavaliers and Chows with, in later years, an occasional Pug. During the 1939–45 war numbers were reduced 'to a mere handful'. Mrs Pitt's prefix Ttiweh is her husband's Christian name, Hewitt, reversed. Her husband was a distinguished solicitor.

Mrs Pitt told Evelyn (Janey) Booth that she considered Ch. Little Dorrit of Ttiweh the nearest to the ideal Cavalier she had ever owned. She told Miss Turle that, for conformation, she considered the heavily-marked, speckled-faced Ch. Comfort of Ttiweh was the best.

Jupiter of Ttiweh was the youngest Cavalier, at 6 months and 30 days, to win a CC. In fact the first three youngest CC winners were all Ttiweh bred. Champion Daywell Roger bred by Lt Col and Mrs Brierley, but owned by Mrs Pitt's daughter Jane (now

Bowdler), won the first dog CC in the breed, and also holds the record for progeny winning most CCs (i.e. 73 CCs). Mrs Bowdler has recently stood down after completing several years service as President to the Cavalier Club. She still continues as the Club's Historian, and the Pitt tradition of service to Cavaliers therefore continues.

Many people have given a great deal to Cavaliers over the years, and long may this continue, but it is widely accepted that the one truly outstanding person was Amice Pitt. As a breeder she still holds the record for the number of English Champions. But she is remembered even more for her role as charismatic leader, mentor and inspiration to the breed for fifty years. Her knowledge, drive and personality were phenomenal. What a person, and what a debt the breed owes to her.

Supreme Best in Show – Crufts

Alansmere Aquarius

Before we consider his appearance at Crufts a brief introduction regarding his breeding and personality is enlightening. It also helps in creating a better understanding of his performance on that momentous day.

Aquarius (a Blenheim) was born 10 September 1971 and came right out of the top drawer as regards breeding. His sire was

Champion Vairire Osiris, and his dam was then the bitch breed record holder for number of Challenge Certificates won (fifteen), namely Champion Alansmere McGoogans Maggie May.

Like most if not all great characters, be they canine or human, Aquarius had a distinctly individual personality. He showed an aptitude for obedience and was highly responsive and proficient. He was not kennelled during the day but was allowed to wander loose about the place and was entirely reliable. However he had to be kennelled on his own at night because, given the opportunity, he was an inveterate ear and coat chewer and could easily destroy another dog's show chances overnight. Both John and Alan, his owners, say that 'his general personality made him a delight to have around'. He was full of self-confidence and his pet name of 'Chirpy' was most apt. Now to Crufts.

Picture the Scene:

LONDON – 10 February 1973

Cruft's Show held at Olympia – a venue rather cramped for space. Over two days 48,000 visitors attended, including many from overseas. The trade stands provided a colourful, market-place atmosphere. Spectators were six to ten deep around each of the thirty-three show-rings.

Dog World described it thus: 'Carp, grumble, blather and blaspheme as we will, Cruft's is still a great show. Though at times it is difficult to see the dogs for the people, there is still that atmosphere, that tension, that great expectancy that no other show can raise. No matter what is said to the contrary, Cruft's is the greatest, and the one we all want to win.'

The 1973 Crufts Show was rather special as it celebrated the centenary year of the Kennel Club. A total of 7,581 dogs were entered, making 11,203 entries. For those who may not know, each dog has to qualify by winning a specified award at a championship show before it can compete at Crufts. It is the cream of dogs, including the really big winners, that appear at Crufts. For instance, I know two Dachshunds were there, each with more than forty Challenge Certificates, a Pyrenean with twenty-nine CCs, a Cocker with thirty-two CCs who won Reserve Best in Show at Crufts two years earlier, and a Pointer with twenty-two CCs who came Reserve BIS this year. Competition is hot!

Breed Judging

There were 123 Cavaliers entered in 12 classes. The judge was Mr Vivian L. Bennett, who had travelled 6,000 miles to judge the breed. Before Crufts Alansmere Aquarius had won one CC, but during his career he went on to win a total of twelve.

First class in the ring was Special Junior Dog with thirteen entries. The winner was Alansmere Aquarius, aged seventeen months. That success was great, but Hall and Evans could have had no idea what a truly unique day they were to experience. Further success was quickly theirs with another dog when Alansmere Sullivan Snuffles won the Undergraduate Dog class. As the judging progressed Aquarius beat Champion Ottermouth Back Badge for the Dog CC. Back Badge had won Best of Breed at Crufts the previous year. The bitch CC winner was Crisdig Florida, who first won a strong Open Bitch class. Second to Florida in the class, and winner of Reserve Bitch CC, was another of Hall and Evans' – namely, Alansmere Ellgee Crystal! Aquarius and Florida met to decide which should be Best of Breed and Aquarius triumphed.

The judge, Mr Bennett, said of Aquarius: 'My most heartfelt congratulations to Messrs Hall and Evans for producing such a wonderful Cavalier. This is the type that all breeders should try to produce, wonderful conformation, the most perfect movement I think I have ever seen in a Cavalier, gay right to the last, a beautiful silky coat, and the softest of eye, and worthy in every way of becoming The Supreme Champion of Cruft's.'

Group Judging

The judge for the Toy Group was Mrs Judy de Casembroot. Aquarius was now required to compete against the Best of Breed from fourteen other toy breeds. Mrs de Casembroot declared it 'an outstanding group' and narrowed the fifteen down to six, from which to make her final selection. The six were a Maltese, Griffon, Yorkshire Terrier, Italian Greyhound, Miniature Pinscher and Aquarius.

In awarding Aquarius best in the Toy Group Mrs de Casembroot said:

Before the Cavalier went into the last round (for Best in Show) I said on television: 'This one has star quality', and so it proved. Even when I joined the celebrations afterwards and drank his health in champagne he was still showing beautifully. He captured everyone by his charm and personality, but not only that, this Cavalier, aged only 17 months, is a splendid specimen of the breed in conformation and coat, and he moved faultlessly. Alansmere Aquarius ... is not only named after a star, he is himself a star. This big occasion with the crowds and spotlights could be unnerving to any dog but Aquarius stood up to every test. I was captivated by his head and expression and his perfect body. In a long experience I have seen few to compare with him.

Judging for Best in Show

This is the summit, the climax, of the whole show. The crowds around the 'Best In Show' ring are enormous and the atmosphere is highly charged. Each of the six group winners were paraded and then examined by the judge, Mr A. Owen Grindey. Let me remind you, these final six had won through from 7,581 dogs. The six were a Pointer, Bulldog, Kerry Blue, Greyhound, Pembroke Corgi and Aquarius. It did not take long for Mr Grindey to choose his Best in Show, although for a brief moment there was a little confusion for ringsiders as to which dog he had chosen. Then it became clear. Aquarius had done it – he had won Supreme Best In Show at Crufts! It still brings a 'tingle' just thinking about it. The award was very warmly received by ringsiders. Aquarius had shown for all he was worth all day and well deserved his success. I am sure that his superb presentation and top class handling also contributed in no small way to the success.

He was, and still is, the only toy dog ever to win the honour. Cavalier enthusiasts were 'over the moon'. I wonder when, or indeed if, a Cavalier will *ever* repeat the success.

Top Stud Dog – Ch. Homaranne Caption

Caption won the Cavalier Club's progeny trophy, i.e. Pargeter Sugar Bowl, for seven consecutive years (1980–6).

He was born 13 June 1976 and lived to the ripe old age of fifteen, dying on 23 June 1991. He was bred by Anne Coaker (now Reddaway), and owned by her mother, Molly Coaker.

Many of his forebears, and his progeny, have been or are long livers. For example his daughter, C. Homerbrent Bewitched, is now fourteen and a half, and I currently have another daughter, Ch. Crieda Rosella, aged thirteen.

Caption had a very successful show career, winning thirteen Challenge Certificates and three Toy Groups. When winning his thirteen CCs he was only beaten twice for Best of Breed. I was privileged to do this once at Southern Counties in June 1980 with Alansmere Rosetta of Crieda, who thus gained her second Challenge Certificate and then quickly went on to win her crown. This was the show at which Caption won his thirteenth and last Challenge Certificate. The photo shows Caption and Rosetta. The judge was Michael Quinney.

Whilst Caption had a brilliant show career, even that did not match his success as a stud dog. His record of siring sixteen English Champions is going to be very difficult to beat. Surprisingly, twelve of his sixteen champions were bitches. Of the sixteen champion progeny, four were bred by Molly Coaker, one by Anne Coaker, four by Gordon and Norma Inglis and seven by other individual owners. He threw his type to many different lines, and to bitches of various types, but one form of line breeding which frequently proved successful was Caption to Rosemullion progeny.

Caption's pedigree was:

		Ch. Rosemullion of Ottermouth B.
	Ch. Bredonvale Bernard B.	
		Bredonvale Ttiweh Lavengro B.
Aust. Ch. Homerbrent Henry B.		
		Eng. & Irish Ch. Tnegun Charivari B.
	Homerbrent Dolly Gray B.	
		Crisdig Betsy B. Ch. Crisdig Merry Matelot B.
	Homerbrent Crisdig Reflection B.	
		Crisdig Genevieve B.
Ch. Homerbrent Captivation T.		
		Crisdig Mr Patch T.
	Homerbrent Nolana T.	
		Belmont Nell B.

It can clearly be seen that Caption had top class breeding behind him including several Crisdig lines, a dash of Ttiweh, plus that great sire Champion Rosemullion of Ottermouth. Readers may be interested in my brief recollections of some of Caption's forebears.

Captivation	– heavily marked, but probably the best constructed tricolour bitch I have seen. Lovely head, great mover, superb character and a true toy spaniel.
Nolana	– rather ordinary to look at but very well constructed and good in movement. The dam of two champions, she lived to almost fourteen.
Merry Matelot	– as a veteran sat on my knee and still looked classy and wonderful. Beautiful temperament.
Bernard	– last saw him when he was eleven years old but he looked much younger. Was then quite lively, his pigment was still jet black and his colouring very rich.

Rosemullion   – most beautiful head with gorgeous eyes. Looked the proud stallion type and in fact he proved to be one of the most successful Cavalier studs of all time.

Caption was given the pet name of Caper as this was felt to be the best name that could be obtained from Caption. However until the age of three or four months he rather belied this name, as he was rather dull and characterless. Then his litter brother was sold, and suddenly Caper blossomed and became the great extrovert that everyone remembers him to be. He was not the easiest puppy to show, and his liveliness often marred his chances in the show-ring. As a result he only won one first at championship shows as a puppy. But then he began to settle, and regular successes followed. As a veteran he was never beaten from the age of seven until he retired at the age of twelve and a half. In the ring when he won and was praised, he used to jump in the air and turn, so that Molly could catch him facing outwards. As Molly said, 'he never considered I might not catch him!'

When Caption was twelve years old Molly Coaker had all her stud dogs hip scored. At this ripe old age Caption had the excellent score of 3:1, total 4.

Caption's great achievements speak for themselves:

1. Thirteen Challenge Certificates and three Toy Groups.
2. Sire of sixteen English champions, and twenty-one of his progeny together won a total of sixty-seven challenge certificates, plus many of his grandchildren have been big winners here and abroad.
3. And finally many of his offspring, like himself, are living to a good age – something very important for the breed today.

In short, Caption has become a breed legend. In a personal communication Molly Coaker states: 'I always felt so privileged to have been the owner of such a dog and so wish I could breed another of his like, but know they only come once in a lifetime.'

Cavalier Winning Most Challenge Certificates

Champion Spring Tide at Alansmere born 6.10.89

Bred by Roger Calladine

Owned by Alan Hall and John Evans

Champion Spring Tide at Alansmere

To fully appreciate Spring Tide's achievement it is helpful to recall the previous record. This was held by Miss Pam Turle's Champion Aloysius of Sunninghill, a tricolour, with nineteen Challenge Certificates. Aloysius won his challenge certificates between May 1957 and May 1960 and the record then stood for thirty-three years. In fact, during the whole of that time it was never seriously challenged.

However in May 1991 the young Blenheim dog Spring Tide at Alansmere won his first Challenge Certificate. This began an amazing series of Challenge Certificate winning performances by Chuckles, as he is known at home. On 27 March 1993, less than two years from winning his first challenge certificate, I awarded him his nineteenth, which equalled the breed record.

My critique on that date stated:

OPEN DOG (11 entries – all present)
This class included 3 multiple Group Winners plus 2 other Champions.

1st. Hall & Evans Ch. Spring Tide at Alansmere.

From his head to his tail he fits the Standard so closely.He has the elegance, gracefulness, type and high quality of a top ranking dog. His head, whilst masculine, exemplifies the desired soft gentle expression. He has a good body, correct forequarters and lovely turn of stifle. His bone is correct. No one in the class surpassed his movement. His markings are well broken and he is extremely glamorous. His owners are probably the breed experts in presentation, so that every assistance is given to him. He was a worthy winner of the CC (and B.O.B.) and it is going to take an exceptional dog to beat him.

A few days after the show John Evans told me, 'We think he is our best ever.'

Spring Tide has since won more challenge certificates, the total at the end of 1994 being twenty-seven, and, as a relatively young dog, he may well win even more. On 4 March 1995 Spring Tide won Best in Show at Parent Club Championship Show, thus taking his record number of CCs to twenty-eight. On this high note he has been retired from the show-ring. He has also won four Toy Groups, including a prestigious Group triumph at Crufts 1994.

Spring Tide was bred by Roger Calladine, who resides with John Evans and Alan Hall. Spring Tide is a combination of Alansmere and Homerbrent bloodlines – two of the very best. His pedigree is:

			Ch. Homerbrent Festival
		Fr. Ch. Homerbrent Jester	
Sire			Dalvreck Highlight of Homerbrent
Homerbrent Jeremy at Cottismeer			Eng. & Ir. Ch. Ronnoc Rhum of Sancem
		Homerbrent Juliet	
			Ch. Homerbrent Samantha Alansmere Lamplighter
		Alansmere Pierre	
Dam			Ch. Alansmere Michelle
Alansmere Angel Song			Ch. Kershope Sandonpark Icebreaker
		Selsey The Snow Crystal	
			Amantra Pan Yan Pickle

At home Chuckles is a quiet dog and hardly ever barks, whereas his brother can be a little noisy at times. Chuckles loves both his food and his daily walk. He is eager and competent in his stud work.

His show career has been wonderful and I understand he will continue to be shown very occasionally. It would be marvellous if he could also achieve similar distinction as a stud dog, thus benefiting the breed greatly.

Epilogue

The little boy was excited at having seen his friend's litter of Cavalier puppies. He was telling his mum all about them and said with some authority, 'There were four. Three boys and one girl.'

'How did you know whether they were boys or girls?' asked his mum.

He replied, 'Easy. They just tipped 'em upside down and it must be stamped on the bottom.'

Bibliography

Alston, George G., *The Winning Edge* (Howell Book House, New York, 1992)

Cavalier King Charles Spaniel Champions 1928–1988 (The Cavalier King Charles Spaniel Club, 1989)

Crighton, G.W., 'Thermal Regulation of the New Born Dog', *Journal of Small Animal Practice*, 9, 463 (1968)

Elliott, Rachel Page, *The New Dogsteps* (Howell Book House, New York, 1983)

Ford, Grahame, *Cavaliers at UK Championship Shows 1946–1992* (Grahame Ford, Hampshire, 1993)

Häggström, Jens, K. Hansson, Clarence Kvart & L. Svenson, 'Chronic valvular disease in the cavalier King Charles spaniel in Sweden', *Veterinary Record* (12.12.92)

Jackson, Frank, *Dog Breeding* (The Crowood Press, Wiltshire, 1994)

Jones, Olwen Gwynne, *The Popular Guide to Puppy Rearing* (The Popular Dogs Publishing Company, London, 1953)

Lyon, McDowell, *The Dog in Action* (Howell Book House, New York, 1950)

Lytton, *Toy Dogs and Their Ancestors* (Duckworth, London, 1911)

Priester, W.A., 'Sex, Size and Breed as Risk Factors in Canine Patella Luxation', *Journal of the American Veterinary Medical Association*, 160: 740–742 (1972)

Robinson, Roy, *Genetics for Dog Breeders* (Pergamon Press, Oxford 1990)

Secord, William, *Dog Painting 1840–1940* (Antique Collectors' Club, Suffolk, 1992)

Shook, Larry, *The Puppy Report* (Lyons & Burford, New York, 1992)

Willis, Malcolm B., *Practical Genetics for Dog Breeders* (H.F. & G. Witherby, 1992)

Wimhurst, C.G.E., *The Book of Toy Dogs* (Muller, London, 1965)

Appendix

Cavalier King Charles Spaniel Clubs Worldwide

There has been a steady expansion in the number of Cavalier breed clubs in other countries. America, Australia, New Zealand and Canada each have several, and there are active clubs in other countries. Many of the overseas clubs are enthusiastic and lively, and show a great deal of vision and concern for the future development of the breed.

Cavalier Clubs in Great Britain and Ireland

THE CAVALIER KING CHARLES SPANIEL CLUB
Mrs Lesley Jupp, 60 Roundway, Copped Hall, Camberley, Surrey GU15 1NU
Telephone: 01276 683282

THREE COUNTIES PEKINGESE AND CAVALIER SOCIETY
Mrs S. Jones, 7 Wellesbourne Road, Coventry CV5 7HG
Telephone: 01203 462816

SCOTTISH CAVALIER KING CHARLES SPANIEL CLUB
Mrs Morag Donaldson, The Bungalow, Langlees Farm, By Newmills, Fife KY12 8HA
Telephone: 01383 880336

CAVALIER KING CHARLES SPANIEL CLUB OF IRELAND
Mrs Evelyn Hurley, 14 Grange Park View, Raheny, Dublin 5, Eire
Telephone: Dublin 481621

WEST OF ENGLAND CAVALIER KING CHARLES
SPANIEL CLUB
Mr J. Evans, The Sheiling, Gloucester Road, Standish,
Stonehouse, Glos. GL10 3DN
Telephone: 01453 822599

NORTHERN CAVALIER KING CHARLES SPANIEL
SOCIETY
Miss B.M. Henshaw, The Orchard, Wharf Lane, Sedgwick,
Kendal, Cumbria LA8 OJW
Telephone: 01539 560360

MIDLAND CAVALIER KING CHARLES SPANIEL CLUB
Mrs Mary Rees, 'Little Oaks', 114 Hawkes Mill Lane, Allesley,
Coventry CV5 9FN
Telephone: 01203 403583

EASTERN COUNTIES CAVALIER KING CHARLES
SPANIEL SOCIETY
Ms Maryann Hogan, 1 Foster Close, Old Stevenage, Herts. SG1
4SA
Telephone: 01438 317071

THE NORTHERN IRELAND CAVALIER KING CHARLES
SPANIEL CLUB
Miss M.E. Elliott, 8 Glengariff Park, Bangor, County Down,
Northern Ireland BT20 4UY
Telephone: 01247 463166

SOUTHERN CAVALIER KING CHARLES SPANIEL CLUB
Miss M. Morrison, 3 St Wilfred's Road, Broadwater, Worthing,
West Sussex BN14 8BA
Telephone: 01903 230939

THE SOUTH AND WEST WALES CAVALIER KING
CHARLES SPANIEL CLUB
Mr A. Close, 'Lamont', Claude Road West, Barry, S. Glamorgan
CF62 7JG
Telephone: 01446 737733

HUMBERSIDE CAVALIER KING CHARLES SPANIEL
CLUB
Mrs Diane Jenkins, Churrasco House, 40 Noel Avenue,
Oakham, Leics. LE15 6SQ
Telephone: 01572 723116

Cavalier Clubs Overseas

AUSTRALIA
CAVALIER KING CHARLES SPANIEL CLUB OF NEW
SOUTH WALES
Secretary: Mrs M. Temby, 9 Hillside Road, Blacktown, New
South Wales 2148

CAVALIER KING CHARLES SPANIEL CLUB OF
VICTORIA
Secretary: Mrs K. Hollingworth, 1814 S. Gippsland Hwy, Five
Ways, Victoria 3977

CAVALIER CLUB OF SOUTH AUSTRALIA
Secretary: Mrs D. Morgan, 44 German Town Road, Red Banks,
South Australia 5502

CAVALIER KING CHARLES SPANIEL CLUB OF
CANBERRA
Secretary: Mrs R. Lane, 35 Macnaughton Street, Holt, ACT 2615

CANADA
CAVALIER KING CHARLES SPANIEL CLUB OF
CANADA
Secretary: Frances Bowness, 860 Anderson Avenue, Milton,
Ontario L9T 4X8

Three Regional Clubs have recently been established in Canada.
They are:
CAVALIER FANCIERS OF SOUTHERN ONTARIO
CAVALIER KC SPANIELS OF BRITISH COLUMBIA
CAVALIER KC SPANIEL CLUB OF MID-WESTERN
CANADA

FINLAND
SUOMEN CAVALIER KING CHARLESINSPANIEL-
IYHIDSTYS RY
Dr A. Paloheimo, Jolkby, 02400 Kirkkonummi

FRANCE
CLUB DES ESPAGNEULS NAINS ANGLAIS
(KING CHARLES ET CAVALIER KING CHARLES)
Pres: M.J.C. Metans, Villa Bel Air, Rue P. Curie 83660
CARNOULES

NETHERLANDS
CAVALIER CLUB NEDERLAND
Secretary: Mrs P.C. Zwaartman-Pinster, Doornweg 3, 3235 Nj
Rockanje, Westvoorne

NEW ZEALAND
CANTERBURY CAVALIER KING CHARLES SPANIEL
CLUB
Mrs J. Higgins, 260 Marshlands Road, Christchurch 6

EAST COAST CAVALIER KING CHARLES SPANIEL
CLUB
Mrs J. Tonkin, 50 Dover Road, Flaxmere, Hastings

OTAGO-SOUTHLAND CAVALIER KING CHARLES
SPANIEL CLUB
Mrs M. Allum, 111 District Road, Green Island, Dunedin

TIKI CAVALIER KING CHARLES SPANIEL CLUB
Mr G. Duncan, PO Box 5619, Hamilton

CENTRAL CAVALIER & KING CHARLES SPANIEL
CLUB
Mr W.T. Murdoch, 41 Nicholson Road, Khandallah, Wellington

SWEDEN
SPECIALKLUBBEN FRO CAVALIER KING CHARLES
SPANIEL (CAVALIERSALLSKAPET)
Secretary: Birgitta Nystedt, Adolf Lemons vag 21, 183 42 TABY

UNITED STATES OF AMERICA
CAVALIER KING CHARLES SPANIEL CLUB USA
Memb. Secretary: C.K.C.S. USA Inc., Box 360, Newtown, PA
18940-0360

CAVALIERS OF THE NORTHEAST
Susan Adams, 11714 Manor Road, Glen Arm, MD 21057

CAVALIERS OF THE SOUTH
David A. Frederick, 1302 Lowell Drive, Huntsville, AL 35801

CAVALIERS OF THE MIDWEST
Patricia Hutchins, 1258 W. Borton Road, Essexville, MI 48732

CAVALIERS OF THE WEST
Harold Letterly, 661 Woodlawn, Devore Heights, San Bernadino, CA 92407

Index